Free F___ll

REDISCOVERI___

Chris Bainbridge & Cai Ross

Based on their acclaimed(ish) podcast

Published by
QUOIT MEDIA LIMITED
www.quoitmedia.co.uk

QUOIT

This edition first published in 2023 by Quoit Media Limited,
Brynmawr, Llanfair Caereinion, Powys, SY21 0DG

For more copies of this book, please email quoit@quoitmedia.co.uk

ISBN 978-1-911537-23-6

Cover design by Cai Ross and Alan Hayes.
Internal design by Alan Hayes.
Cover and internal illustrations by Jemima Duncalf.
Cover and internal photos © Chris Bainbridge and Cai Ross,
except photo of Patrick McGoohan statue on page 7 © Alan Hayes,
photos on pages 126 and 127 © Y Cymro,
and Patrick McGoohan photo on back cover © Y Cymro.

A CIP catalogue record for this book is available from the British Library.

Printed and bound in Great Britain by Clays Ltd, Elcograf S.p.A.

For Claire and Liss

Useful Numbers

Free For All

The *Free For All* podcast was launched across the streaming platforms in December 2021 as a weekly examination of Patrick McGoohan's enigmatic TV series *The Prisoner*. Each week, screenwriter Cai Ross and media lecturer Chris Bainbridge delved into an episode of the series, interpreting it in their own unique way.

In addition to speaking with such luminaries as Alex Cox, Dave Barrie, Robert Fairclough and Rick Davy, Chris and Cai have interviewed notable cast members Jane Merrow and Derren Nesbitt.

Having covered all 17 episodes of *The Prisoner*, the podcast continues with special episodes that have since looked at Patrick McGoohan's work on *Columbo* and *Danger Man*.

Free For All is a light hearted, funny, critical and sometimes analytical exploration of McGoohan's televisual magnum opus.

https://podcasts.apple.com/gb/podcast/free-for-all/id1594717945

Who Are We?

Chris Bainbridge is a lecturer in creative and broadcast media in beautiful north Wales. Chris has worked in theatre, broadcasting, IT, and more recently in education. In 2010 Chris retrained as a secondary school teacher, before moving on to work in further and higher education; in 2019 he became a Senior Fellow of the Higher Education Academy. Chris is also a musician, having played bass guitar for several original and cover bands since the 1990s. Chris' main passions are vinyl records, travelling in his  VW camper and being creative, which he has Cai to thank for keeping him on track! Chris lives with his family in Snowdonia, and is currently studying for a PhD in Film at Bangor University.

Cai Ross has written for film and food magazines like *BBC Good Food*, *Cinema Retro*, *Scream*, *Fire & Knives* and *Calibre*, as well as *HeyUGuys* and *Film Inquiry* online. His path to scriptwriting glory took a circuitous turn when he briefly took over his parents' bistro, Paysanne in north Wales, only to stick around for the next twenty years and counting. His cookbook based on the bistro's thirty year history was published in 2018, and a new cookbook will be published in 2024. He also  provides scripts and narration for audio guides at several prominent tourist sites, and his short film *Bang-Zoom*, co-starring the estimable Chris Bainbridge, was nominated for Best Short Film at the 2023 Gog Awards.

Preface

Having decided over a few beers that making a podcast about *The Prisoner* might be a fun idea, old friends Chris Bainbridge and Cai Ross set about revisiting the classic 1960s television series afresh.

Despite being *Prisoner* fans since it was screened on Channel 4 back in 1992, this was the first time either had seen it for over ten years. This was to be less a cursory watch and more of a deep dive.

The result was the *Free For All* podcast, which first aired in December 2021. Every week, each of the seventeen episodes of *The Prisoner* was forensically examined and given a critical going over. In their quest, they were delighted to be able to enlist the help of *Prisoner* experts and even cast members, who very kindly came on board to share their experiences.

This is the result of Chris and Cai's tireless ordeal to answer some of the many enigmas and solve at long last the countless riddles that Patrick McGoohan weaved throughout his magnificent opus. Well, more accurately, it was two old pals chatting about something they both loved and making tenuous links to The Beatles and the 1980s sit-com *Duty Free*.

In so doing, they discovered elements about *The Prisoner* that had hitherto eluded them. There's the extraordinary prescience; filling the Village with the furniture of science-fiction, only for it all to become the stuff of everyday reality. They analysed the extent to which *The Prisoner* alluded to McGoohan's inescapable fame and his discomfort with it. It all built up to the notorious climax, 'Fall Out', derided by many but revealed by Chris to be an autobiographical masterpiece with its foundations built upon the theories of Plato and Socrates.

Free For All: Rediscovering The Prisoner captures the results of all their hard work. Moreover, it gives them the chance to correct a few mistakes and replace a few 'Ummmm, not sure's and 'It'll come to me…'s with the actual information that may have eluded them at the time of recording.

This then is a love letter to a work of art which has been quietly obsessing them for over three decades; one that has become more fascinating as it has aged alongside them.

Introduction

CAI: *The Prisoner* played a fundamental part in how Chris and I first became friends. I was 17, and I became obsessed with *The Prisoner* after it was rebroadcast in 1992. I'd been to Portmeirion and gone to the Prisoner shop and bought pens and stickers and a No. 6 badge. I used to wear this badge on the lapel of an especially awful (fake) leather flying jacket which I fondly imagined made me look like Maverick from *Top Gun*, but more accurately had me resembling someone who sold pirate VHS tapes from the back of his Yugo at car boot sales.

I wore this jacket and badge combo to a party and naturally, every imbecile in the room took turns staggering up to me and asking if it was my sixth birthday. Chris saw it though, and in a flash gave me the eye salute and said, 'Be seeing you!' 'Thank God,' thought I. 'I can be friends with this guy.' We chatted about *The Prisoner* for about an hour, and thirty-odd years later, that conversation still hasn't finished.

CHRIS: For me, my first introduction to *The Prisoner* was in WH Smith's[1], when I saw a VHS of two episodes on the *Channel 5* label. I remember thinking, 'This is right up my street,' but it was something like twenty quid! It

---

[1] WH Smith is a British chain of shops that sells books, stationery, magazines, newspapers, entertainment products and confectionery.

was only when Channel 4 broadcast it in 1992, that I set the video to record it and never missed an episode. Paused all the adverts, but kept those wonderful bumpers before and after with the penny farthing, which of course you don't get with the DVD and Blu-ray versions. Every time I watch 'Arrival' and Guy Doleman says, 'I think we have a challenge on our hands...' I still expect that bumper to appear.'

CAI: It was already inveigled into the public consciousness by that point, through things like rock videos and car adverts. There had been an especially referential car ad for Renault fairly recently that explicitly referenced *The Prisoner*. My first direct exposure was a series called *TV Heaven*, presented by the great Frank Muir, which was mainly a repeat of various ITC shows, broadcast in 1991. *The Prisoner* episode they chose to show was 'The Girl Who Was Death', which has practically nothing to do with the rest of the series. Nonetheless, I was hooked; never seen anything like it before. We were both hooked actually, and I'll bet that any 17-year-olds watching it now would feel the same way.

CHRIS: I take a lot of my film students to Portmeirion and ask them to replicate shots from the series to get some practice in, and you'd be amazed how many of them go to the shop and buy the set because they are simply intrigued by it and want to know more. It's like what JJ Abrams said about

'The Mystery Box.' He gave a very interesting TED[2] Talk once and spoke about this mystery box that his grandfather had bought him, back in the 60s when he was a little boy. A bit like the Paul Daniels Magic Sets that we had in the UK in the 80s.

CAI: I had one of those. The wand didn't work.

CHRIS: With this magic box, you don't know what's inside it. There's no list of contents, so Abrams has never opened it. To him, this box holds all this symbolism and mystery. Like any great magic trick, once it's explained, it loses all its power: you'd think that Abrams would have remembered that lesson when he made *Lost*. With that, he borrowed a lot from *The Prisoner*: a mysterious setting from which there is no escape, the branded goods in the shop etc. Nevertheless, he answered a lot of the questions raised in the show. McGoohan never did. In the 2017 Chris Rodley documentary, *In My Mind*, McGoohan does give a little bit away, explaining his thinking, but of course, we don't need an answer. The fact that audiences have been making their informed interpretations about it is one of the reasons it has endured for so long.

---

[2] www.ted.com/talks/j_j_abrams_the_mystery_box

CAI: McGoohan said that it was 'A question about a conundrum, and if you answer the conundrum, then it's no longer a conundrum.' I think that is specifically why it still has the power to fascinate. Every time I see it, I see something new. It's been going on 30 years since I first saw it and it's a different experience watching it as a 30 or a 40-year-old than it was when I was 17. Fascinating in new ways each time.

CHRIS: When the Paramount channel came out in the US, *Star Trek: Voyager* was going to be their flagship show but one of the others they put out was a show with Bruce Greenwood[3] about a Number 6-type character who has his identity removed and his family and friends no longer knew him, was he going mad? That was very *Prisoner*-ish. There was a resolution, which was very similar to the one they used in the *Prisoner* remake in 2009.

CAI: …Which we won't dwell on. Ian McKellen was the only highlight of that, wasn't he? And I remember at the time he said, 'We'll be answering a lot of questions in this one, which you couldn't really say about the original,' which rather missed the point. He was the only Number 2 in that. One of the lovely things about the original series is seeing all those wonderful character actors lining up to take a crack at playing Number 2.

CHRIS: You can imagine who'd they use today. Stephen Fry did play Number 2 in a very funny show called *The Laughing Prisoner* with Jools Holland, Siouxsie and the Banshees and XTC, all playing in Portmeirion. That happened a lot, actually; pop stars coming up to Portmeirion to make videos. Supergrass for one recorded their *Alright* video there. The *Doctor Who* episode 'The Masque of Mandragora' (1976) was filmed in Portmeirion too, as were episodes[4] of *Danger Man*, which is when McGoohan first encountered it. He drives into the entrance, up past where the shops are now, and everyone there is pretending to be Italian; pretending that it's hot and sunny.

CAI: That was a regular ITC trick, that. A typical episode of *The Saint* for example would start with all this stock footage of Rome and the Colosseum

---

[3] *Nowhere Man*. Broadcast on the United Paramount Network between 1995 and 1996.

[4] The two prominent episodes were 'View from the Villa' (1960) and 'Under the Lake' (1961). Portmeirion also features in 'The Honeymooners' (1961), 'Find and Return' (1961), 'The Journey Ends Halfway' (1961) and 'Bury the Dead' (1961).

and all that, then cut suddenly to the standard alley set in Pinewood, covered in Italian film posters, while Warren Mitchell wandered over and pretended he was called Luigi.

CHRIS: One thing that always amazes me about *The Prisoner* was that it was made at a time when we had no video recorders. If you missed it, that was it, gone. Yet it was designed to be re-watched, like any piece of art so that it could be reassessed and re-evaluated. All these tiny background details would have barely been noticed. Some of them I've only discovered now, 35 years later. It was shot on 35mm, so there might have been a sense that it would last back then, the BBC was still wiping shows like *Doctor Who* and *Dad's Army* to reuse the tapes. Even so, shows were designed to be watched once, but I think McGoohan had the prescience to deliberately create something that could be watched and re-watched.

Which is precisely what we did...

episode one
Arrival

An unnamed man resigns from his job and is promptly kidnapped. He wakes up in a seemingly pleasant Italianate village with its own curious set of rules, where everyone is known only by their number. He discovers that the people in charge are determined at all costs to find out why he resigned. He also discovers that escaping from this Village is seemingly impossible.

The Prisoner made its (British) debut on ITV on Friday the 29th of September 1967 at 7:30 pm. Back in the day, the introduction of colour TV was not yet widespread, so many people would have watched this series in black and white, denied all the colour and vibrancy. Viewers would have missed the extraordinary shot when the doors to Number 2's room slide open and McGoohan's face is suddenly bathed in bright purple light; essentially the moment when this 'Spy Show' edges more into science fiction territory.

In 1967, there were also what was known as regional variations. ITV was a conglomerate of several different stations all based in different locations around the UK. Scotland and the North would have Grampian and Tyne Tees, for example. Wales had HTV, London had Thames TV and LWT (London Weekend Television) and so it was all over Great Britain, with inconsistent broadcast dates as a matter of course.

According to Andrew Pixley's magnificent book[5], *The Prisoner's* debut was first shown in the Midlands and Grampian, so viewers in Scotland and Birmingham got first dibs. Welsh viewers on HTV, where it was filmed, didn't get to see it for another three years!

It had a very respectable eleven million viewers in its first run, a testament to Patrick McGoohan's status as the biggest and best-paid TV star in the world.

What was it up against? Well, on the same night that *The Prisoner* first aired, BBC1 offered The Hippodrome Circus in Great Yarmouth, presented by Bobby Roberts of Liberty Horses, the Svensons, The Four Angli, and Zelka! On BBC2, which was still relatively new[6], we had *Outlook For Friday: Towards World Government?* presented by Erskine Childers and David Morse. Let's face it, *The Prisoner* was by far the most entertaining option that night.

This was originally titled 'The Arrival,' as evidenced by photos of clapperboards from the set. From the off, Number 6 is completely clueless, alone and vulnerable. We drop in with him and know as much as he does, which is precisely nothing. From the get-go, we are utterly intrigued.

---

[5] *The Prisoner: A Complete Production Guide* by Andrew Pixley. 2008.
[6] If you haven't seen the footage of the disastrous opening of BBC2, do look it up on YouTube. It's like a *Monty Python* sketch.

Let's start at the very beginning: the title sequence. In 'Arrival', we get an extended sequence which would be shortened for the rest of the series (excepting episodes where it wasn't there at all).

CHRIS: My favourite moment of this is when the Prisoner arrives at the car park barrier in his Lotus 7. We get a lovely bit of character-building here because the car is so low that he could easily drive under the barrier without even having to duck... but he doesn't. He stops and takes his ticket. He plays by the rules. I love it; it's semiotic, giving that kind of non-verbal communication about this character and what he stands for.

This little grace note was subsequently cut from the regular titles sequence but each week, to the pounding beat of Ron Grainer's main theme, the show would start with a montage of increasingly iconic images. The Lotus zooming towards us like a sped-up Omar Sharif in *Lawrence of Arabia*; the endless corridor, and McGoohan, a vision in black, flinging open a pair of doors and filling the screen, arms outstretched.

He resigns, by hand, to none other than George Markstein himself, taking care to spill his tea in the process. That whole office set, where McGoohan quits his job, was built in the car park where they were filming[7].

CHRIS: One thing that always impressed me, and I show this to my students and they never fail to be impressed, is the matte shot of the filing cabinet stretching out into the far distance. It is a little bit betrayed by new HD transfers, but matte shots and matte paintings are brilliantly used here.

It was George Markstein, by most accounts, who suggested to McGoohan the concept of a retirement home for ex-spies. The story that Markstein told was that he knew about these retirement homes, specifically one in Scotland called Inverlair Lodge. He'd posited this idea as the seeds of a plot to McGoohan during his *Danger Man* days. Because of this, Markstein remained convinced that *The Prisoner* was the continuing adventures of John Drake.

---

[7] The car park and office scenes were shot on location at the Cumberland Gate underground car park beneath Hyde Park and Park Lane, W2 2ET. As of 2023, the car park is now known as the Q-Park Marble Arch.

CHRIS: There's a place near Portmeirion by coincidence, called Nant Gwrtheyrn, which is a village for Welsh learners, where people only speak Welsh. It has all the amenities, a local pub, local shops and all that, but it's exclusively in Welsh. I'm not suggesting for a second that it's like 'the Village' in that respect! But it does remind me of those places in Russia where spies were trained to be English[8]: villages which were mini-Britains where everyone spoke English and they learned how to speak slang and order the right things in restaurants. How to blend in.

Markstein's concept of a Village in which everybody knows too much, and from which nobody can escape, is incredibly strong, simple and robust. It also ensured that no episode could end with the escape of the central character so each adventure could be resolved with the protagonist remaining essentially where he is, ready to give it another go the next week.

In that respect, *The Prisoner* shares a lot of its storytelling DNA with *The Fugitive* (1963), the US TV show starring David Janssen. Likewise, the main character's central quest (in his case to prove his innocence and clear his name) can never come close to a resolution until the final episode. Until then, every single episode is resolved but he remains on the run.

CHRIS: It pretty much stayed that way until the mid-90s. *Star Trek: Deep Space Nine* (1993) was one of the first shows to have a serialised arc, rather than just stand-alone episodes; it's syndication though. You need a show that you can broadcast out of order and you can do that with *The Fugitive* and even, barring three episodes, *The Prisoner*.

McGoohan categorically denied that Number 6 and Drake were the same man. Then again, one might suspect that McGoohan was happy initially for audiences to suspect that this might be the case, simply because it would have helped to sell the series.

CAI: I also think he would have enjoyed the muddying of expectations and the arguments and counterarguments that later ensued.

---

[8] See *Danger Man* episode 'Colony Three' (1964) directed by *Arrival* director Don Chaffey.

CHRIS: Markstein would certainly have wanted to see this as a continuation of *Danger Man*, simply as a means to sell the show. He wasn't especially a fan of surrealism and allegory. Realistically, he thought that all of that nonsense hurt the sales. This wasn't shot as a 'cult show,' it was a big-budget affair, possibly (one of) the biggest-budget TV shows of the time, destined for prime time slots around the world.

The Prisoner looks cinematic, much more so than any contemporary TV show of the time. One might put that down to the presence of Don Chaffey[9] in the director's chair. Chaffey had only just come off *One Million Years BC* (1966), which was a huge hit for Hammer Films. A prolific director, one of his other big hits had been Disney's *The Three Lives of Thomasina* (1963), starring Patrick McGoohan. He was equally comfortable directing television shows (overseeing fifteen episodes of *Danger Man*), which was becoming common for many feature directors in the 1960s.

A quick scan of the crew list reveals a whole roster of eminent talents from the British film and television industry. Chief among them is David Tomblin whose role in shaping *The Prisoner* was of incalculable importance. The question of authorship very often boils down to the McGoohan / Markstein dynamic, but Tomblin can claim to have produced the series, was responsible for a lot of the Portmeirion-shot footage, was there from beginning to end and even directed two episodes[10].

He also co-founded Everyman Productions with McGoohan. A telling, important detail in the context of *The Prisoner*, in that Number 6 *is* an everyman; he represents everyone. This indicates that from the very beginning McGoohan and Tomblin had a far more ambitious artistic reach than just making an action-based spy series.

CHRIS: There is a little bit of hoodwinking the audience, in that it is set up to be just that, another spy series.

---

[9] Don Chaffey (1917-1990) was a British director, writer, art director and producer, famous for directing the big-screen epics *Jason and the Argonauts* (1963) and *One Million Years BC* (1966). In his later years, Chaffey went on to direct episodes of popular American television shows including *Airwolf*, *Charlie's Angels* and *T.J. Hooker*.
[10] The episodes in question were 'Living in Harmony' (1967) and 'The Girl Who Was Death' (1968).

CAI: That's one of my favourite aspects of the whole thing is that it's an extraordinary allegorical artwork... that's been Trojan-horsed into millions of living rooms, disguised as a big, colourful ITC caper series.

Audiences at the time, especially the all-important younger *James Bond* viewers were primed for excitement by all the usual temptations like the Mini Moke Dinky Toys. The 7:30 pm broadcast schedule suggests that this would have been a bit of a treat for the kids in the house to be allowed to stay up and watch in their pyjamas and dressing gowns. Their appetite for action and excitement would have been well sated by this opening episode. There's an escape attempt, a pursuit across the beach, and an attempted break-out via helicopter, plus all the usual fisticuffs. Threaded in around all the usual staples, something else was going on.

CAI: The first time I realised that there was something different going on when I first saw it, something more than just entertainment, was the insert shot of Guy Doleman's static, unblinking face that is cut in, almost subliminally at the moment Number 6 angrily smashes the metal cloche onto his breakfast.

CHRIS: It's so jarring. There are a lot of crash zooms in this episode, but this is just a split-second shot of a non-reaction from Number Two[11].

CAI: And he's staring at 'you' straight down the lens.

This unusual editing style is used brilliantly to discombobulate the audience from the moment Number 6 wakes up and starts scampering around his new home town. A brilliantly edited scene is where he spots someone in the clock tower, then runs up to find nothing up there, but a view that makes so much sense to him that lasts no longer than five seconds.

CHRIS: The original *Prisoner* theme was a far more avant garde, esoteric take; more Stockhausen or even John Cage than Mike Post. That said, the first few minutes of 'Arrival' make great aural use out of having no score at all, just a ghostly wind sourced from the same library of stock 'sounds' where

---

[11] Episode 1, 'Arrival' at roughly the 11:42 mark.

they found the thunderclap which starts each episode. This absence of diegetic sounds effectively intensifies Number 6's sense of isolation.

The world-building in 'Arrival' could hardly have been better. Like Number 6, you are constantly wrong-footed all the way through. By the end of the episode though, you know everything you need to know, but you still know nothing. You know he's trapped there, and you can't trust anybody.

CHRIS: He then spies the café owner and heads over, and I found myself looking at this in the context of 1966 when it was very difficult to get on television with a regional accent. There was still a tradition of received pronunciation[12]. Here, the waitress is played by Patsy Smart, performing with a very authentic northern tone.

The couple who later walk past McGoohan and merrily quip, 'Beautiful day!' were local residents from Penrhyndeudraeth[13], their north Walean accents conspicuously absent.

Cordless telephones. Now, anyone under the age of thirty might have to take a seat while they process this, but at one point, a 'phone' was something one merely used to speak to someone else. That's it. Moreover, this so-called 'telephone' would have been, until roughly the early 1990s when mobiles or cell phones became more ubiquitous, very firmly secured to the wall via a cord. If you were an American living in a situation comedy, this cord could be anything up to thirty metres long. The cordless telephone, in 1967, was the stuff of science-fiction fantasy.

Imagine Number 6's amazement then, when he picks up a cordless phone to place a call to London, and hears a dialling tone... As with the Bose-like wireless speaker in his room, this is technology from the future decades before it became commonplace.

---

[12] Chris recommends the 1952 film *Hindle Wakes*, partly filmed in Llandudno, for anyone who wants to hear what a broad Lancastrian accent sounds like after several months of received pronunciation vocal coaching.

[13] If you're interested, the phonetic pronunciation is *Pen-rin-day-dry-th*. Chris once had to write this down for popular Emu puppeteer, Rod Hull during a Christmas 1996 pantomime.

CHRIS: In his vision of the Village, McGoohan tried to avoid anachronisms. He's made everybody very colourful and not the fashion of the time. He's tried to make things timeless, as best as he can, whereas a show like *Space: 1999*, ironically, could only have been made in 1975.

Whilst seeking to avoid elements that would date the series one could argue that there's a lot in the show that is, conversely, 1960s *The Prisoner*'s visual touchstones hark back to an Edwardian aesthetic which was extremely popular in many shows from the 1960s, especially *The Avengers*, whose hero John Steed was a model of 1920s politesse; impeccable in manners and tailoring.

CHRIS: It was very much in the air back then. Look at the Teddy Boys, whose very name is a reference to Edwardian fashion. William Hartnell's *Doctor Who* and Patrick Troughton's to a certain extent wore very Edwardian-style smoking jackets and frock coats. Carnaby Street was full of these very militaristic tunics, frilly shirts and jackets, the kind of thing Jimi Hendrix used to wear.

The miraculously cordless telephone is item one in a lengthy roster of ubiquitous future tech presaged with uncanny prescience but its foresight goes deeper than just lucky guesswork.

CHRIS: There's something else going on here that you can only see clearly from a 21st century viewpoint. It's not just the phone. He's predicting on-demand culture. It only really occurred to me when he pushed the button at the taxi rank and it immediately arrived. The instantaneous nature of Uber, Spotify, Netflix, Deliveroo and so many others, was science fiction back in 1967 but McGoohan could see it around the corner.

When the taxi arrives, the driver asks where he would like to go, firstly in English, then in French. In one version, Number 6 insinuates that being a taxi driver is an odd job for a woman, but wisely it was cut from the final edit. The driver talks of Czechs and Poles. 'What would Czechs and Poles be doing here?' It's one of the very few references to the bigger picture of contemporary world affairs that informed all spy shows of the age, namely the Cold War.

CAI: It's a genuinely unclassifiable creature, *The Prisoner*. Is it a Cold War spy show? Is it sci-fi, or fantasy? There are allusions to the Cold War. Why, thinks Number 6, are there Eastern Bloc citizens here? This all helps to keep him shrouded in the mist of intrigue. By the end of the show, we and Number 6 still have no idea who the masters are.

CHRIS: *The Prisoner* depicts a world in a microcosm. There's global imagery all over the place, throughout the series. Rover, the seats, the globes in Number 6's apartment, the map of the world on his wall. The abandoned 'Pop!' image that was originally meant to close each episode showed the world exploding; the end-times.

Number 6 then enters the Village Shop, where the shopkeeper (Denis Shaw), having spoken to one of his customers in a foreign language, kindly instructs her to help herself to a pineapple.

CHRIS: One thing that's always intrigued me about this scene is that if you look at the clock in the shop, you'll notice that the time is 5:50; ten to six. Is it 5:50 am? Almost certainly not, not even in the Village. It can't be 5:50pm because he's about to have breakfast with Number 2. Excepting the explanation that it's just shoddy work from the set-dresser, this is a lovely reminder that he isn't quite '6' yet. He hasn't been given his badge. He's still in his old clothes.

Number 6 is there to get his hands on a map and is duly handed one: a completely useless, coordinate-free leaflet that simply details the mountains and the sea surrounding the Village in the vaguest terms. A 'bigger' map is requested 'Only in colour. Much more expensive.' which is only bigger in terms of the paper size. Number 6 doesn't actually buy a map, which would have come as a relief when he discovered that a free copy had already been left in his new house.

The celebrated, honey-larynxed *Carry On*[14] actress Fenella Fielding makes her first appearance as the reassuring voice of the Village speaker system.

---

[14] A long running British comedy film series that ran from 1958-1978, with a one off return in 1992.

(Fielding was such a memorable part of the audioscape of *The Prisoner* that she was invited back to Portmeirion as part of the 50th-anniversary celebrations in 2017, which sadly proved to be her final public appearance.)

CAI: I hear the echoes of Fielding's Village voice in so many pre-recorded announcements these days. That pleasant, soothing, ultimately banal and empty tone, is often used to tell us all terrible news in the nicest possible way so we don't all get mad.

While the speaker alerts the Villagers to the weather forecast and announces that today's ice cream flavour is strawberry, Number 6 notices an unusual signpost, directing people to 'Walk On The Grass.' It heightens the way that the Village is not playing by the rules, especially jarring for a character like Number 6 who habitually does play by the rules. This is a world turned on its head.

It's also a direct steal from *The Strange World of Gurney Slade* (1960). This was an extraordinary surreal ITV show in which the then-superstar Anthony Newley played Gurney Slade, a character trying unsuccessfully to escape from his own TV show. It was said to have reflected Newley's desire to escape from the suffocating world of celebrity that his life had become. It only lasted one series, but Patrick McGoohan was said to have been a great admirer.

In the Village, the rules of logic and physics don't apply in the same way. Everything about the Village is about discombobulation; distorting reality for Number 6 and for us as the watching audience. The speaker in Number 6's room playing interminable Muzak at an irritating level[15] has no lead or plug glance at your smart speaker and you'll spot another uncanny prediction and Number 6 can't even destroy it without someone arriving within seconds to repair it.

Moreover, Number 6 walks past the repairman in the garden seconds later. Or is it his twin brother? In both cases, he looks very much like the hairless actor Oliver MacGreevy, so effective as a heavy in *The Ipcress File* (1965).

---

[15] The music is actually from the Chappell library titled *Party Dress* by Tony Tamburello (1957). Performed by the Telecast Orchestra, directed by Elliot Mayes.

Because this is the world-building, set-up episode, it is packed full of unsettling touches like this that keep the audience as bewildered and as uncomfortable as our protagonist.

CHRIS: If you watch most of the other TV shows around at the time, especially the action-adventure shows, there is nothing like as much attention to detail as there is here.

Number 6 is invited to have breakfast with 'Number 2' at his office, the Green Dome, in what might be described as his office but which is officially known as the Living Space.

Even more importantly, we also meet the Butler for the first time, played by the diminutive Maltese actor, Angelo Muscat. Muscat had already carved a respectable career for himself by this point and he would later appear in *Willy Wonka & the Chocolate Factory* (1971).

CAI: There was a lovely interview with McGoohan where he said he went to Malta to visit Muscat, who was a big, big deal over there, and he was constantly surrounded by all these beautiful women who thought he was amazing; he was Malta's biggest celebrity.

The Butler is one of the only members of the Village who doesn't wear a badge. He is also often incorrectly cited as the only character apart from Number 6 to appear in all seventeen episodes[16]. A lot of people gradually suspected that he would eventually be revealed as Number 1.

CHRIS: There are various theories, suggesting that he represents the general public: the 'little people.' He also represents the question: if you are not a part of society, do you have a voice? The Butler has no voice. Never says a word. Does this mean that he is on the fringe of society?

---

[16] The episodes that Muscat does not appear in are 'Living in Harmony' and 'The Girl Who Was Death'. The Butler appears briefly in the final shot of 'Many Happy Returns' holding an umbrella but this is a reused piece of footage and he is not credited.

The casting of Muscat eschews the classic 'butler' part which in practically every other TV show you can imagine would have been played by someone who looked and sounded like John Le Mesurier. Or John Le Mesurier himself. Because he is there in nearly all the episodes, ever-present, silent, diligent and reliable, Muscat increasingly comes to seem like a rock of stability, particularly in later episodes when Number 2s start to become unhinged.

The very concept of a butler was omnipresent in British literature and television up until this point but was very much on the wane by 1967. Having a butler was an aristocratic trope, soon to be looked upon as nostalgia in the 1970s TV show *Upstairs Downstairs*.

If the post-war years in the UK were about anything, it was about trying to get rid of the rigid class system. Anyone who was anyone in the world of music or theatre in the late 50s and early 60s was either from a working-class background or pretended to be, and their art reflected that. It was a societal shift that came with a lot of pushback from the upper decks. Famously, a lot of MBEs were returned in disgust from Brigadier So-And-So and company when the Beatles were awarded theirs.

The Prisoner did straddle the volcano-crater of the 1960s at its most incendiary. Filming first started at the end of 1966, when the Vietnam War was starting to meet with vigorous resistance from the home crowd, and finished in 1968, the flashpoint year of protests, riots and assassinations. Despite being shot a year before, *The Prisoner* also manages to pre-emptively capture a lot of the psychedelic mood of 1967.

Instantly, Number 2 is the establishment. Even when he is replaced and more often than not, it is 'he' who replaces 'him' there is a continuity of an old-boy network maintaining stability. Their outfits are a satirical mish-mash of establishment 'must-haves,' the blazers, the Oxbridge scarves and the shooting sticks.

CAI: What Number 2 represents is the various different types of mindless bureaucrats that continue to bedevil us all. The privileged, the psychotic, the useless, the cruel, the seemingly benign, the toadying, the delusional…

CHRIS: He's almost like a Prime Minister, in that he's a replaceable boss who nonetheless answers to a higher power.

Breakfast is always a rather sumptuous treat in the Green Dome and Number 6 is passing up a fine meal by not grabbing as much of it as he can. The bacon and eggs look especially good. It arrives instantaneously. This is not simply superb service; this is a show of power. This is Number 2 undermining Number 6 by showing him that he already knows what he's going to order.

This is something that Number 2 makes clear when he shows Number 6 a montage of photographs taken surreptitiously while on a mission somewhere in Europe. There is much to be gleaned here. For a start, Number 6's birthday is revealed to be the same as McGoohan's, the 19th of March, 1928. The photos of Number 6 as a child are of the young Patrick McGoohan.

'You were about to meet Chambers, late of the Foreign Office, hoping to change his mind before the big boys found out.' Who is Chambers?

CHRIS: I see this as alluding to one of the reasons why he resigned. In 'The Chimes of Big Ben', he talks about a matter of conscience. There was an incident perhaps? Was this what he wanted to talk to Chambers about? In any case, it's another show of power, as he is telling Number 6, basically, we know everything anyway.

There are ominous parallels here between the collection of personal data, everything there is to know, except the specific time of his birth and contemporary data collection. All the personal information we have has been gradually siphoned off or given away freely so that algorithms can be created that help companies sell us their stuff more effectively and push us into echo chambers of political inflexibility and subvert democracies.

The idea that someone can have that amount of personal data about you is presented here not as liberating and helpful but as threatening and sinister, and rightly so.

Taking pride of place in Number 2's office is an antique penny farthing, the very emblem of the Village embossed on its badges and flags. McGoohan from the get-go was reluctant to reveal the meaning behind any of the *Prisoner* imagery, but was always clear that the seemingly benign penny farthing was an explicit warning that we were evolving too quickly. He told Alain Carrazé that it represented 'Progress: one has only to be in a traffic jam for hours on the highway to know what that meant. In the traffic jam, in the immobile cars, one is a statistic, a number, futile, a prisoner.'

He believed that we need to stop and take a moment to assess where we are and where we've come from. Technology has moved on too fast and keeps pushing us forward and we never take a breather to see what it is doing to us.

CHRIS: The smartphone is the perfect example of this. If you have one in your pocket right now, you'll have a phone, a camera, a film studio, a television, a radio, a notepad, a tracking system, etc etc. You can access the sum of all human knowledge; read anything, listen to anything. It is essentially magic... but all we do with it is make silly videos of ourselves dancing and lip-synching, and then post them on social media.

CAI: All this tech has only been around for a few years. Post-smartphone technology. I can remember downloading a film trailer, I think it was *Planet of The Apes* (2001), and it took half a day. iPhones, Facebook, Twitter etc are all products of the early 21st century. This is *Star Trek* stuff. There is more technological ingenuity in my mobile telephone than has existed in all of human evolution, and as a society, we have never taken a moment to ask ourselves, 'What is all this doing to us?!' God, we sound like grumpy old men don't we?

CHRIS: It seems that we are far more obsessed with attaining technology than exploring it. It is more important to buy the latest version of our phones, even though they are pretty much exactly like the versions we already own, than by using all this extraordinary technology to better ourselves as a nation or even as a species. We'd rather just get 'likes' and have the perception of looking good for owning the newest gadgets. And yes, we do sound like grumpy old men!

McGoohan's scepticism about technology and its questionable benefits was shared by a lot of artists and writers at the time. It was something of a trope, particularly in *The Avengers* whenever someone invented an amazing machine that did the work of a hundred people or would render the need for human involvement obsolete, you can bet that it will have run amok and been destroyed by the end of the episode, taking the 'mad scientist' along with it as will happen later in *The Prisoner*.

Number 2 takes Number 6 on a tour of his new home. Keep your eyes peeled and you'll see the extras in the scene by the fountain suddenly start to move as though snapped into action by the director. You might be wondering where Number 2 disappears to; why he's suddenly standing on a balcony up ahead with a loudspeaker covering his face. We've already discovered that the mechanics of the Village are there to discombobulate you, but in this case, it's because the actor Guy Doleman had to drop out of the scene with, reportedly, a terribly bad back.

This scene marks the first appearance of one of *The Prisoner*'s most iconic elements: Rover, the bouncing white ball, sheepdog and sentry, sent to smother and quell any dissenters.

CHRIS: Production designer Bernard Williams was looking for any opportunity to reuse footage. One of the reasons 'Arrival' was such an annoyance to him was that McGoohan isn't wearing the classic piped blazer, he's wearing his civilian suit and therefore his scenes here can't be edited into any future episodes. Of course, when that poor guy gets suffocated by Rover,[17] it is clearly McGoohan under the rubber. This same shot is used, regardless of who the victim is, every time Rover gets his victim.

Rover was originally designed as something of a robotic monster on caterpillar tracks that would pursue its victims across all terrains, including water. It was actually built too but proved to be completely useless. McGoohan said, 'This thing was like a hovercraft and it would go underwater, come up on the beach, climb walls… it could do anything.'

Some photos of this first iteration have survived. Chris described it as looking like a pie, or a flying saucer on a go-kart chassis. Neither of us could work out what this Rover would do to you once it got hold of you.

When Rover Mk. I made its debut, chasing McGoohan into the sea, 'It went down into the water and stayed down, permanently.' In our chat later in the

---

[17] The Villager in question was played by the third assistant director, Seamus Byrne. Byrne went on to become a production manager for the 1992 Tom Cruise and Nicole Kidman film, *Far and Away*.

podcast, Six of One co-founder Dave Barrie said that he saw the remains of this mechanical disappointment junked by a wall, ready to be taken away and scrapped; divine inspiration was required. It came, so Bernard Williams maintained, when he looked up in the sky and spotted a white weather balloon floating above. Quick as a flash, he set off in a land rover, headed to the meteorological station near Penrhyndeudraeth, picked up as many weather balloons as he could and had them brought to the set[18].

While this idea solved certain problems and gave the series its most unforgettable icon, other problems came along with it. Filled with a mixture of air, helium and water, the balloons had to be guided with a fishing wire. In the final scene of 'Arrival', McGoohan has a balloon attached to his jacket. Many of them burst at the very brush of a sharp object.

Rover's debut was ingeniously staged: a ping-pong ball was balanced upon the waters of the fountain, and was then shot away by an air rifle and at that moment, the camera zoomed in to frame Rover pulsating away at the top of the building. It's a brilliant shot that must have been a nightmare to get right.

Originally, Rover sounded a little bit like Darth Vader, or someone with an aqua-lung, combined with a sinister heartbeat. It was eventually replaced by an ungodly, otherworldly roar.

CAI: The roar is genuinely terrifying, a horrible primal noise which is completely at odds with the delightful tweeness that has been all we've heard since the titles finished. It reminds me of a couple of effects from a BBC sound effects album I used to have, Death & Horror. It's like a Gregorian chant of animal noises[19].

Adding to the tension, we have our first death (or at the very least a near-fatal injury) as the dissenting villager is cornered and smothered, screaming in agony as Rover overcomes him. This is also our first whiff of rebellion…

---

[18] There are many versions of this story but only McGoohan and Williams were present at this moment of divine inspiration.

[19] According to sound editor Wilfred Thompson, the composite sound effects used for Rover included an inflated inner tube with gunshot pellets rolled around, a slowed down recording of a man screaming in a lecture hall, and a reversed monks' chorus.

CHRIS: ...or is it all staged? Another show of power? Is the villager conditioned to make a run for it so that Number 2 can show off his powers? And what the hell just happened? 'That would be telling.'

Having witnessed the Village at its most oppressive and destructive, we now move on to the banality of bureaucracy. He is taken to the Labour Exchange, which one suspects does not function anything like any Labour Exchange or Job Centre that you and I might have once frequented. Here he meets Number 20 played by Christopher Benjamin, which would have been something of a treat for fans of *Danger Man*, in which Benjamin played Potter.

Number 6 is given a quick aptitude test to perform while Christopher Benjamin plays with an elaborate wooden toy. Number 6 has to pass a square rod through a round hole; a play on the expression denoting someone who doesn't fit in. In this case, though, the square hole adapts by becoming a round hole and grips the peg. The implications are quite clear: you will conform, no matter how much you try not to fit in. The square / circle is a vivid motif which shows up repeatedly throughout the series.

Quizzed on his hobbies, likes, dislikes, family illnesses and politics, Number 6 destroys Number 20's toy with one swipe of his hand, and storms off; a perfectly reasonable response to anyone who wants to ask us too many personal questions.

Back at 'home,' Number 6 discovers that he can't even find sanctuary in his diary which, chillingly, has already been filled in by someone else: 'Arrived to-day. Made very welcome.'

He then, like any good secret agent, makes observations of his new surroundings. He inspects the own-brand cans of food, perhaps to make sure they're real. While he does this, we can get a good look at the reproduction of his actual flat and perhaps gauge something of this character from his choice of decoration.

There's a military theme running through a lot of his decor; there is global iconography everywhere and with it the inference of a well-travelled life, including the tiger-skin rug, which suggests the spoils of an African safari. The map of the world is set in curious counterpoint to the only maps available in the Village, which implies that there is no 'world' as such anymore, only the Village itself.

Having met the electrician's twin in the garden, Number 6 makes his first bid for freedom. It is here that we first see the statues, rotating busts direct their gaze at unsuspecting escapees; their eyes doubling as cameras.

CHRIS: I find the busts intriguing. Who are they? Are they the Village founders? If so, how long has the Village been there?[20] It's a question that pops up later on in 'Dance of the Dead' when he is told that it's been here for a 'long time.' 'Before the war?' he asks. '*Which* war?' he asks again, only a little louder!

Watching on the other side of the screen is the Supervisor, played by Peter Swanwick, one of the few actors to play a recurring part throughout the series. He is credited as The Supervisor but he is never actually addressed as such. He also has a number, 28.

Jack Shampan's extraordinary construction of the surveillance room, with the enormous manned camera slowly and forever turning at its centre like a centrifuge, is somewhat unbelievably the same set as the Living Space in the Green Dome, just redressed it also featured as the interior of the art gallery in 'The Chimes of Big Ben'.

So as not to give Shampan too many sleepless nights, though he confessed to several, most of the shots of The Surveillance Room were taken in this episode and largely reused throughout the series. Whenever Swanwick intones his infamous announcement, 'Orange alert, orange alert,' it's the same shot each time.

The Surveillance Room also gives us our first look at the mechanics behind the Villagers' incarceration. Until now, we've only seen the charming veneer; the ultra-hospitable, albeit occasionally terrifying exterior world in which they live.

---

[20] Note: See Alan Moore and Kevin O'Neill's *The League of Extraordinary Gentlemen: Black Dossier* (2007). The Village is referenced in connection with Big Brother's Thought Police from George Orwell's *1984*.

CAI: You're only about twenty five years here since actual wartime prisoner camps which would have been very simple caged affairs with sentry-manned gun towers and spotlights. The Surveillance Room by contrast is an incredibly futuristic, super-efficient system of incarceration. In an episode where everything has to be set up for the audience, this is the scene where you are shown just how impossible it will be to break out of there.

CHRIS: They have to establish the rules of the world they're creating, and you want to see your protagonist challenge those rules or push against them, almost like a child in a classroom pushing the boundaries, and then the teacher pushes back. He's learning these rules along with the audience.

Number 6's escape doesn't go especially well. He overpowers some villagers in a Mini Moke and drives off to the beach where Rover is waiting for him. Having foolishly tried to punch his way through the great rubber sphere, he is rendered unconscious. When he wakes, he is in the Village hospital.

CHRIS: What I like about the doctor who attends to him when he's going through the check-up, is that he goes to a computer, a classic 1960s computer with huge reel tapes. These days, if you have an appointment with your doctor or GP, they will go onto their computer and access your prior medical history. This wasn't common back in 1967, even in the US. McGoohan has the prescience here to say, 'This is what is going to happen.'

Some of the other patients recovering at the hospital seem to be beyond the help of medicinal assistance. There's a surreal, almost Dadaist nature to Number 6's brief tour of the wards. One patient, who seems to be immobilised while serenading a small ball with a never-ending gibberish song, is straight out of a Reeves & Mortimer[21] comedy sketch.

It's all scored with an underlying nursery rhyme soundtrack, pleasingly copyright-free, which only makes things creepier. In one room, a patient undergoes a form of aversion therapy, something close to the Ludovico technique in Anthony Burgess' *A Clockwork Orange*.

---

[21] Vic Reeves (Jim Moir) and Bob Mortimer (AKA *Vic and Bob*) are a British comedy duo famous for their surrealist and absurdist sketch comedy.

It's in the hospital that Number 6 meets an old friend, possibly a comrade-in-arms, Cobb, played by Paul Eddington. Alongside innumerable TV appearances, Eddington has played opposite McGoohan in *Danger Man*, which short-hands a rapport. In no time at all, their relationship feels genuine and lived-in.[22]

With Cobb dead, having leapt out of a window (conveniently off-screen), Number 6 is discharged and to Bernard Williams' delight, is given his famous blazer and trousers combo that he will be wearing for pretty much the rest of the series.

CHRIS: Number 6 gets into a Mini Moke taxi, and the driver's badge is 66. The chess-playing General at the end of the episode is also Number 66, so clearly this Number 66 badge has been doing the rounds. Much as I'd love to read something into this, let's be honest, this is just an oversight in the props department. Who'd have even noticed such a thing on the kind of small black and white TVs that most people had back then? I think Lew Grade had a good vision for the legacy of his ITC shows. Most of his shows had at least one American star in there which meant that they could be sold to US networks. His aim was syndication, possibly indefinitely, which is about right. They still show all these shows somewhere even today.

Number 6 attends Cobb's 'funeral,' almost like a show funeral, which takes place on the beach. He meets Virginia Maskell's character, Number 9 (an interesting choice; almost like a ying / yang). Number 9 is the only genuine ally in the episode. She might well have played further helpful roles in the series, but sadly, Maskell was battling severe depression, a fight she would tragically lose in January 1968.

Number 6 is duped into thinking that he can escape by stealing the Village helicopter which arrives and departs at regularly scheduled appointments. One look from George Baker's new Number 2 tells us he'll not be airborne for long.

---

[22] In their youth, McGoohan and Eddington were members of the same Sheffield Repertory company.

CHRIS: It's another show of power. They deliberately deflate him. They actually let him steal the helicopter and let him take it up just long enough to think he might succeed. That's real cruelty.

There's a chess match to conclude the episode. For the first handful of episodes, chess is an ever-present visual metaphor.

CHRIS: When you get to 'Checkmate', you realise that it's not just about being pawns or being black or white pieces, it's about being two or three moves ahead and trying to outthink your opponent. To defeat the Village, Number 6 will have to consider all the possible outcomes of his actions.

Number 6 ends up a prisoner once more. Cobb, it transpires, is alive and well and working for 'new masters,' though which ones we don't know. His departing 'Auf wiedersehen,' gives a clue but it's still an opaque one. Of Number 9, her fate is, alas, far more certain. 'We'll take good care of her,' states Number 2. Cobb replies, 'That's what I'm afraid of.'

Who's the Two?

The first Number 2 is played by Guy Doleman, another *Ipcress File* alumni (he played Michael Caine's world-weary boss, Colonel Ross in the first three Harry Palmer movies). A New Zealand-born actor, Doleman's stock in trade was withdrawn, silent types with a hint of menace, ideal for a character described in the script as 'Dangerously charming.'

CAI: He'd already done two of his Harry Palmer films before this came out, so in audiences' minds, he instantly had a natural, headmasterly authority about him, along with an enjoyably dry, laconic wit.

CHRIS: There's a nice bit of foreshadowing with his avuncular line, 'You'll be the death of me,' because shortly afterwards, he's vanished and been replaced. What happens to the Number 2s once they're done? Are they disposed of, or do they just trot off back to the House of Lords? I have to confess, Doleman's line, 'Everybody's very nice,' is one of my favourite line readings in the whole series!

Perhaps his most famous rolé apart from this was as the villainous Count Lippe in the James Bond mega-hit, *Thunderball*. Another Bond actor was George Baker, who would go on to play the genealogist, Sir Hilary Bray in *On Her Majesty's Secret Service* and dub the actor George Lazenby for about half the film, as well as a naval captain in *The Spy Who Loved Me*. His Number 2 is a marvellous blend of bonhomie and dead-eyed inflexibility. When Number 6 makes his doomed escape attempt in the helicopter, he breaks out into the kind of smile a cartoon cat would wear having spotted a mouse with a limp.

Scores

CHRIS: It was a five for me. A high score, but there are issues mainly continuity issues if I'm going to nitpick

CAI: It sets up the world well, plays with us and our expectations, and gets everything off to a good start, but the series hasn't quite found its feet yet. It was a 5 from me too, so a solid 10 for *The Prisoner*'s first adventure.

Cai: 5 out of 6
Chris: 5 out of 6

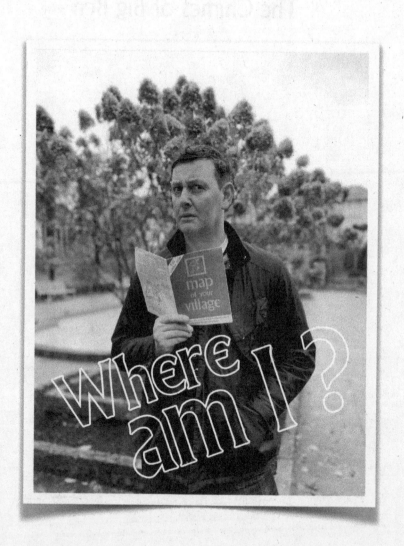

map
of your
village

Where
am I ?

episode two
The Chimes of Big Ben

Number 6 is browbeaten into looking after Nadia, a new abductee. He agrees to take part in the Village arts festival, but only so that he can construct a method of escape under his captors' noses, and take Nadia with him to freedom.

The first thing to say about this second episode is that in no way does it work as the second episode. The reason for this is that it was the fifth episode to be shot. This discrepancy between the shooting dates and the broadcast order is something that has bewitched and bedevilled Prisoner fans for decades. Several elements in 'The Chimes of Big Ben' indicate that it was shot a long way into production. A very nostalgic Number 2, when Nadia is brought in, says to Number 6, 'Ah, seems like old times.'

CHRIS: 'Once upon a Time' was actually the next episode to be filmed after this, which is pretty extraordinary[23]. Leaving such madness behind, this is an absolute knockout of an episode. The sucker-punch ending is one of the very best in the series.

CAI: I have heard some people rather sniffily dismiss the ending. "Oh, obviously, you know what's going to happen..." I bloody didn't! The way it's done too, with the heightened audio of the traffic suddenly cutting out, and the penny drops like a guillotine blade. It's heartbreaking, and he looks utterly broken at the end, moping out of there in his blue tracksuit. Some episodes end with something of a mini-victory when he wins a battle in an ongoing war. This is a complete victory for the Village.

It's an odd start. If you watch the first few shots, there are some curious editing and cinematography choices. As soon as it opens, there's a very shaky zoom, and some of the edits seem a little 'off.' The ersatz nature of a lot of the set-based locations, particularly the beach, is exposed in the light of the mainly location-shot 'Arrival' not that anyone would have noticed things like the panto-cloth background as Number 6 walks into his house when they were watching this in black and white on a small TV screen in 1967.

One of the main reasons for the high quality of this episode is the writer, Vincent Tilsley, who was one of the most prolific and highly regarded television writers in Britain at the time, with over 150 writing credits to his name. His association with McGoohan went back to the unforgiving days of live television drama. He co-wrote (with his brother, Frank) *The Makepeace Story* for Sunday Night Theatre in 1955 and starred McGoohan.

---

[23] 'Once upon a Time' was the sixth show to be produced and the penultimate episode to be screened.

There doesn't appear, at this time at least, to be a show bible, or a format document as they were known at the time in the UK. Every new TV drama series will have a show bible which details the overarching plot and various themes, the characters and their characteristics, and details of the world they inhabit. Apocryphally, McGoohan had prepared reams of fastidiously typed-up information about his *Prisoner* idea for his pitch with Lew Grade, who said, 'Just tell me what it's about, Pat.'

A show bible is essential for any new scriptwriters hired to write episodes, who may not be familiar with the lore or mythology they are about to describe.

CHRIS: You need to have as much background detail as possible and the show bible fleshes all that out, like Captain Picard from *Star Trek: The Next Generation* for example, who drinks Earl Grey tea and keeps a lion fish. The tiniest details like that, which the writers can pick up and use.

When Vincent Tilsley came to write this episode, the best Markstein could do was to show him the script for 'Arrival'. Writers and directors who had no real idea what was going on are not restricted to this episode by any means.

Several interesting characters and interesting actors make an appearance here. Christopher Benjamin pops up again, as does the great British character actor Finlay Currie as The General. Famous for roles in Powell & Pressburger's *I Know Where I'm Going!* and as Magwitch in David Lean's *Great Expectations*, he will forever remain in Chris' mind as the grumbling Councillor Duxbury in *Billy Liar!*

CAI: He was possibly the greatest ever 'In my day, lad...' actor.

CHRIS: Even though he was probably only 30 years old. It's unbelievable how young these ancient-looking actors were back then. Peter Swanwick was only forty-six when he made this!

CAI: It's what a steady diet of fried bread, forty cigarettes a day and wartime service can do to you, I suppose.

Time for tea! Tea is something of a recurring character in *The Prisoner*. Being Brits, tea is part of our cultural makeup. Number 2 knows from Number 6's file that he doesn't take sugar in his tea, Guy Doleman's Number 2 hadn't updated this minor detail. In response, Number 6 plips the first two, then a third sugar cube into his tea. 'Everything he does is an act of defiance!

Enter Nadia, played by Nadia Gray, who was a widely known actress in Europe, most famously in Fellini's *La Dolce Vita*. Perhaps this was another reason for pushing this episode forward? To capitalise on Gray's European fame?

CHRIS: On a promotional level, it's got Leo McKern, it's got Nadia Gray; you can sell that. It's a strong episode and you want a strong episode because you want to grab and keep your audience.

Number 2 makes Number 6 bear witness to Nadia's own 'arrival,' forcing him to relive his own debut, still fresh in the audience's mind. Of course, this is all just part of the grand plan, but here are some contradictions, though. When Nadia starts to swim, Number 2 is alone when he notes in her file that she is in fact an olympic-level swimmer, but no one is there to witness it, especially not Number 6, so why is Number 2 concerned in any way shape or form? Then again, could that imply that at this stage, Nadia is not complicit in Number 2's plan? Perhaps they get her in the hospital?

From Tilsley's perspective, we are meant to be rooting for Nadia and empathising with her as a victim caught in the same web as Number 6. The audience has to trust her, so we can see why McKern's scene was there: for the audience's benefit.

CAI: It's still shoddy storytelling!

Without that scene though, we would have been denied the strange spectacle of Rover and his two mini-Rover extensions, which are deployed to drag Nadia back to the beach. Ignoring the question of how smothering Nadia by pressing her face underwater didn't kill her, the mechanics of the three-part Rover are beyond intriguing. If it makes no sense, it might be because when Vincent Tilsley wrote it, he imagined Rover to be the amphibious robot, complete with hypno-light, which had yet to prove itself practically useless.

Not that Nadia Gray herself was in any danger of floating out to sea. Her beach scenes were all filmed on a not-especially convincing set at Borehamwood. Performing the actual offshore swimming was local actress, Heulwen Vaughan-Hatcher (who many *Prisoner* fans got to meet across the years when she ran the *Prisoner* shop in Portmeirion).

Upon recovering, Nadia is subjected to an almost Pavlovian set of experiments in the hospital again, duly witnessed by Number 6. She is given a bowl of water which she uses to determine which parts of the floor are electrocuted and which will give her safe passage out of the room. Instead, she makes what looks like an attempt at suicide and a panicked Number 2 aborts the exercise.

CHRIS: Number 2 has a dictaphone! He talks into a very small box, using it to amend Number 6's notes 'Must add sense of humour.' That technology didn't exist in 1967, certainly not recording devices of that size. Where would you even store the tape or the battery?

Perhaps it's Number 2 who isn't in the know at this point a touch of plausible deniability? which would explain the query about Nadia's swimming skills. We know that someone is staging it, but it is still pretty convincing. It's certainly enough to convince Number 6, who demands that they 'Let her go!'

In exchange for releasing Nadia into his care, Number 6 agrees to the barest minimum of collusion, he will enter the Village Arts Festival. To create his artwork, Number 6 heads into the forest and via a combination of unconvincing set-work, ill-matched stock footage and *The Shadows*-style guitar music, has soon felled and hollowed out an incredibly thin-looking tree using what looks like a penknife, which Number 2 kindly allows him to use despite the ownership of such tools being against regulations.

CHRIS: It's a very elaborate plan, this. There are a lot of questions in this episode, and I know that questions are a burden to others and answers a burden to oneself, but what was the goal? To get him to enter the Arts Festival? Because they don't know he's going to construct a means of escape. He could have just made a ceramic ashtray or a nice tea towel. Was Nadia the goal? To get him to form a relationship with her, fall in love with her and perhaps get him to confide in her? I think they're improvising here, to see what'll happen next.

There's a healthy amount of ridicule at the expense of modern art in all its intellectual emptiness in this scene. There's even a potentially scatological reading in the fact that everything on display is literally number two.

Every piece exhibited is a portrait in some form or other of Number 2, all except Number 6's postmodern abstract piece, 'Escape.' 'I don't understand,' questions one of the judges. 'Where's Number 2?'

Is this sycophancy? Are they afraid of Number 2? Are they trying to curry favour with him? Or is it a sideswipe at the kind of iconic propaganda beloved by 20th century despots and dictators?

That said, one can also enjoy the parallel between modern art's openness to every permutation of interpretation and McGoohan's desire for *The Prisoner* to be critiqued in the same way, 'It is what it is.'

There's a lot of relationship-building in this episode, all very deftly done. There's a lovely scene where she visits him at his house and he makes them breakfast. Unusually for Number 6, he is clearly enjoying her company. His relationship with Number 2 also appears to be one of mutual respect, however much both parties are lying to each other.

Outside Number 6's house one balmy evening, *The Prisoner* comes as close as it will ever come to featuring a romantic scene, as Number 6 and Nadia spend a few moments bonding across a café table under the stars.

CAI: It's all very *Lady & The Tramp*, isn't it? McGoohan all but nudges a meatball towards her with his nose.

This is quite a famous scene in *Prisoner* lore, largely for what doesn't happen. McGoohan was noted for his refusal to engage in anything remotely lascivious in his television roles. If Roger Moore had been cast as Number 6, there would have been at least one romantic tryst per episode. In this scene, Number 6 brushes Nadia's hair off her shoulder. That's your lot. (A pretty unlikely rumour circulated that McGoohan had his own daughter sit in for Nadia Gray's reverse shots, to entirely remove even the tiniest vestiges of romance from the scene.)

As they bond (or pretend to), Nadia refers to Big Ben in London as 'Big Bill,' which seems like a desperately unlikely pocket of cultural ignorance for an intelligence officer so important that she warrants capture and immobilisation in the Village. It does, though, allow her to humanise Number 6 by giving him a playful nickname.

Their relationship builds still further during their escape when they are both hermetically sealed in a large, two-berth crate. Nadia probes him for more personal details, flirtatiously asking if he has a wife back home. All very sweet, and all the more heartbreaking for us at the crushing finale.

One of the very first special features on the 1992 Polygram VHS release of *The Prisoner* was an alternative version of 'The Chimes of Big Ben', which tantalisingly suggested all manner of wonderful new scenes. Sadly, there's only really one, in which Number 6 uses an ancient astronomical device called a triquetrum to divine the location of the Village from the position of the stars.

CAI: There's a nice story about the 'stars' in that scene. They were borrowed from the effects department of *2001: A Space Odyssey* which was shooting at Borehamwood at the same time. I'm not sure if Stanley Kubrick knew about it!

Using Number 6's artwork, which he reassembles as a small boat to which he mischievously adds a Number 2 tapestry as a sail; Nadia and Number 6 make their escape, aided by a pair of Nadia's contacts. Number 6 borrows a watch from one of them, to help calculate the time of his journey home.

Despite the intervention of Rover, who it seems does not care for being shot at, there is already a creeping sense that this is not going to end well. There is a half-smile on Peter Swanwick's face when their ruse is discovered, recalling George Baker's look of delight in 'Arrival'. To continue the chess allegory, the Village masters are already several moves ahead of our hero. It's telling that when he is playing chess with the General (Finlay Currie), he isn't playing it very well.

CHRIS: He hasn't foreseen the end result. Maybe they've already planned for contingency in various ways? Perhaps if he hadn't built the boat and stolen the tapestry as a sail, Nadia would have 'stolen' an electro-pass or 'discovered' a secret tunnel?

Number 6 is delivered back to his old office in London. Nadia is escorted out, while Number 6 is gently interrogated by his old comrades in arms. There is much talk of disappearing across the Iron Curtain and swapping sides. The Colonel (Kevin Stoney) appears deeply sceptical about the fabulous talk of villages and numbered residents. Eventually, Number 6 is persuaded to explain why he resigned. 'I resigned because for a long time now, I... wait a minute...'

They were just one chime away from getting it out of him. It's all a marvellously convoluted con. Number 6 never left the Village. His old office has been reconstructed there and the sounds of London are being piped in via a recording. Were it not for the fact that his borrowed watch was set to Polish time, which didn't correspond to the chimes of Big Ben in the recorded soundscape, he would have elaborated at length about the matter of conscience he briefly alludes to.

He leaves, broken and dejected, opening the doors and walking back out into the prison he's been living in since his capture. Moreover, Nadia is revealed to have been playing him all along.

Had this denouement taken place in London, with the scam taking place there, it would set the seal on the theory that MI5 or the British were the ones running the Village, but because Number 6 has never actually left the Village, a certain ambiguity remains, despite the presence of two faces familiar to Number 6. They would have been familiar to *Danger Man* fans too; The Colonel played by Kevin Stoney supporting a tremendous moustache, and 1950s British comedy film stalwart Richard Wattis as Fotheringay. Nothing explicit is said, but who's to say that these two aren't double agents? They're never seen again even in later episodes featuring Number 6's old comrades.

CHRIS: It raises an interesting possibility. If everything that is taking place is an allegory, then it's like a dream. From a fantastical individual's perspective, he is casting characters and using situations from his own experience. He's taking a face from someone he doesn't like and applying it to Number 2, as

47

he'll later do with Patrick Cargill[24], for instance. It's something of a solecistic interpretation: he's the only person in the universe and everyone else is a construct designed to facilitate his being a bit like *The Truman Show*, which as far as I'm concerned is a contemporary *Prisoner* remake in all but name and much more effective and ingenious than the actual remake in 2009.

CAI: The use of 'love' as a means to destroy agents, foreign and domestic, was standard fare in a lot of Cold War spy dramas. Most of John le Carré's spies had their lives upended by lovers who were often working for the other side. This is the only time the Village uses love as a weapon to trick Number 6 into the big reveal, and it's telling that this is as close as they ever get to getting it out of him.

At one point, Number 2 memorably justifies the Village. 'When both sides are facing each other, suddenly they realise that they're staring into a mirror and they'll see that this is the pattern for the future.' There are allusions here to what was going on in Britain at the time, leading up to the application to join what was then known as the Common Market.

CAI: It was very much in the air back in the late sixties. Was it a good thing? Was it a bad thing? Surprisingly, there were several voices on the left like Tony Benn who was very much against it, so there are interesting questions to be asked about this. I wonder, did McGoohan see this as a good thing

CHRIS: Or was Number 6 a secret Brexiteer?!

This was Don Chaffey's final episode in order of production; he had already directed 'Dance of the Dead' and 'Checkmate'. All of them shot largely in Portmeirion. It has been suggested that by the time of the fifth episode, McGoohan himself was directing many of the scenes being shot at Borehamwood. It has also been hinted that by this point, the relationship between the director and star was starting to fray at the edges.

---

[24] The episodes being 'Many Happy Returns' and 'Hammer into Anvil' in which Cargill appears both times.

Who's the Two?

Sydney-born Leo McKern is still perhaps best known in the UK for his signature role, Horace Rumpole QC in *Rumpole of The Bailey* (1978-92) but his CV is full of memorable, often scene-stealing performances. He was an effective scheming Thomas Cromwell in *A Man For All Seasons* (1966). Equally impressive was his bullish newspaper editor Bill Maguire in *The Day The Earth Caught Fire* (1961), and on a lighter note, proved a delightful comic foil as Klang, the cult leader pursuing The Beatles and Ringo in particular, in *Help!* (1965).

He enjoyed the actor's gift of an extraordinarily expressive face with thousands of tales chiselled into it. Further to that, he is possessed of the great authority of immense intelligence, which is desperately hard to fake. This is something he brings to his Number 2. Despite all his bonhomie and friendliness, he can turn on a sixpence to reveal an all-too-dark alter-ego. He has only to growl the word 'whimpering' to let us know that there is nothing he won't do to defeat his quarry.

He had an unexpected athleticism to him, he walks as if he is on springs. Look at the way he bounds onto the podium in the arts festival scene.

CHRIS: One thing that I really love about his performance in this is his swing from a sinister authority figure, mellowing into a more friendly companion when he feels like Number 6 is starting to acquiesce to the task, winking a 'blind surveillance eye' at Number 6's minor transgressions. There are, very subtly, lots of different sides to him and they have a genuine rapport.

CAI: Or is it all, absolutely all of it, play-acting? By appearing in three episodes, a record for Number 2s, he alone is given something of a character arc. His three episodes do make a certain sense as a three-parter. He is a company man, 'a lifer,' in 'Chimes', conflicted, determined and somewhat betrayed in 'Once upon a Time', and swaps sides in 'Fall Out'.

CHRIS: You could argue that he is the closest thing to an actual nemesis. He represents the Village, but there's also a lot of McGoohan's character in there too. He thought (in this episode at least) that Number 6 had accepted his place, while he determinedly has not. Also, I have to say, he reminds me so much in this episode of actor Matt Berry, who seems to have carved out an entire career by channelling Leo McKern's Number 2.

He made such a huge impact in this role that he became synonymous with the part. In much of the fan-fiction and *Prisoner* spin-offs (the DC produced graphic novel *Shattered Visage* being the best example), it is McKern who represents the office of Number 2. Compounded by his key role in later episodes, 'Once upon a Time' and 'Fall Out', McKern can lay claim to being the definitive Number 2.

CHRIS: One thing that amused me was that in Spotlight, the actors' directory, McKern and McGoohan were listed right next to each other for years, despite having never met.

CAI: There's an oft-repeated anecdote about the first time they did meet on the set, presumably later on in the pub. 'Patrick McGoohan's first words to him were apparently, 'You're a funny little fucker, aren't you?'

The two actors did become very close, McGoohan often spoke about 'Leo' and how wonderful he was in later interviews. They shared very similar ideas about the freedom of the individual and, unlike perhaps one or two other members of the *Prisoner* crew, understood exactly what McGoohan was shooting for.

At the time of his casting, McKern was on the London stage performing Ben Jonson's *Volpone*. When casting director Rose Tobias-Shaw picked McKern, his Spotlight photo depicting him immaculately clean-shaven, she hadn't realised that he was now wearing a full-grown *Volpone* beard, which needed to remain intact for later performances. This proved an interesting challenge to the art department, who had already created several McKern-based props for the arts festival scene, all of which had to have beards very quickly added to them, even the chess piece!

CAI: Do you think McKern got to take any of that stuff home with him? What else are they going to do with it? 'Sorry mate, we need this huge tapestry with your face on it for an episode of *The Champions*. No can do.'

CHRIS: Hardly any props from *The Prisoner* ever pop up on sites like eBay, curiously. Some things surface occasionally but there's rarely any provenance.

He's under surveillance himself. He's the most complicated of the Number 2s; a genuinely fascinating character as opposed to a stock villain.

Scores

CAI: I thought this was a firm 5.

CHRIS: I gave it 5 and a half. Or 5.6. I prefer this episode over 'Arrival' and I gave that 5. I prefer it for many reasons, especially that twist.

CAI: It's wonderful. It's a very well-put-together episode. It's intriguing, interesting, you see a slightly different side to Number 6 here, you have the definitive Number 2. It's a high five.

Cai: 5 out of 6
Chris: 5.5 out of 6

A. B. and C.

The Village scientists have developed a technique for watching and even manipulating people's dreams. Number 2 uses it on Number 6 to try and learn the identity of a mysterious double-agent.

'A Play in Three Acts' was the original title of the episode, then '1. 2. and 3', until finally they settled on 'A. B. and C.'. It is an interesting tale in many ways, least of all in its unlikely positioning as the third episode. More fascinatingly, it's the only episode to deal with the oneiric theme of dreaming. A scientist has discovered a means to witness and even manipulate someone else's dreams. Number 2 (Colin Gordon) unleashes this potentially dangerous, not quite perfected technique on Number 6, to uncover the identity of an elusive spy.

Number 2 suspects that the reason Number 6 resigned was that he was about to sell secrets to the 'other side.' On that line of enquiry, Number 2 has whittled the suspects down to three possible turncoats. While under sedation, Number 6 is encouraged to 'meet' each one, and hopefully give away his motives in his sleep.

CAI: We don't know what the third spy looks like but the first looks a lot like Peter Bowles, sporting one of his most luxurious moustaches in a long career that boasted several superb soup-strainers.

This was first broadcast in the UK on Friday the 13th of October 1967, reaching an audience of 10.9 million. It was directed by Pat Jackson, who was a popular ITC helmer though he was brought in at the eleventh hour to replace Michael Truman.[25]

CAI: Pat Jackson was viewed as a safe pair of hands, which has connotations of faint praise, but he was far more accomplished than that.

CHRIS: What I find lovely about Jackson is that he was pretty much a cinematic polymath. He was a director, producer, writer, cinematographer, actor, a production designer and an editor. He'd worked with the GPO Unit in the war making propaganda films for the British. He had a Hollywood contract, scoring a hit in 1944 with *Western Approaches* which was the one that put him on the map.

CAI: Katherine Kath described her time making this episode as 'joyous,' and a lot of that can be put down to Pat Jackson's professionalism and his

---

[25] Actress Katherine Kath (Engadine) suggested that Truman had a nervous breakdown.

ability to run a non-conflicted set. He was something of an unsung hero in the *Prisoner* story.

It's a sort of proto-version of *Inception*. There are also echoes of a *Danger Man* episode called 'The Ubiquitous Mr Lovegrove' (directed by Don Chaffey), which was a classic 'it's all a dream in the end' story. John Drake initially doesn't realise that he's in the middle of a dream. As in 'A. B. and C', characters are created within this dream world and concerns and worries manifest.

CHRIS: This was never one of my favourite episodes. I wouldn't say that I used to skip it, but I certainly never gave it much status. Watching it again with fresh eyes, I enjoyed it.

CAI: I did too, and I remembered it as being a sort of filler episode and I think it was made with similarly unambitious intentions. I've read that David Tomblin, with money on the wane and an episode still required, basically grabbed writer Anthony Skene and asked him to write an episode that could be put together using lots of stock footage.

At the time of production, the crew had limited access to Portmeirion so the shots of McGoohan walking around are almost all of his stunt-double Frank Maher walking away from the camera. Maher is in this episode so much he really ought to have been given a separate credit!

Seeking inspiration, Anthony Skene went for a walk around Borehamwood and found a film crew shooting *The Dirty Dozen*. He decided to write his story to accommodate these pre-existing sets. It was heavily influenced by one of his scripts for a TV show called *Counterstrike*, starring Jon Finch. His episode, 'Nocturne' was never used, so was retrofitted for *The Prisoner*.

Such a desperate-sounding provenance hardly sets one's anticipation to the maximum, and yet Tomblin and George Markstein both regularly cited this as one of their favourite episodes.

Number 6 is repeatedly drugged and taken to a secret laboratory where his dreams can be played out on a large screen for the benefit of Number 2 and Number 14. Interestingly, he is dreaming the title sequence from a third-person perspective, taking the recycled footage policy into a subconscious dimension.

CHRIS: This is the closest thing in the series to being a 'bottle episode,' that is to say an episode that takes place in a restricted location largely as a way to keep costs down. It certainly would have been one of the cheaper episodes to make. All the sets they shot on were already there.

As 'A,' Peter Bowles is one of the highlights of a guest-star-heavy episode, giving a sinister, possibly coded homoerotic performance as a villainous traitor, making a huge impression with only a brief appearance. He purringly talks about spies who have defected recently and 'made world news.' Robert Fairclough in his superb book, *The Prisoner: The Official Companion to The Classic TV Series* establishes a link to the notorious Cambridge spy scandal of the early-1960s, with 'A. B. and C' representing Guy Burgess, Kim Philby and Donald Maclean.

The heavy emphasis on spycraft and espionage could be seen as something of a sop to the *Danger Man* fans in the audience and might help to explain why an episode shot so late in the running (it was the 10th episode to be produced) was slotted in so early in the broadcast schedule.

'B' is played by Annette Carell, a German actress with several British TV credits to her name before her appearance here. Sadly she died a week after the first UK airing of the episode. Georgina Cookson (Mrs Butterworth in 'Many Happy Returns') also appears playing a nameless guest at the central party, another case of an actor turning up more than once in the series as different characters; or are they the same character?

CHRIS: My interpretation is that it's an internal casting by the individual character. The only person who is real in Number 6's mind is Number 6. He represents the individual in society so to play out this psycho-drama, he is casting from his own experience; putting faces onto these characters from people that he knows and perhaps doesn't like. Or it could just be a matter of which actor was available at the time.

CAI: I prefer your first theory!

CHRIS: It reminds me of a serial killer film called *Identity*, starring John Cusack. The twist (spoiler alert!) is that the characters within the story are all facets of the killer's personality. Maybe, in *The Prisoner*, the characters are all elements of Number 6's psyche? His fears, his concerns, his passions, his insecurities? By defeating these authority figures each week, he is breaking down his own failings. This is very much the Jungian theory!

Each spy is represented in Number 14's laboratory by a thick red box folder which contains their photograph and the reel of film which spools into Number 6's thoughts. These red folders are clearly the property of the ITC props department, two of them (B&C) reappeared in the 1969 episode of *Randall & Hopkirk (Deceased)*, 'A Disturbing Case'.

The red symbology continues with the telephone, which has never looked so threatening as when picked up reluctantly by a lip-trembling Colin Gordon. It must be said that in purely utilitarian terms, the design of this phone is a disaster, so cumbersome and elongated that holding the receiver to the ear leaves the mouthpiece half a metre from one's chin. Steve Jobs would never have green-lit such an unwieldy design!

So much for the form, but the function is to dominate Number 2 which it certainly does simply by ringing and visually, by being much bigger than Colin Gordon's head. Whomever is at the other end of the line is clearly not one who takes bad news well. The insinuation that it is Number 1 calling in for results is curious, given what we will discover in 'Fall Out'. In this episode, Number 1 is more of a Markstein creation; an unseen Blofeld variant, finger hovering above the button that drops his underlings into the piranha pool.

CHRIS: Like a bad manager, Number 2 is forever blaming others for his mistakes. Despite several warnings that the technology has not been perfected yet, he insists that Number 14 presses on and warns her that any failure will be her fault. This cocktail of narcissism, paranoia and ineptitude would resurface later on with Patrick Cargill's version of Number 2 in the episode 'Hammer into Anvil'.

Playing Madame Engadine, the hostess of this grand party is esteemed French actress Katherine Kath, giving a wonderfully broad and flirty performance in a billowing diaphanous ball gown. Kath was predominantly a respected movie actress in her native France but was not above making appearances in a 1957 episode of *The Benny Hill Show*.

Her party is a gloriously groovy sixties 'happening' which wouldn't have looked out of place in an episode of *The Man From U.N.C.L.E.* It's an effectively vibrant location to thrice stage the same 'dream memory.' Each time Number 6 is made to revisit this soirée, things alter slightly, as he fights for control of his mind. In one incredible shot, facing a mirror, McGoohan grabs the frame and starts to turn the room on an angle, and we the audience with it.

CAI: In perhaps the most quotable line of the episode, McGoohan barks, 'It's a pretty dreamy party,' in a way that only he would ever have attempted; unique in its staccato delivery and the way he says 'party' in a manner one imagines a hallucinating parrot might try.

Towards the end of the episode, we are treated to a marvellous moment of self-awareness, as the dream version of Number 6 speaks directly to Number 2 and Number 14, but is essentially talking to us. The much-vexed question of 'Who is Number 1?' threatens to be answered but the shocking reveal turns out to be a bluff. In exposing 'Number 2' as the ultimate villain, in doing so revealing that he's been onto him the whole time, he proffers Colin Gordon towards not just his captors but us, the TV audience. This rather cheeky riposte would have worked a lot better had this been a much later episode, after weeks and months of speculation about the identity of Number 1 was reaching fever pitch.

Perhaps the spectacle of McGoohan dressed to the nines in an immaculate dinner jacket could be another Easter egg in plain sight; a taste of what his James Bond might have looked like had he not famously turned down the role.

Finally, Number 6 teases Number 2 with the answer to the biggest secret of all: why he resigned. For a brief moment, Number 2 sees all his problems vanishing as he grasps the possibility of the ultimate success, only for Number 6 to reveal that he was simply going on holiday, as suggested by the rather convenient photos of palm trees thrust into his case each week in the opening credits.

CHRIS: I think that this is McGoohan slyly letting us know that we're all barking up the wrong tree. If you're concerned by the mystery and the motives, if you think this is a John Drake show, you're missing the point.

Who's the Two?

Born in Ceylon (formerly Sri Lanka), Colin Gordon was essentially a 1950s British Army Major type from central casting, though he was equally at home playing officious, mid-level bureaucratic authority figures like bank managers or foreign ambassadors, though in the Boulting Brothers' *Heavens Above!* he was promoted up to Prime Minister.

He had a great gift for straight parts in broad comedies, allowing big-performance actors like Peter Sellers to bounce off him effectively in *Casino Royale* and *The Pink Panther*. Gordon's work in several movies and television shows stands up to this day, mainly because he never looked any different in any of them.

He was 55 when he played Number 2 in *The Prisoner* but, in contrast to pretty much everyone else in the cast, seems much younger. In one scene when he wakes up (in the middle of the day!) blonde streaks in his hair are visible making him seem even more youthful.

Gordon was the only actor apart from Leo McKern to have been given two cracks at playing Number 2. His trademark is his ever-present glass of milk, suggesting either a healthy appreciation of the benefits of calcium or more likely the presence of a stomach ulcer brought on by stress.

In a slight but telling change to the opening titles, Colin Gordon intones 'I am Number 2,' as opposed to 'I am the *new* Number 2.'

CHRIS: I have a theory about this. In 'The General', which was shot after this episode, he goes back to saying 'The new Number 2,' suggesting that this was supposed to go out after 'The General', which makes sense in many ways. In 'The General', his character is very confident and cocksure, completely certain about the success of his plan. In this, following 'The General's explosive failure (pun intended), he is a bag of nerves, constantly staring in horror at the colossal phone, as though this was his second and very last chance to get it right.

Just as one tries to decode this alteration, Gordon distracts your attention with easily the most forced and unconvincing end-of-titles maniacal laugh of the entire series.

'A. B. and C' is a fun, perfectly enjoyable, and ingeniously put-together episode that belies its budgetary shortcomings; put together with extraordinary competence. The concept that 'they' can get you, even in your dreams, is a precursor to iconic films like *Inception* and the *Nightmare on Elm Street* series. *Pulp Fiction* co-writer Roger Avary is clearly a fan. In his 1995 movie *Killing Zoe*, one of the characters lists 'A. B. and C.' as his favourite *Prisoner* episode. But did we…?

Scores

CAI: I gave it a 4, and not in a bad way. It's fun escapism and well-made… but it *is* filler. Good filler and better than I remember, but it is inescapably disposable.

CHRIS: It was a 4 from me too. It doesn't drive Number 6's character arc. It's there to provide an extra episode and to appeal to the *Danger Man* crowd with some sci-fi-tinged spy tropes, but it was better than I remembered.

Cai: 4 out of 6
Chris: 4 out of 6

episode four
Free For All

Number 2 convinces Number 6 to run against him in the Village elections. Sensing an opportunity to escape, Number 6 agrees, but his maverick tendencies lead to him being brainwashed. Victory in the election leads only to unexpected revelations making escape seem more impossible than ever.

Brilliant title, I think you'll agree. The fourth episode to be broadcast but the second to be shot was written by one Paddy Fitz, who was better known to his pals as Patrick Joseph McGoohan (Fitzpatrick was his mother's maiden name). We talked in previous chapters about why such pure entertainment as 'The Chimes of Big Ben' and 'A. B. and C' were front-loaded in the schedule to help build and maintain a large audience. 'Free For All' was designed to be the second episode and it makes sense as the second episode, with lots of references to Number 6 being 'new here' but if this actually was the second episode, we suspect the effects could have been severe on the viewing figures.

CAI: It is such a brutally pessimistic episode that I think a lot of the core ITC crowd would have been so unnerved by it that they might not have come back for more. It's that good!

CHRIS: They needed a buffer zone of espionage tropes before they got here, but there is so much depth in this episode. You can rip apart every scene. There's no chaff.

This was written and shot in an election year when Harold Wilson and the Labour Party were returned to power. It's actually hard to pinpoint where McGoohan stood politically. He appears neither left nor right, and not even centrist, objective politics viewed through a greater lens.

Patrick McGoohan also directed this episode, credited under his own name, but it's something of a contentious credit. Don Chaffey was the original director and did indeed shoot many of the scenes, largely the ones set in Portmeirion. ('Free For All' is one of the very best Portmeirion episodes, benefitting from reams of footage shot there with all the guest stars in attendance.) However, according to several reports, when the interiors were shot at Borehamwood, McGoohan was the one holding the bullhorn yelling 'Action.'

Film librarian, Tony Sloman said in 1999, "'Free For All' particularly, was directed by Don Chaffey, and Pat didn't like it. Don and Pat were very close and Pat really wanted to take over 'Free For All' and shoot new material." It's worth saying that this wasn't an irreparable Kinski / Herzog-style fallout, a rapprochement suggested by Chaffey's director credit in the very McGoohan-shot 'Checkmate'.

In 1983, McGoohan stated, 'When I write my scripts, I do them very fast. The three I wrote for *The Prisoner*, I did in 36 hours at a stretch for each one.'

CAI: One wonders where the hand of George Markstein lay in this episode because he would, I suspect, have been pretty cold on this one. If he had anything to do with it, it would have been adding a speedboat chase so the *Danger Man* fans watching might have been able to get their bearings a little.

Continuing *The Prisoner*'s uncanny prescience, Number 2 appears in Number 6's room on the television, via call screen, much like we do today on interminable Zoom meetings, but certainly not back in 1967. Continuing the reality-defying logic first seen in 'Arrival', Number 2 is able to turn up in person at the front door seconds after Number 6 has turned off his screen. The mountain does, as instructed, come to Mohammed.

'Everest, I presume?' Like two cats unknown to each other, Numbers 6 and 2 now circle each other cautiously, sizing the other up in a scene filled with delightful and fascinating dialogue. One reference that neither of us, nor I suspect many seventeen-year-olds were aware of on first viewing is Number 6's expression, 'According to the rules of Hoyle,' whilst setting terms with Number 2[26]

In a rather sweet moment, the discussion about Number 6 running for the Village election opposite Number 2 spills over into breakfast, and Number 6 offers some toast for his apparently benevolent captor. Breakfast has already played a major role in *The Prisoner* thus far. This is the third excellent breakfast that our hero has been offered; today kippers are on the menu.

Although there is an apparent moment of detente, the chess match is ongoing. In each shot of Number 6, we can see him working out his next move in his head. His entire body language turns suddenly on a sixpence, his eyes flickering surreptitiously when he spots a potential opportunity for escape. 'What happens if I win?'

---

[26] Edmond Hoyle was an 18th century writer and the ultimate authority on the rules of card games, so much so that "according to Hoyle" became a widely used phrase signifying strict adherence to the rules of the game.

If he wins, promises Number 2, 'Number 1 will no longer be a mystery to you.' An interesting proposition, knowing what we know about the final episode. In a way, this line very quietly pre-empts and makes succinct everything that McGoohan would eventually say about what Number 1 really represents.

Following Number 2 around and attending to his every whim is his maid, Number 58, played by Rachel Herbert. Herbert had worked with McGoohan in *Danger Man* and he had noted her great skill with accents, which she deployed magnificently here, fluently speaking a language made up entirely of gibberish. Apparently. McGoohan himself made up the language and Herbert played it backwards and learned to speak the results! 'She doesn't even speak English!' barks Number 6 at one point.

Number 2's aside that She may be a *mere* 58...' suggests for the first time that there might be a hierarchy of numbers, which shows just how valuable the single-digit Number 6 is to the Village.

That he was going to run for office was never in doubt, certainly not to Number 2. The shutters open to reveal a Village full of political campaigners, many of them carrying placards pledging their loyalty to the brand-new candidate (including Nadia Gray's body double, Heulwen Vaughan-Hatcher[27]).

The election process itself throws up all manner of issues. If Number 2s are only elected once a year, how is it that Number 6 has to do battle with so many of them? In fact, in *It's Your Funeral* we even have an incumbent Number 2, with a new one ready to take over. Perhaps by that episode, they've decided that dictatorship is the way forward after all, as Number 6 says here, 'everyone votes for a dictator.'

CHRIS: It plays into the idea of each episode standing alone rather than being part of a narrative arc. It's almost like you can take every episode as a self-contained standalone, so the rules of one episode don't necessarily have to inform another. The fact that we don't confront many of the constructs of

---

[27] Heulwen Vaughan-Hatcher appeared numerous times in the series including appearances as the bikini clad girl at the swimming pool in 'Arrival' and the Spanish dancer in 'Dance of the Dead'. In later years, Heulwen took over the running of the *Prisoner* shop at Portmeirion.

'Free For All' in later episodes creates a narrative problem, but I think that it's by design.

For an episode that ultimately ends in hopelessness and cynicism, 'Free For All' is not without its lighter moments. In fact, it might well boast some of the sharpest humour of the entire series. Harold Berens, a great favourite of McGoohan's, wrings some marvellous comic mileage in his role as political journalist Number 113, replacing Number 6's repeated 'no comment' with anodyne slogans. When Number 6 snaps, 'Mind your own business,' 113 quotes him as saying, 'No comment.'[28]

CHRIS: It's a fabulous precursor to the fake news of today; putting words into people's mouths and misquoting them as 'alternative facts.' Another way of looking at it is that fake news is nothing new.

As soon as his 'interview' takes place, it is already printed in the latest copy of the *Tally Ho!* Much as with social media or the twenty-four-hour rolling headlines of today, the news is reported instantly in all its sensationalist, factually dubious glory.

There's something of a conflict in the etymology of the phrase, 'Tally Ho!' Some people believe that it's derived from a Saxon war cry "Taille Haut," meaning 'Swords up,' but the French had been shouting 'taïaut!' at their hunting hounds since the 18th century, which makes it the most likely antecedent of the classic British fox-hunters cry.

CAI: There's a sly implication from the name *Tally Ho* that the newspaper does what all tabloid newspapers do, it hunts people. There's a predatory aspect to the tawdry end of the tabloid news; these disgusting paparazzi people chasing people with cameras. Already a megastar by now, McGoohan would I'm sure have developed a distaste for that aspect of being a famous actor.

Number 6 makes the first speech of his campaign to an audience who are at first scornful, then suddenly completely won over by his words. 'I am not a number. I am a person. In some place, at some time, all of you held positions

---

[28] 113 is ably assisted by a photographer, 113b played by Dene Cooper, the only known instance of a sub-number in the series.

of a secret nature and had knowledge that was invaluable to an enemy. Like me, you are here to have that knowledge protected or extracted. Unlike me, many of you have accepted the situation of your imprisonment and will die here like rotten cabbages. The rest of you have gone over to the side of our keepers. Which is which? How many of each? Who's standing beside you now? I intend to discover who are the prisoners and who are the warders.' Immediately, the square is full of 'Vote For Number 6' placards passionately waved by devoted followers; the photo used is one of McGoohan's publicity stills.

While Number 6 makes his speech, Angelo Muscat's Butler holds up dummy cards telling the crowds what to shout in response. At one point, they are prompted to shout 'Progress! Progress! Progress!' The entire scene encapsulates McGoohan's dismissive view on the manipulative and empty nature of party politics, the partisan nature of the press and even the willing participation in all this phoniness of the voters themselves who know so little that they have to have their own opinions spoon-fed to them by their masters.

We came across some rather wonderful testimonies of what it was like to work with Patrick McGoohan during the filming of this episode. Many actors and extras said that McGoohan was the perfect gentleman, very professional and encouraging, but there was a local extra named Samuel Owen Hughes, who accidentally stood on McGoohan's foot. He apologised immediately, at which McGoohan retorted angrily, 'Shut up! It's a *scene*!' It sounds like he was a friendly, genuine person until one got to the technical intricacies of making a television show, and then he expected a high level of proficiency and professionalism. You have to be on your game, and ideally not step on his foot.

CHRIS: He surrounded himself on this project with people that he knew would deliver the goods and could be relied upon for their professionalism. In the world of television production, in which McGoohan was now steeped, you have a limited budget and a certain amount of time to shoot. You might want to do a hundred takes but you simply don't have the time.

CAI: Rachel Herbert said that he was an absolute darling, calling her to make sure her room in Portmeirion was comfortable enough for her. A true gentleman, but… just make sure you're on the set on time.

Number 6 is then presented to the council. The councillors themselves may as well be, as Number 6 says, 'tailor's dummies.' They are completely passive and unresponsive, even when Number 6 questions them with understandable irritation. They seem to be there to represent an unelected body with a complete absence of power. Like most parish councillors in the UK, they don't have any actual 'power.' There's a sense of it, possibly the illusion of it, but ultimately it only amounts to suggesting where certain shrubberies should be placed and suchlike. Number 6 calls them a '20th century Bastille that pretends to be a pocket democracy.'

Number 2 is the only actual power here, save that of the glowing eye above his chair, an extremely curious addition to the set design, namely the eye within a triangle logo denoting … The Illuminati? (sinister organ chord). So much nonsense has been written about the Illuminati and their supposed control over everything that we'd rather not take you down that road, but it does reinforce the central conceit of this scene: is democracy a delusion? Are the outcomes the same regardless of who we vote for?

Even Number 2 is ultimately a replaceable figurehead serving under an absolute ruler, rather than someone with his hands gripping the levers of power. When Number 6 does eventually do a Liz Truss[29] and becomes Number 2 at the end of the episode for the briefest possible time, it turns out that he has no actual power at all.

Having enraged the council and Number 2 with his impertinence, Number 6 is literally taken for a spin and subjected to a hallucinogenic freak-out, eventually finding himself entertained in a subterranean chamber by the new director of the labour exchange, Number 26, played by George Benson (the delightful veteran character actor rather than the acclaimed jazz singer and *Give Me The Night* hitmaker). Number 26 interrogates Number 6 with a very Village-like combination of warmth, charm, courtesy and sinisterness. 'That shows that you're afraid!' he chirps in delight at the revelation of Number 6's reduced (and once again wildly inconsistent) sugar intake.

CAI: There's a fantastic line, worthy of *Yes Minister* when Number 2, watching all this unfold onscreen, is asked where they found Number 26 and he replies, 'The civil service. He fit right in.'

This doesn't quite explain why he's wearing a morning jacket; hardly standard civil service garb. Morning suits were traditionally worn by country gentlemen in the morning before a day's horse riding. Tally ho?

Number 26's examination of Number 6 involves the return of the circle and square motif first seen in 'Arrival'. Here, they are shown in silhouette lined up towards Number 6's mind. Lies will mean the shapes shift closer to his brain, truth will keep them at bay. Neither of us has any idea how this works in practice, but the image is certainly striking. There is a suggestion of some kind of telepathy or some kind of mental manipulation. Whatever is happening, it's all too much for Number 6, who passes out exhausted in his chair.

Following this 'treatment,' he wakes up a new man. A very different man. Transformed into the ultimate blandly insincere political candidate, his first thought is to shake Number Number 26's hand and ask, 'You will be voting

---

[29] Liz Truss (Conservative) was one of the shortest serving British Prime Ministers with a total of only 49 days in office.

for me, I hope?' He takes on the slogans and the vocabulary of the establishment.

CHRIS: This is something that's become incredibly noticeable in the UK and the US in the last few years, well, twas ever thus really, but it's intensified of late. Politicians will turn up on TV or the radio just repeating slogans along party lines. Repetition, repetition, repetition *ad nauseam*, as if it was any kind of answer. In one scene during his 'campaign,' Number 6 is simply reading this nonsense from a prompt card being held up for him.

Having been driven to the brink of madness by Rachel Herbert's manic gobbledygook, Number 6 briefly snaps out of his brainwashed trance and makes a break for it. Cue an action-packed sequence involving a speedboat chase and some not-especially-convincing stunt doubles.

CAI: I think Markstein would have insisted on something like this. There's a certain amount of expectation in an ITC show. Even in one as rich in allegory as this episode... at some point, you still need to have a foot chase and someone getting punched in the face.

Number 6 is eventually apprehended by Rover, who is then seen for the only time returning to the bottom of the sea, scored by some memorably Hammer horror-style music. This smothering encounter leaves Number 6 in the hospital. As he rests there, he has a dream which recaps the events of the episode thus far. Strangely, the dialogue spoken by Number 2 in the council chamber is different: he complements and congratulates Number 6, rather than banging his gavel and chiding him. This is clearly by design, the Village is manipulating his thought processes. To a certain extent, Number 6 as we know him, is absent from this episode for huge swathes of the narrative. From the moment he wakes up in his chair and shakes George Benson's hand, he is a brainwashed robot controlled by others.

CHRIS: You need to take Number 6's true intentions out and replace them with something else to emphasise the falseness, hypocrisy and two-facedness of politics.

Number 6 spends the evening in the Village pub, The Cat & Mouse, making its sole appearance in the series. Despite the fact that alcohol is not allowed in the Village, he appears quite addled; most likely a result of his mind manipulation. Kudos to the extra in the wide-brimmed floppy hat throwing some marvellous shapes in the background. She is dancing to music being played by instruments with no band. It's a minor detail but such an elaborate one to have set up.

CHRIS: It's predicting, once again, where technology will be heading. It's predicting the automation of live music. Why pay musicians when you can just plug in this contraption and Bob's your uncle? This removes the pesky and costly human element. Someone recently invented an algorithm[30] that has created every melody that could possibly be written, to try to end music copyright law. That's where we're heading. It's the kind of 'progress' McGoohan warned us against.

In his quest for actual booze, Number 6 is taken to a mysterious cave where ITC regular John Cazabon (credited as 'Man in Cave') is cooking up some moonshine. To Number 6's surprise, one of his fellow drunkards turns out to be Number 2. Slurring and in good, over-sharing form, Number 2 reveals his own contempt for the Village and its ways. He proudly shows off Cazabon's work as a chemist, his workings scribbled down on a blackboard. The ramifications of this development are wide-reaching. Number 2 talks about 'managing the Village's exports.' What exports? What is the Village making? Is Cazabon Big Pharma?

Or is it all just staged nonsense? Number 6 is drugged and passes out, and Number 2, with a delicious swish of his robes, reveals himself to be a very deliberate and very sober manipulator.

Number 6 wins the election by a landslide. Rather creepily, he goes through the motions in dead-eyed silence. Having won, he greets the voters, who stare back at him impassively, the wild fervour of the election campaign completely forgotten, replaced instantly by cynicism, suspicion and apathy.

---

[30] In 2020, lawyer / musician Damien Riehl and musician / programmer Noah Rubin developed a program that recorded every possible melody (all 68.7 billion of them) in an attempt to help avoid accidental copyright infringement cases.

Number 2 leaves his scarf and shooting stick behind, emphasising the fact that these props really are part of the 'Number 2' uniform.

With a childishly excitable Number 58 at his side, Number 6 is taken to his new office. Still brainwashed, Number 6 seems to struggle to take it all in, pushing random buttons out of curiosity and like most real-life politicians, winging it. Number 58 initially acts like a child in a toyshop, but very soon her demeanour takes on the countenance of a sinister hypnotist. 'Tick. Tick. Tick...' She snaps him out of his hypnosis, slapping his face violently.

In a desperate act, Number 6 takes his chance and pushes as many buttons as he can, telling the Villagers, 'I have command. I will immobilise all electronic controls!' The Villagers are free! Free to go!! And yet no one moves. They have been reduced to an ovine, cattle-like state of blind acceptance.

There's just time for one more regulation ITC action scene as Number 6 fights off a pair of guards and makes a last-ditch escape attempt. In his bid for freedom, he chances upon one of the strangest sights of the entire series, a chamber in which four villagers sit transfixed in the presence of Rover, seemingly worshipping the great white inflatable orb.

CHRIS: This is often known as The Cult of Rover, but I have another suggestion. What if they're controlling Rover? Is this the Rover control hub? It's a strange room to have right next to Number 2's office. They're not seated in a worshipping position. It could just be their annual general meeting.

After a scrap with the guards that would have been longer and more violent but for the ITV censors, Number 6 is dragged before the true villain, who's been in plain sight for the whole episode, Number 58. The tilting shot reveals Rachel Herbert as the new Number 2, replete with the scarf; perfect.

This revelation would have been even more unexpected in 1967 when a woman in high authority was a rare sight, certainly in the UK. There were even banks that didn't let women into the building right up to the 1970s. In *Star Trek*, which was made at around the same time, the network didn't think that anyone would buy the idea of a female first officer and so Majel Barrett's first officer 'Number One' never made it past the pilot episode.

Just as Eric Portman was merely pretending to be an affable chap, Number 58's bizarre language was just another character prop. Speaking in immaculate English, her words are few but the threat could not be clearer or more sincere. 'Will you never learn? This is only the beginning. We have many ways and means but we don't wish to damage you permanently. Are you ready to talk?'

CAI: One of the aspects I enjoyed most was that when you get to the end, you realise that the entire episode has been one long, very complicated plot, not necessarily to get any information out of Number 6 but to completely break him; to take away the vaguest whiff of hope that there's a way out of this for him.

Who's the Two?

Technically, there are two Number 2s in this episode, three if you count Number 6's very brief tenure. Eric Portman was a very distinguished actor with a long career behind him. Arguably, he was one of the very best actors to have worn the signature scarf. He is probably most famous for his work in the 1940s with Michael Powell and Emeric Pressburger, for whom he was something of a good luck charm. He played a pivotal role in their magnificent ode to pastoral England, *A Canterbury Tale* (1944), and was an effectively soldierly Nazi, leading his men through the Canadian wilderness in *49th Parallel* (1941).

Such was his fame that he has a blue plaque dedicated to him in his home town of Halifax, West Yorkshire. As a youth, he was quite the matinee idol, cutting a dash in films like *We Dive At Dawn* (1943) and *One of Our Aircraft Is Missing* (1942). He sadly died, aged 68 in 1969, making one final performance as Elleston in *Strange Report* for ITC[31].

Despite his avuncular charm, his Number 2 is one of the most successful manipulators of 'The Game' that Number 6 encounters. One suspects that the entire concept of the Village elections was his idea, all a ruse to break Number 6, just for kicks.

---

[31] *Strange Report.* Report 0649: Skeleton - 'Let Sleeping Heroes Lie' (1969)

Rachel Herbert's filmography really doesn't reflect the breadth of her talent. She had only given a few performances on TV before her unforgettable role in *The Prisoner*. One of her previous roles was in *Danger Man* when she appeared on McGoohan's radar. In 1967, she played a memorable witness to the titular *Robbery* in Peter Yates' compelling thriller, but she spent the rest of her career in television. She appeared three times in the slightly forgotten police drama *No Hiding Place* and became something of an ITC mainstay.

Scores

CHRIS: 6 out of 6. For me, this is the quintessential *Prisoner* episode. I couldn't find fault.

CAI: Same. I think if this was the second episode, there might not have been a third! But if I had to give a first-time viewer an episode to watch, I'd give them this one. It perfectly captures an impotent anger that was in the air, a slow-burning fuse that would hit the dynamite sticks in '68.

Cai: 6 out of 6
Chris: 6 out of 6

episode five
The Schizoid Man

Number 6 wakes up one February morning and is shocked to find that he's grown a moustache overnight and is no longer right handed. He's even more unnerved to be tasked by Number 2 to impersonate his most prized prisoner and destroy his sense of identity. The prisoner? Number 6!

After the soul-crushing denouement of 'Free For All', here comes some much-needed relief. 'The Schizoid Man' is one of the 'plot' episodes, a result of George Markstein reaching out to his bevvy of writers looking for strong episodes with a big hook. In this instance, the writer was Terence Feely, who duly delivered something strong, big and tremendous fun (written, apparently, in under two weeks).

It wasn't just a welcome change of pace for the viewers either. Such were the pressures of filming 'Once upon a Time', that co-star Leo McKern suffered a nervous breakdown. The bulk of this episode was filmed while the poor fellow recovered. One suspects that even McGoohan might have appreciated the relief of this comparatively light caper.

The central conceit of TV stars playing opposite themselves or being cloned was very popular in the 1960s. Plastic surgery gives John Steed some evil doppelgangers to work with in *The Avengers* episode 'They Keep Killing Steed'. Captain Kirk too went up against himself in the *Star Trek* episode 'The Enemy Within', and Roger Moore gave perhaps his greatest-ever performance(s) in 1970's *The Man Who Haunted Himself*.

Perhaps it was the irresistible play on words of 'double-agent' that was such catnip to writers? 'Where'd they get you,' asks Number 12 of his mirror image, 'A people copying service, or are you one of those double agents we hear so much about these days?' Perhaps it was the technological developments in filming that allowed for that ultimate special effect of showing an actor playing opposite themselves?

CHRIS: We're still talking about a static camera and an optical process where you expose half the shot, leaving the other half unexposed and then expose the other half when you reshoot the actor in the next take. You can see a slight variation of lighting on the crease-line but that wouldn't have been an issue on small 1976 TVs. You can see it more now, the Blu-ray pause button is no friend to such things.

This technology goes back to the days of special effects pioneer Georges Méliès, in particular his groundbreaking 1898 film *Un Homme de Têtes*, or *The Four Troublesome Heads*, in which the director repeatedly pulls his head off and lines them up on a pair of tables.

Actors playing opposite themselves continued to be a popular idea with audiences, perhaps even more so as advances in special effects technology made it so seamless[32]. David Cronenberg's 1988 classic *Dead Ringers*, with its double helping of Jeremy Irons seemed to kick-start the idea and soon we had twice the Jean-Claude Van Dammage in *Double Impact*, and multiple Michael J Foxes in *Back To The Future Parts II* and *III*. These days CGI means that in the likes of *Legend* and *Gemini Man* (and the 2023 TV adaptation of *Dead Ringers* starring Rachel Weisz), you simply can't see the joins.

At the time 'The Schizoid Man' was being filmed in 1966, we weren't there yet, but ITC *had* perfected the technique of having an actor's stunt double appear in the same shot, whilst keeping his face away from the camera at all times. Frank Maher very much earned his money on this episode!

We start with an interrogation in process. Not the usual drilling for information but some mind-control practice between Number 6 and a young girl, Alison (played by Golden Globe Award nominated Jane Merrow, who very kindly spoke to us for our 'Schizoid Man' episode). Much like in a similar scene from *Ghostbusters*, Number 6 stares intently at some cards while Alison reads his mind and guesses what's on them. It seems that these two have a keen mental connection.

The scene is superbly framed; a seated student with her teacher raised on a dais, looking down on her. Theirs is an avuncular, paternal relationship. The age difference between McGoohan and Merrow made any possible romantic tension unlikely. Nonetheless, Feely had initially suggested a liaison between them, Alison would be able to tell which one was the real Number 6 from his kiss but McGoohan nixed that immediately and it was eventually replaced with the telepathy idea.

When Feely asked McGoohan about his absolute aversion to kissing scenes, he claimed that McGoohan replied, 'I have this tremendous guilt inside me and if I did, I would not be able to look my wife in the eye that night.'

A clumsy accident results in poor Number 6 getting a blood blister on his nail. No matter. 'It will heal itself.' That night he goes to bed, only to be

---

[32] We're forgetting David Hasselhoff's performance as Michael Knight's evil twin, Garthe, in *Knight Rider* (or trying to).

hypnotised via a pulsator, or what appears to be an electric, illuminated crème caramel being lowered onto his face.

We don't yet know what the Village has done to him but something has clearly happened. For one thing, he has woken up with a finely combed moustache. Moreover, he has woken up in someone else's bed.

A call from Number 2, who seems to know him unusually well even if he does think he's called Number 12, invites him to breakfast at the Green Dome. Once there, another peerless breakfast of bacon eggs is presented but Number 6 isn't keen. He's far more interested in the dish of folded pancakes provided as an alternative. Apparently his nickname used to be Flapjack Charlie. Cheery and friendly though Number 2 is, his inability to tell the difference between a pancake and a flapjack remains one of the great mysteries of the episode.

As far as Number 2 is concerned, he is talking to an old comrade called Curtis, now referred to as Number 12. It is Curtis' mission to impersonate the Village's 'Prize Prisoner,' Number 6. 'Take his sense of reality away. Once he begins to doubt his own identity, he'll crack.'

According to the calendar on his desk, the date that Number 6, or "Curtis" is supposed to have awoken from his slumber is Wednesday, February 10th. This proved to be something of an issue for Chris.

CHRIS: Alison takes her photo of Number 6 when really she's taking a photo of the calendar for plot purposes, two purposes, in fact, if you count the bruise on his fingernail. Going back (with the luxury of hindsight and the internet), and looking at all the February the 10ths which fall on a Wednesday, the only years in which February the 10th does fall on a Wednesday are 1960, 1965 and 1971. This begs the question, what year is this set in? 1960 is too early so it's either '65 or '71. Or maybe they did this on purpose to discombobulate Number 6? This is a guy after all who can count clock chimes with his peripheral hearing! Dates aren't usually plucked out of thin air on TV shows, so I wonder if there is a special reason for this.

Number 6 finally meets his look-alike. Identical in all but his blazer which, in a nice touch is his own in negative: white with black piping. Number 6's various attempts to prove to Number 2 and more importantly himself, are repeatedly thwarted by mysterious new developments that he cannot account for. He is suddenly left-handed, which means that he is bested in marksmanship, fencing and even boxing, a call back to McGoohan's favourite school sport.

He can't even smoke his usual brand of cigarettes without hacking up a lung. To compound things, the ace up his sleeve, his telepathic bond with Alison turns out to be not quite as simpatico as he thought. For a while, our hero genuinely seems to be cracking under the strain, until he spots the one thing his captors have overlooked: the blood blister, which has somehow grown all the way up his nail in less than 48 hours.

A flashback reveals the lengthy process that the Village went through over many weeks, long enough for Number 6 to grow a bushy moustache. Still hypnotised, he was subjected to a relentless Pavlovian experiment that gave him electric shocks for reverting to type and rewarded him for using his left hand and eating pancakes (not flapjacks).

This is the first episode in which Rover is referred to by name. It seems that Rover can easily be outfoxed and confused. Confronting both McGoohans at the end, Number 6 is the first to give the password 'Schizoid Man'. When Curtis uses the same password, Rover smothers him to death. Thank God he asked Number 6 first.

McGoohan plays Curtis with a wonderful pompous smarminess. He has an arrogance that betrays his status as one of 'them.' Overconfidence is a trait one rarely associates with Number 6 throughout the series. As Number 6, McGoohan beautifully suggests the fragile character starting to crack beneath the skin, until he uses an electric shock to get his mojo, and his right-handedness back.

As Number 2's accomplice, and giving Peter Swanwick a week off as his Supervisor, Earl Cameron makes his only appearance in the show and in doing so becomes the only black actor to earn a credit in the series. Cameron was very much a pioneering actor in British cinema. His role in *Pool of London*, Basil Dearden's social drama about interracial romance, helped break new ground. In *Doctor Who* circles, it is a beloved bit of trivia that Cameron's suit in the 1966 episode 'The Tenth Planet' was also worn by the bounty hunter Bossk in *The Empire Strikes Back*.

Given *The Prisoner's* tendency to focus its gaze on specific social elements like politics and education, it's perhaps something of a sin of omission that race and racism aren't really mentioned at all throughout the series. Then again, in 1967, the sight of a person of colour in a position of power was still extremely rare.

CHRIS: At the time, Nichelle Nichols was almost recast in *Star Trek* because people were complaining that a communications officer was being played by a black actress. We forget sometimes, with the benefit of 21st century eyes, that it was a really big deal for a black character to be shown in a position of authority. We imagine that such things had been addressed by the end of the '50s but it was ridiculously prevalent even in the late '60s.

In Cameron's scene with Number 2, there is an intriguing moment of pluralisation when Number 2 talks about 'our masters.' This is most likely an inconsistency due to the lack of a show bible to keep things constant.

Similarly, Number 2's remarks about 'Reporting to the General,' despite their tantalising foreshadowing of the very next episode are best overlooked.

Having outwitted his captors and fooled them into thinking that he is Curtis, Number 6 is driven out to meet a departing helicopter by Number 2. There is a well-known expression: it is sometimes better to remain silent and be thought a fool than to open one's mouth and remove all doubt. Perhaps, Number 6 is trying to channel Curtis' cockiness, but rather than keep schtum, he allows himself to fall into Number 2's trap.

CAI: I love the fact that Number 2 actually allows him to get into the helicopter and take off so that he can imagine he's made it for about thirty seconds, before landing again. He didn't need to let him board the helicopter. It was just an extra bit of soul-crushing. That said, after the 100% defeat of 'Free For All,' I think this can be counted as a draw. He did beat the system, but they had the last laugh.

Terence Feely was a particular type of TV writer who wrote in a more unconventional way than most espionage writers at the time. McGoohan has stated that whenever an episode seemed to be heading down a standard path, he would demand that the writer bend it out of shape.

One of the hardest-working TV writers of the time, Feely was seemingly in constant employment across the ITC production roster. In 1980, he created his own hit ITV show, *The Gentle Touch*, an innovatively female-led cop show starring Jill Gascoine as DI Maggie Forbes. A spin-off show in 1985, *C.A.T.S. Eyes* was equally successful. His script for 'The Schizoid Man' ingeniously builds upon the idea of removing the essence of someone to the point that they genuinely don't know who they are anymore. In one of McGoohan's most vulnerable performances, he really does start to crumble and question himself.

CAI: It's such a fascinating idea: if you were relentless and persistent enough, could you eventually convince someone that they're actually someone else? With all the tools at their disposal, including threading a wire through his cigarettes, they take everything off him. Taking away his possessions and even his freedom is one thing, but taking away his identity is so much more potent. His identity, and his right to assign himself his own identity, is one of the defining themes of *The Prisoner*.

McGoohan told Feely, 'Look, this is a series where you can do anything you like. I don't know what it's about. The writers will decide what it's about when they start writing.' Feely said, 'Do you mean a kind of surrealistic television where we can get away with anything? McGoohan said 'Yes. I think that is what I'm talking about.'

CHRIS: You can take that a number of ways, and of course, our memories tend to change facts over the years. I don't believe McGoohan would have said, 'I don't know what it's about.' Perhaps he might have said something similar to give Feely more freedom, but he certainly knew what it was all about.

CAI: It would have worked well as an extended or feature episode. In fact, there was talk that that was actually an option at one point. It feels like there are huge, fascinating ideas here being squeezed into one hour, as opposed to a weak idea being stretched out to fill the time, as was sometimes the case with ITC shows.

CHRIS: You can argue that you can take many of the episodes as allegory, and enjoy the others as spy thrillers. They're more grounded in reality. Number 2 talks about being 'Stuck in admin.' This, like many others of the syndication episodes, could have worked equally well as episodes of other ITC shows. There's also a nice counterpoint between this episode and 'Do Not Forsake Me Oh My Darling'. Number 6 loses his identity and he starts to feel diminished. In 'Do Not Forsake Me', he body-swaps, and loses his own reflection, but maintains, indeed strengthens his own identity.

In terms of the episode's prescience, it does look forward to the very 21st century concept of identity theft. The theft of Number 6's identity may come from a specifically nefarious Village agenda, but it's alive and well today in the form of credit card cloning, stolen bank account details, fake social media accounts and even the completely terrifying rise of Deepfake videos.

The influence of 'The Schizoid Man' can also be felt keenly in the second coming of *Star Trek*. An episode of *Star Trek: The Next Generation* (Season two, episode six) titled… 'The Schizoid Man'. It features a character called Dr Ira Graves, played by W. Morgan Sheppard, a part written with McGoohan in mind. The writers were desperate to land McGoohan for the role but to no avail. There was also an episode in the sixth season called 'Frame of Mind.' Here, Commander William Riker (much like Number 6) becomes convinced that he is not who he thinks he is, in this case by a malevolent alien species.

This is undeniably filler; the first episode created for Lew Grade's mandate for syndication but it's terribly good filler. It also gives McGoohan the great ego-massaging challenge of playing opposite oneself; something he rises to with barely disguised relish.

Who's the Two?

Anton Rodgers wasn't quite yet a star by the time he made 'The Schizoid Man' but he had already made an impression both in supporting roles on TV and in the theatre, where he'd been working since he was 15. He'd made uncredited appearances as school pupils in Peter Ustinov's *Vice Versa* (1948) and Anthony Asquith's *The Browning Version* (1951) and spent the next two decades building up a commendably thick resumé. Even so, he was still one of the youngest Number 2s of the series, his *Where Eagles Dare* co-star Derren Nesbitt pipped him by two years.

He made multiple appearances in ITC shows and was especially good in the *Man in a Suitcase* two-parter 'Variation on a Million Bucks', which reunited him with director Pat Jackson. (Years later, he would be one of the small handful of co-stars to be remembered fondly by star Richard Bradford.)

There's something of ex-Prime Minister David Cameron about Rodgers' characterisation of Number 2. Wonderfully charming, slick, couldn't be more helpful, always asking after your wife, telling you you've lost weight and can I get you anything? Oh, also, I'm also completely ruthless and I have a terribly short temper when I don't get my way, don't you know. So lovely to see you.

There seemed to be two phases of Anton Rodgers' career, without wishing to sound rude. There's the whippet-thin young blade of the 1960s and 70s, and then a beloved and noticeably filled-out sit-com mainstay of *Fresh Fields*, *French Fields* and *May To December*, all of which helped to make him a household name in the 1980s. He finished that decade with a delightful role in *Dirty Rotten Scoundrels*, deploying the French accent that served him so well playing various European villains in the ITC years. As Inspector Andre, he quips the immortal line, 'To be with another woman, that is French. To be caught, *that* is American.'

He was a lovely actor and when he passed away in 2007 at the age of 74, the grief from everyone who'd ever worked with him was palpable.

Scores

CHRIS: This was quite a hard one to score. I was between 4 and 5 on it but went with a 4 in the end. A solid 4 though. It's a return to the spy form.

CAI: 4 is like a B. An admirable score. I think this was full of really good ideas but they didn't quite have time to expand on it. I thought it was like a seriously good B-side... but it is a B-side, so I gave it a 4 too.

Cai: 4 out of 6
Chris: 4 out of 6

The General

The Village is under the spell of 'Speedlearn,' a miraculous process that teaches people vast amounts of knowledge in mere seconds. Number 6 suspects that the professor behind this 'miracle' is not all he seems, and plots to expose the mysterious 'General' making it all possible.

Patrick McGoohan wasn't the only creative working on *The Prisoner* with a fondness for pseudonyms. Joshua Adam, the credited writer of this episode was actually Lewis Greifer, paying a sweet little tribute to his children, Joshua and Adam. It was the education of these two lads which gave Greifer the idea for 'The General'. His kids were at the age of O and A-Levels and were complaining to their father that they were fed up of 'learning by rote' and being tested. Greifer channelled this frustration into his *Prisoner* script, which married up very well with McGoohan's fears that technology would dilute education rather than broaden it. 'Speedlearn' represented what Greifer and McGoohan feared was the natural progression of education in a world of ever-advancing technology.

CHRIS: As someone who works in education, the points being raised here resonated with me a great deal. There's a difference between being knowledgeable and being able to recall information. That isn't education, that's remembering a fact and regurgitating it. There's no synthesis of that information. If I teach someone how to bake a cake, for example, they will pick up skills in that process that they will be able to apply when doing something else. That's the application of knowledge and giving it context. The whole learning-by-rote system is archaic. People on quiz shows who know who won the FA Cup in 1971[33]: that isn't being knowledgeable, that's memory-recall. That, I think, is what Greifer is challenging. Everyone suddenly 'knows' all these dates and facts but, so what? Number 6 calls them 'a row of cabbages.' 'Knowledgeable cabbages,' Number 2 corrects him.

Greifer was best known as a TV writer. He wrote several episodes of *Emergency Ward 10*, which featured Peter Howell, who plays the Professor here. Greifer had enjoyed a decade-long career as a writer before writing 'The General'. Markstein and he were long-time friends having worked together as journalists several years previously. After writing 'The General', he contributed scripts for *Special Branch*, *Fraud Squad*, and he co-wrote one of the most celebrated episodes of *Doctor Who* from the Tom Baker era, 'Pyramids of Mars'. It wasn't long after that he emigrated to Tel Aviv to become a teacher.

Making his debut as a *Prisoner* director was Peter Graham Scott, a name that will be familiar to fans of 1960s espionage show credits sequences as he

---

[33] Arsenal (2-1 against Liverpool)

directed four *Avengers* episodes and was a regular *Danger Man* director. He also made a rather fine Hammer horror movie, *Captain Clegg* (aka *Night Creatures*) in 1962, and could claim to be something of a multi-tasker, with writing, producing and even acting credits on his resumé. McGoohan was once asked why he came to hire Scott and replied, 'Because he was quick and he was cheap.'

Another director had indeed been lined up initially but left before filming began and Scott was parachuted in at the last minute, barely given enough time to read a script he struggled to understand. It is conspicuously one of the more Borehamwood MGM-set episodes, laced with stock footage of Portmeirion including the opening shot where the staff members' cars are clearly visible in the car park, though one could argue that it's simply where the Village maintenance staff park up while they attend to the cleaning and the filling-in of new arrivals' diaries. One has to be a little bit forgiving about such 'gaffes.' Portmeirion was still a working tourist attraction at the time. Search about on YouTube and you'll find some extraordinary footage of Patrick McGoohan filming his scenes in 'Arrival'... with a small crowd of onlookers standing three-deep just across the path staring at him in wonder, Nikon cameras in hand.

Rover has been given the week off. It's the villagers themselves, all but wielding pitchforks and flaming torches, who are doing the pursuing, chasing the errant Professor across the beach in a scene of mob justice that prefigures similar crowd violence in 'Dance of the Dead'. One of them, played by the hirsute Michael Miller, is perhaps the most visible 'Villager' of them all, turning up again in 'A Change of Mind' (screaming 'Believe me!' to great effect) and also in 'Fall Out'. Number 6 refers to him and his cronies disdainfully as 'Prefects,' which is a subtle use of schoolyard terminology that Greifer repeats throughout the episode. Number 6 is very often described as being 'naughty' and 'playing truant,' sewing classroom associations into the dialogue.

The Professor's escape bid seems a little out of place, given that in his television appearances and on the many posters around the Village, he is an enthusiastic supporter of Speedlearn, a revolutionary process that gives viewers 'a three-year course in three minutes... one hundred per cent entry, one hundred percent pass.'

The prefects are looking for the Professor's tape recorder which Number 6 has discovered and is now hiding. When Number 2 comes looking for it, he takes the opportunity to enjoy a little victory by revealing just how much information about the Treaty of Adrianople Number 6 has memorised without even knowing it.

CHRIS: This is precisely what bothers me about education techniques today, which are as infuriating to me as they were to Greifer. Memory recall means that a student can pass an exam, then the examiners get to tick a box and the stats look great for another year, which leads into the culture of 'statistics' which has dominated education for years. Students become numbers represented on a database for things like attendance, retention, attainment, and successful completion, all these numbers become a string of data which end up determining budgets and costs.

CAI: It's the fallacy of the labour-saving device and how they liberate us. If you think about it, practically every invention of the past 75 years has taken something we already had but made it smaller, faster, and more convenient, removing all the unnecessary obstacles and giving everybody more me-time. Even the internet is basically a library, only one that you don't have to drive to and whisper within. And yet, we have less free time, are more stressed than ever and have in many instances forgotten how to do basic things like how to cook.

CHRIS: I think it's one of the problems we have with the government in the UK, any of them regardless of party; it's the system that lets our children down. Let's say you were having heart surgery. Would you want someone who'd never been to medical school and knew nothing of human anatomy, or would you want a trained heart surgeon? The answer's obvious, it's B, by the way, and yet in the highest echelons of government, we're happy to put people in place to run all the great departments of state who have absolutely no experience in those spheres. Education Secretaries should be specialists in that specific area with years of experience in the field of education, but in reality, they're just ministers going up or down a career ladder.

The intention of the Professor may well have been good, and he certainly isn't written as the villain of the piece, but his intentions are subverted by another malign force, the Village.

To the Village, Speedlearn is an experiment, which echoes back to a point raised in 'Free For All', namely the exports. They're trying out this new system on the guinea-pigs they have at their disposal before shipping it out to the wider world. It's a rather neat Marksteinian spy-trope hiding in plain view. Many critics and commentators have speculated that the Village might well be a test centre, a petri-dish where all manner of experiments can be carried out on its subjects before being safely unleashed onto the public.

Number 6 raises the issue of precisely what information is being burned into the memory of the 'students.' Are these simply dates from history, or can something far more sinister be beamed into someone's mind while they watch television unawares? 'For the time being, history will have to do,' states Number 2 proudly, 'but shortly we shall be making our own.'

It's usually left to Fenella Fielding or Robert Rietty to make Village service announcements, but in the case of Speedlearn, the programmes are presented by Al Mancini, the first American to appear in the show.

CAI: I think he won the part by coming first in a Ringo Starr look-a-like competition.

Mancini would have only just finished his role as one of *The Dirty Dozen*, filming in the same studio, and which would probably remain his most famous part, though he popped up all over the place on British TV throughout the 1960s. His brash, confident American tones help to open up the Village internationally, and further muddies the vexed question of who runs it.

John Castle would go on to enjoy a rather lengthier career in film and television after his sole *Prisoner* appearance, as the Village 'Prefect' Number 12, who turns ally and helps Number 6 to overthrow The General. Castle had a decades-long career in television but also appeared in classic films like *The Lion in Winter* (with Jane Merrow), *Blow-Up* and as the chief baddie in the not-very-classic *Robocop 3*.

We have of course met Number 12 before, last week in fact, when he was played by Number 6 being made to think he was Curtis... still with us? Curtis was smothered at the end of 'The Schizoid Man', so perhaps this new Number 12 isn't just a matter of the costume department rummaging through a box of *Prisoner* badges and tossing John Castle the first one they could grab.

He has only recently joined the Village, 'How long have you been with us?' asks Number 2, suspiciously.

He is also one of the very few genuine allies in the series. At this point, only 'Arrival's Virginia Maskell and Alison in 'The Schizoid Man' have genuinely had Number 6's best interests at heart. Perhaps after the duplicity of Nadia, Number 6's trust has been forever broken, but then such absolute scepticism will come back to haunt him in 'Checkmate'.

CAI: Having seen him being let down by all the duplicitous turncoats of the past, as a viewer we are waiting for the big reveal, it's a trap! But then again by this point in the series, that reveal would not have worked as a reveal because by now we're assuming that everyone is trying to trick him.

Number 6 decides to get to the bottom of the 'abomination' of Speedlearn and pays a visit to the Professor's wife, who is running an art class which Number 6 attends. His militaristic cartoon of the Professor's wife, all epalettes and medals, does not go down well at all. It does reveal further proof of Number 6's mercurial artistic skills; we already know that he is an award-winning abstract artist.

Number 6's benefactor on that occasion, Leo McKern's Number 2, is given a little tribute in the Professor's house as one of the busts that Number 6 unveils. A nice 'Easter Egg' for fans and confirmation of the fact that those bespoke props were not offered to McKern as a thank-you gift after all.

CHRIS: Certain words we use in our vocabulary have different meanings which can be used in different ways. The 'General': automatically one's mind drifts to the image of a man in a green uniform covered in medals and ribbons. Generally, general could mean literally anything.

Number 12 stages an electrical fault in Number 6's house to allow a very quick secret briefing, before Norman Mitchell arrives to repair it. McGoohan had been in rep with Mitchell. He might not be a household name but he might well have the longest CV of any actor in Britain, save possibly Sam Kydd. You name it, chances are Norman Mitchell's made at least one appearance.

Number 12's plan is for Number 6 to infiltrate the control room and substitute the next scheduled Speedlearn broadcast for the Professor's taped warnings and his demand that The General must be destroyed. To sabotage the broadcast, Number 6 must insert a metal rod, a precursor to a USB stick into what appears to be a large satellite-cum-artificial solar system. The periscope he peers through adds another spoonful of militaristic imagery. This switcheroo, for unfathomable reasons, involves the various members of Village Security dressing up as undertakers in (very cool) sunglasses, and being given access to the control room via an Addams Family-style toy piggy bank[34].

CAI: From this point on, the episode does get a little bit… silly. There are moments when it creeps into *Our Man Flint* territory.

The undertaker reference is not new of course. It's an undertaker, arriving in a hearse, who fills Number 6's London house with gas in every title sequence. This has led to many theories that *The Prisoner* is a story about purgatory (a theory that Patrick McGoohan regularly shot down). Are the undertakers threshold guardians, going back to Joseph Campbell?

CAI: It could have been McGoohan, sensing that this episode was heading in a rather conventional direction, who decided to shake things up by making everyone dress up in costumes that would have fans discussing the allegorical aspect again.

CHRIS: Sometimes you can really spot the push / pull dynamics of two very different kinds of artists working together. You get the same thing in music with Lennon and McCartney or Roger Waters and David Gilmour. Each works as a contrary sounding board to the other and, often incredibly begrudgingly, they will create something amazing that they could not have achieved by themselves. McGoohan and Markstein fit very comfortably into that pattern. Look at the difference between the George Lucas of *Star Wars* (1977), surrounded by all manner of talented people questioning and challenging him, and the godlike, untouchable 1990s George Lucas who made *The Phantom Menace*, a boring kids' film about trade delegations.

---

[34] Aka, a Morris Costumes Black Box Money Trap

To this end, McGoohan had a superb coterie of professionals to offer their honest opinions and, perhaps rein in any megalomaniacal tendencies, initially at least, specifically Bernard Williams, David Tomblin and Jack Shampan, who was even more of a workaholic than McGoohan; almost always on set before the main star arrived.

Finally, the curtain is pulled back and the identity of The General is revealed to be a massive 1960s computer. Reportedly, it was cobbled together from whatever spare electronic equipment that they could find. This tradition of recycling was nothing new for ITC, the Professor's study features the same shelving units from the 'London' offices in 'The Chimes of Big Ben'.

CHRIS: The set of the General is amazing, it looks fantastic, but it's so impractical. The wheelchair access is a plus. Having it so high up does give it some appropriate dominance.

The revelation that the General is in fact, a giant super-computer may well have been an unexpected twist in 1967, but in retrospect, it feels like a sixties spy trope stolen from the plot of a late-period episode of *The Avengers*. The titular star of the third *Harry Palmer* movie, *Billion Dollar Brain* turned out to be another mechanical mastermind, this time with a robotic monotone.

Number 6 challenges Number 2's assertion that the General can answer any question it is asked by asking it a question so profound that it explodes, electrocuting the Professor and Number 12 in the process.

CAI: It's quite odd to actually see people get killed like this in *The Prisoner*. It's not a shoot 'em-up series, so it's quite shocking (literally) when Number 12 and the Professor both end up being electrocuted.

CHRIS: Joseph Campbell called it *Apotheosis*, in *The Hero's Journey*, which is usually demarcated, in most film and TV shows, by someone getting killed and elevated to a new almost godlike status[35]. A plot point to move things forward. But yes, it very rarely happens in *The Prisoner*.

CAI: The 'Question' asked by Number 6 is… 'Why?' When I was 17, I thought that was an absolutely brilliant moment. Now, having grown up with

---

[35] See Gandalf the Grey and Obi-Wan Kenobi.

computers, even terrible ones like my old Commodore Vic 20, I just thought, 'It wouldn't blow up.' The worst that would happen would be a flashing cursor and a flashing 'System Error' sign.

CHRIS: A paper clip pops up and asks, 'You're trying to ask an insoluble question. Would you like some help with that?'

Who's the Two?

It's our old chum Colin Gordon again. Apart from Leo McKern, he is the only actor to play Number 2 twice. Initially, he was meant to die in the explosion that kills the Professor, but it was rewritten so that he could reappear. This cements the fact that this was evidently meant to be broadcast before 'A. B. and C.'. In that episode, he is terrified, paranoid and aware at every turn that he has one chance left or he is finished.

In this episode, his first, despite claiming that he and Number 6 are 'old friends,' he is on his game. Right up until the point where Number 6 exposes the sleeping Professor to be a wax effigy, Number 2 is a confident, strutting antagonist, in no doubt as to who will come out on top. He doesn't even seem to care about why Number 6 resigned; the subject never comes up. He still enjoys his milk, but it seems to be more for pleasure and the calcium intake than to deal with a Number 6 related stomach ulcer.

Scores

CHRIS: I liked the message, I liked the theme, it's a good idea, but there are aspects of the final delivery that needed work and haven't aged well, so I gave it 4.

CAI: I agreed, but went one lower and gave it 3. There are elements of it that I found frustratingly undercooked.

CHRIS: Ironically, it probably would have worked better as an expanded episode or TV movie version. There are a lot of strong ideas here and they needed room to breathe. It doesn't land. But that said, it does still chime with a lot of what I believe as someone who works in education. McGoohan and Greifer's take on it is that it's the application of technology that makes it easier. As a result, the teachers are taken out of the equation. Speedlearn becomes an automated system. It's a bit like an online test. There's no human involvement; no formative or summative assessment, which is something only a human being can really do. A computer can ask you a question, but it lacks the intelligence to analyse your answer. It will give you a multiple choice and your answer has to be one of those options. If you were going to remake *The Prisoner* today, I think that this is a theme which would be explored: the dehumanisation of the processes. Not just in education but in everything. Look at supermarkets, where you have self-service checkout tills. It's human beings that have been replaced, and their jobs with it. In education terms, automation can help with certain things but it cannot replace having a teacher in the classroom to offer practical guidance and I don't think it ever will, whatever they tell you about AI and where it's heading.

Cai: 3 out of 6
Chris: 4 out of 6

Many Happy Returns

When Number 6 awakes to find the Village completely deserted, he wastes no time in making an escape bid. He builds a raft and navigates successfully back to England. When he gets there he finds his old employers in a sceptical mood, and someone else living in his house.

This episode has a very special place in our hearts because it had just been broadcast as part of the 25th Anniversary repeat run on Channel 4 when we first met, and we were both so tickled pink by it that we spoke of nothing else for about half an hour.

For the first 20 minutes or so, 'Many Happy Returns' is pure cinema. Not a word is spoken, just diegetic wind effects and occasional bursts of non-diegetic music. In a lovely moment, just before Number 6 makes his escape bid, the sound of crockery breaking snaps him and us out of this reverie... but it's merely a cat being careless with a cup and saucer. And so, Number 6, his bags packed with as much as he can carry, heads out to sea once again.

Playing said cat was this week's special guest star, Tammy. The story goes that the producers had hired a professional acting cat, which refused to perform on the day. A local couple volunteered the services of their pet cat, Tammy, who knocked it out of the park. A black cat breaking a cup and saucer doesn't add up to much of a good omen as Number 6 embarks on his journey.

This is his last escape attempt of the series in production order, at least before he changes tack and concentrates more on playing mind games with the Village.

CHRIS: I think this one just pummels him by the end of it and it left him thinking, 'You know what? I'm going to play them at their own game after this.'

This was the last of the initial block of episodes to be shot, before McGoohan headed off to make *Ice Station Zebra* with Rock Hudson. This was also the last episode made with the cooperation of George Markstein, who bailed after this (though he does make a nice little cameo, repeating his role from the title sequence as 'Man Who is Handed Resignation Before His Tea is Spilled'). Somewhat unbelievably, Markstein was only 38 years old when he handed in his notice.

Anthony Skene returned to write the episode and the experienced Michael Truman was pencilled in to direct but had been replaced by the time shooting began. Reports say that Truman had fallen ill, so McGoohan took over direction, this time working as one Joseph Serf. *Prisoner* fans and McGoohan-heads have attributed Kafkaesque undertones to this pseudonym but in an interview with Howard Foy in 1990, McGoohan claimed that he was by the sea at the time, saw the surf and thought, 'That'll do' (Joseph was his middle name).

There are echoes of 'Arrival' in the first few scenes of this episode. Once again, Number 6 is walking around a completely empty Village, possibly more confused on this occasion than he was when he arrived. Again, he climbs the clock tower, this time to ring the bell and yet again, he pays a visit to the Village Shop. The camera that he picks up there is a Canon Dial 35 with the logo carefully covered in black tape. Equally obfuscated is the EMI logo on the various records on display, covered up by a Village sticker. A range of cameras does seem like an unlikely thing for the Village Shop to be selling. Perhaps one of the ideas being cultivated by the Village's export division was one-hour photograph development.

CAI: It's nice to be back in Portmeirion again, albeit briefly. For a while, I had been getting used to seeing him in an evident studio setting with Portmeirion painted on a cloth outside his living room set but here he is, in his pyjamas no less.

Not that this episode is free of stock footage syndrome. Anyone who is lucky enough to have visited Portmeirion will be as shocked as Number 6 was to find a Nepalese mountain range just outside of the Village limits, when he commandeers a Mini Moke and tests the boundaries.

Precisely as in 'The Chimes of Big Ben', Number 6's tree-felling episode is scored by the same Hank Marvin-style guitar jangling. The boat he creates this time is far more sea-worthy than his first attempt. It was purpose-built by a local company called Gwynedd Marina. Famously, there was an engine fire on the boat that was towing her, and she came loose and sailed away, never to be seen again.

The scenes of Number 6's sea-bound journey were filmed along the coast of Abersoch and further out into the Irish Sea, which gives them a genuine sense of veracity and jeopardy. So often, especially in TV series of this time, scenes at sea have manifestly been filmed in a studio tank before a blue curtain, with unseen prop handlers throwing the occasional glass of water at the cast.

CHRIS: The shaving scene on the raft is a lovely bit of character development. It's the mark of a civilised man. There's also an element of routine here which goes back to something taught in military institutions all over the world: if you're in a captured or compromised position over a long period, set yourself a routine. Shave at a certain time, eat at a certain time, etc.

Number 6's assembly of his raft and escape kit gives us an insight into the kind of training he would have undergone in his career. He doesn't just build a raft, he designs a compass (using Village® needles) and is able to plot a course and keep a ship's log on the back of a newspaper. It's all dashingly *Boy's Own*, but it tells us much about his almost limitless resourcefulness.

Being born in 1928, he would have been too young to have fought in the Second World War but at the very least he would have done his National Service[36]. His escape suggests that his service was spent in the Navy, a possibility which is reinforced by some of the militaristic decor in his house. The triquetrum scene from 'The Chimes of Big Ben' also tells us that he is capable of navigating using the stars, or would have done had it not been deleted.

Eventually, his raft is spotted by the crew of a boat. Sadly, they turn out to be a pair of German gunrunners, Günther and Ernst (played by Dennis Chinnery and Jon Laurimore).

CHRIS: There's a lovely connection here. John Laurimore returned to Portmeirion (well, went for the first time technically) to film the *Doctor Who* episode, 'The Masque of Mandragora', in which he played Count Federico. I honestly think there's a great book to be written about the micro-connections that link *The Prisoner* and *Doctor Who!*

The gunrunners tip Number 6 overboard and quickly make a feast from his collection of Village brand tinned goods. However, our hero has already climbed back on board and cunningly overpowers them, leaving them tied up in the ship's hold. Displaying their own ingenuity, Günther and Ernst manage to escape through the back of a cupboard. It is telling that while their first response is to drown Number 6 and steal his food, Number 6 takes great

---

[36] In England, National Service was finally phased out by 1963.

care not to kill this pair, even though it would have been very much in his interests to have the boat all to himself.

CHRIS: It's a little bit crow-barred in, the whole gunrunner scene. It's there to inject a bit of tension and action after what is the most serene and passive start to an episode in the whole series.

CAI: Perhaps it was the contractual ITC fisticuffs stipulation. If it was, it was one of the better brawls. Something about the scrapping being in a tight claustrophobic setting reminded me of the train carriage fight in *From Russia With Love*.

Having escaped the boat and his captors, Number 6 manages to swim to shore and finds himself at Beachy Head which, very curiously, he doesn't seem to recognise.

CHRIS: Something bothers me about this scene. He's by a lighthouse, and yet he decides to clamber up the embankment of the cliff when surely there would be a path leading down to the lighthouse where the keeper can travel to and from work.

He ascends the cliff, suddenly sporting a head of wonderfully curly hair. In fact, McGoohan looks more ruggedly handsome in these first England-based scenes than he does in the whole series, something only intensified by his weather-beaten jumper.

In a beautifully shot scene, shot almost in silhouette with something of the fairy tale in its lens. It's only now, after almost 23 minutes, that Number 6 utters his first words; asking the same question he asks at the start of each episode 'Where am I?' He's asking a Romany woman, played by Nike Arrighi, who was making a good name for herself in films like Hammer's *The Devil Rides Out*.

Despite having just wandered past one of the famous landmarks in Great Britain, the Romany couple's language seems to add to Number 6's sense of discombobulation. He isn't sure yet just where he is until the familiar (and oppressively authoritarian) sight of a policeman's helmet leaves him in no doubt. Thinking the police are after him, he smuggles himself into a delivery truck (NetCo, a fictitious company which oddly enough is now a real company).

When he arrives in London, much rested, he finds himself standing on the paving of the Victoria Station courtyard which looks to all intents and purposes like a large chessboard. This motif is replicated in the entrance room floor of his own house, 1 Buckingham Place, where he is greeted in a manner most brusque by a classically snobbish maid (Grace Arnold, who will reappear in 'It's Your Funeral'). The owner of the house is summoned, Mrs Butterworth.

CHRIS: You can take Mrs Butterworth's response to Number 6 in two ways. There's the obvious, flirtatious 'Who is this handsome devil?' reaction. There's also something more sadistic; toying with him like a cat with a mouse. You have to factor in that the Village has pre-empted all his moves; they knew he'd head home. As such, this is gratuitous salt-rubbing into Number 6's wounds.

CAI: They haven't just taken his house, they've wiped him out of history. His name isn't even on the deeds. It's like he hasn't ever existed.

Mrs Butterworth may have moved into his house, but for some reason appears not to have replaced any of the decor. She's even kept his old tiger skin rug! This is prime London real estate so she's clearly got money. Would she not have splashed out on a fashionable interior decorator? Number 6 appears not to hear this alarm bell clanging away.

He gives the lady of the house an alias: Peter Smith. This name will come up again in 'Do Not Forsake Me Oh My Darling' as Schmidt. Perhaps he's used Peter instead of the more obvious John at the last minute? There is a slight but noticeable pause between names. Perhaps, as some people believe, Peter Smith really is his name? Maybe it's an old alias from his spy days?

Taken into the house and given the full charm offensive by his hostess, Number 6 slips her up with a trick question about the solicitors. Strangely, after his experience in the Village, he doesn't flee the house. Instead, he is taken in further by Mrs Butterworth's openness and her sob story about her dead husband. Of course, by now the Village will already know from past experiences that Number 6's soft spot is a woman in tears.

Mrs Butterworth is generous to a fault, it must be said. Number 6 is offered cake and an array of delicate sandwich triangles that would have put Fortnum & Mason to shame. 'That was the nicest fruit cake I have ever tasted,' he says, gratefully. The cake is appropriate, because it's his birthday the next day, March the 18th.

As possibly the best birthday present imaginable, Number 6 is given back the keys to his Lotus 7 and takes it for a spin. 'KAR 120C,' he bellows. 'I know every nut and bolt and cog, I built it with my own hands!' Number 6's Lotus ranks alongside any of the most famous TV cars of the 20th century.

We're then treated to a wonderful pre-meta meta sequence as the title sequence is essentially restaged, with Number 6 returning to his place of business to the surprise of George Markstein. Soon, Number 6 is explaining his work absence to the Colonel, played by veteran actor Donald Sinden.

We also meet Thorpe, played by Patrick Cargill (wearing his own old school tie from Haileybury School in Hertfordshire), whose presence will present something of a continuity conundrum a few episodes down the line. There's an interesting power dynamic going on between Sinden and Cargill. The latter is resolutely unconvinced by Number 6's story 'You resign. You disappear. You return. You spin a yarn that Hans Christian Anderson would reject for a fairy tale.' Yet Thorpe is the underling and he answers to The Colonel and has to look up to him for approval.

CHRIS: I reckon he's H.R. It's a return-to-work meeting.

Number 6's close history with the Colonel is hinted at by the way he calls him 'James.' There's also a line about solving the riddle of which side the Village is on 'If not here, then elsewhere' that sees James change his tone. This all suggests that the two men go back a long way, and gives Number 6 the sway he needs to put his plan into action despite Thorpe's misgivings. 'The dice are heavily in your favour.'

CHRIS: I have no doubt that James is the real deal. He sends a policeman to investigate Number 6's story and interview the Romany family. They even interview Mrs Butterworth. Why would they need to do that if they were part of the Village's machinations?

With the final denouement, it becomes clear that the Village are several moves ahead of Number 6, as always. It does require a superhuman suspension of disbelief to work out how their powers of prediction were so uncanny. How can they possibly have foreseen the specific sequence of events that led to Number 6 deciding to fly back from England to find the Village?

CAI: There is absolutely no way. As a genius plan, this simply doesn't hold up. There are so many variables that they would have had no control over. He could have drowned in a storm. The gunrunners could have murdered him. His raft could have been struck by a cross-channel ferry. He could have overslept in that Netco van, and who's to say it wasn't delivering to the Shetland Islands instead of London? The only mitigating factor is the fact that the Village knew that he wouldn't be able to resist the urge to exact revenge.

The plan to locate the Village is given the green light but for the audience, the tension of impending doom starts to tighten. What just happened with that milkman? What is a milkman doing at an airbase?

With a co-pilot in tow, Number 6's plane takes off. Actually, it's footage of another plane taking off from the classic *Avengers* episode, 'The Superlative Seven'. Using coordinates calculated from his sea journey, Number 6 does eventually spot the unmistakable sight of Portmeirion beneath him supposedly somewhere between Morocco and the Portuguese coast.

This is the closest he gets to victory and it is snatched away from him in an instant. His co-pilot is actually the milkman, who is actually working for the Village. He turns and says, 'Be seeing you!' before ejecting Number 6 into the skies above. After a few moments of hopelessly unconvincing back projection as he parachutes towards the ground, he lands on the beach in a state of utter despair.

Tammy the cat is there to welcome him back. At first, the Village is as empty and non-functioning as it was the last time he was there. No sooner has he got back to his house, but the shower starts to work, the kettle starts to boil, and a big band parades outside the house playing another jaunty theme. The door opens and Number 2 arrives, bringing Number 6 a birthday cake (bearing six candles, naturally). Number 2 is, of course, Mrs Butterworth, so at least we know the cake will be excellent.

CHRIS: Now, I have a theory about all this. When he goes to bed the night before he escapes, the Village ceases to exist, and when he returns, the Village returns. Without him in it, the Village doesn't really exist.

CAI: I think that works really well on a metaphorical level. In practical terms, it's actually pretty ridiculous. How did they manage to sneak everybody out of the Village that night? Were they all hiding behind their sofas like a big surprise party? 'Everybody shhhhh! Don't tell Derek, he can't keep secrets. He's staying with Number 2...'

Markstein intended this to be the end of the first series and also an indicator of the kind of adventures Number 6 could have in the second series; not necessarily within the Village, but always ending up back there.

Who's the Two?

Born in Cornwall in 1918, Georgina Cookson enjoyed a long and varied career that never really took her further than a bit part player, making several appearances across the ITC universe. She also appeared in a show called *A Life of Bliss* alongside her fellow Number 2, Colin Gordon. Seven episodes of ITV's live-screened *Play of The Week* gives you some indication of the theatrical experience she would have built up to repeatedly take on such a daunting proposal.

Her relative obscurity would have been a positive attribute to audiences first watching 'Many Happy Returns'. Had Mrs Butterworth been played by a more famous actress like Diana Dors, her status would most likely give her true identity away. Instead, her delivery of Number 6's cake at the end is an effective final twist of the knife.

Cookson has already appeared as a guest at one of the dreamy parties in 'A. B. and C.', which was shot after 'Many Happy Returns'. Had the episodes been broadcast in that order, it would have lent credence to the idea that his 'dreams' are being populated by characters from his own memory. Alternatively, given that his sleep has been induced, who's to say that it isn't the Village inserting members of their own administration into Number 6's dreams?

Mrs Butterworth also gets a mention in the DC comic 'Shattered Visage' as the Head of Intelligence. Keep your eyes open for a lovely moment after she hands the car keys to Number 6 and steps back, almost knocking over a passing extra.

Scores

CAI: I gave this a 5. It's a very strong episode. I liked the cinematic first act and I loved where it went. It's unique within the body of the series, and the ending is possibly the most brutal gut-punch of the whole show. It was a favourite when I was 17 and it remains so. Ultimately, it shows the Village as diabolically evil: look at just how much effort they put in just to wreck Number 6's birthday!

CHRIS: It's a filler, but a high-quality one. It's got everything you want: Portmeirion exterior shots, a fantastic twist, and great guest stars. It was a 5 from me too.

Cai: 5 out of 6
Chris: 5 out of 6

episode eight
Dance of the Dead

There is a carnival and Number 6 is invited. However, he is more interested in using the body of a stranger, washed up on the shore, as a way to signal to the outside world and send for help.

Directed by Don Chaffey, 'Dance of the Dead' was the fourth episode to be shot but had to wait an interminably long time to get broadcast. Patrick McGoohan wasn't very happy with the footage in the can and it was, to a certain extent, shelved. It was rescued by the editor who presented it to McGoohan, who then saw it in a much kinder light.

McGoohan's sniffy initial view of 'Dance of the Dead' sounds a note of intrigue because it's a Chaffey and one of the first episodes to be shot; as such, people generally assume it to be one of the so-called 'Core Seven' episodes. This is a reference to the fact that McGoohan's original pitch to the ITC was a seven-episode mini-series, which Lew Grade then demanded to be extended into a two-series project that could then be syndicated.

In 'The Official Prisoner Companion' by Matthew White and Jaffer Ali, the original seven episodes were listed, but McGoohan later stated that while that might have been *their* list, it wasn't necessarily his. 'Dance of the Dead' presents a complication to the murky business of what the Core Seven episodes were, and it also split us into two camps.

CAI: I love this episode. It haunted me when I first saw it. I found something especially chilling about it and when I saw it again, in bright Blu-ray sharpness, I thought it had improved, if anything.

CHRIS: I want to like it a lot more than I did. Because it was salvaged, there isn't really a natural flow to the episode. It had to be Frankensteined a little bit to get it into shape.

It is a little low on plot. There's a grand ball on the horizon, the Carnival, and Number 6 will have to attend against his will. His refusal to conform is viewed as petulance by his official observer (Norma West), and something easily remedied via a sinister medical procedure by a cruel doctor (Duncan MacRae). Meanwhile, there's a spin on the *Operation Mincemeat* story, as Number 6 uses a dead body washed up on the shore as a way to contact the homeland (he fills the dead man's pockets with information and shoves him back out to sea like a message in a bottle).

Dialogue like 'I'm new here,' gives away its position as an early episode. Number 6 seems to still be a little gauche and unaware of the full extent of the Village's capabilities. It also ties up a few loose ends in a way that a second episode might, but it makes very little sense as the eighth episode. The problem was, it simply wasn't ready and available for broadcast in time.

CHRIS: I think this is the case with quite a few of the episodes, in terms of the broadcast order; a lot of that was determined by what was ready to go out. 'A. B. and C.' must have been an absolute doddle to edit!

This was very much a writer's episode, and in this case, it was 'Many Happy Returns' writer Anthony Skene. Talking to Stephen McKay in 1988, Skene said, '*The Prisoner* was generally a bastard. George Markstein had seen and presumably liked plays of mine on the box.' Referring to the show bible, Skene said, 'I saw not one piece of paper. The show was a cosmic void. They sat there waiting for ideas. A free hand? Oh God yes.'

Skene made explicit his referencing of French director Jean Cocteau's work on 'Dance of the Dead', particularly *Orphée* (1950). Based on the legend of Orpheus and Eurydice, the dreamlike film shows a contemporary French poet becoming obsessed by some abstract poetry he hears on a car radio, and descending into the underworld.

CAI: During lockdown, I went through a phase of getting up stupidly early and watching films downstairs while everyone else was asleep. One of those was *Orphée*, and watching it at 5.00 am when I really should have been dreaming was a mesmeric experience. There is a specific reference in 'Dance of the Dead': the radio that Number 6 finds on the dead man's body, which still works. He uses it to tune into a voice from outside the Village. For years, I thought that it was Churchill, that it was a reassurance that there was life outside this prison camp.

In fact, the voice is reciting something far more puzzling and enigmatic. 'Nowhere in the world is there more beauty than here. Tonight, when the moon rises, the whole world will turn to silver... If our torment is to end, if liberty is to be restored, we must grasp the nettle even if it makes our hands bleed...'

CHRIS: I picked up a different reference here: a possible allusion to Number Stations, which were radio stations that broadcast various things, music, poetry, recitals, all on a repeated sequence, followed by someone reading out numbers. There was a famous number broadcast called 'The

Lincolnshire Poacher,' which ran from the mid-1960s until 2008. It's all a bit of a mystery but many people think that they're coded government messages intended for their secret operatives. That's what I thought this was!

Because of the free hand, Skene was given to pay homage to his influences, 'Dance of the Dead' feels unique within the *Prisoner* canon. Surreal and dream-like, there isn't another episode quite like it.

We have our third female Number 2, though it's the first time her gender isn't used as a plot twist *'A woman in power?!! Now I've seen everything!!'* Mary Morris is in charge from the off (she is also the only female Number 2 to take part in the opening titles).

CHRIS: I hate her opening dialogue in that title sequence. It feels like she's gone into a vocal booth, had a look at the script, given them one take, and then left. No effort whatsoever. There seems to be an oddness of intonation and delivery that I found quite sinister and remote. Maybe it's just me.

We meet the Night Supervisor in this episode, played by Michael Nightingale. Our false memory would have us believe that Peter Swanwick was the only 'Supervisor' in *The Prisoner* but this re-watch revealed that there were quite a few, distinctive in their green turtle-neck tops. Next week the Supervisor will be Basil Dignam.

Fans of *Whisky Galore!* will recognise the unmistakable features of Duncan MacRae, turning years of affable supporting parts in loveable comedies on their head by playing a particularly nasty doctor. Carrying a dark air of Joseph Mengele, one planned scene that never saw the light, saw him burying the results of his failed experiments. Sadly, in a fate shared by quite a few *Prisoner* actors, MacRae passed away not long after he filmed his scenes, at the age of 61. In fact, 'Dance of the Dead' was broadcast eight months after his passing.

Patsy Smart is back too, this time as a maid who brings Number 6 a little nightcap, spiked of course, to help him drift off.

CHRIS: I'd like to suggest that it's a posset! Traditionally it would have been given to children at night, usually in a bowl. I remember one from an episode of *The Box of Delights* in the 1980s.

Why not make your own Village Posset and help yourself settle in for a fine night's sleep.

You will need...
120 mls whole milk
Half a teaspoon of grated lemon peel.
50g golden caster sugar
1 teaspoon almond extract
1 egg white
50mls dark rum
50mls brandy

Gently heat the milk, lemon peel, sugar and almond extract in a saucepan until it starts to rise up and froth. Take it off the heat, then beat the egg white and stir it in, followed by the rum and the brandy.

The reliably scene-chewing Aubrey Morris (Mr. Deltoid from *A Clockwork Orange*) appears as the Town Crier. A master of the comic pause, he bellows his invitation to the Village Carnival, 'Turn back the clock!! There will be music, dancing, happiness, all at the Carnival... by order!!'

Even the crew get a look-in. The dead man who washes up on the beach is played by Roy Cannon, the props man, making a sterling acting debut. In amongst his 'wallet luggage' is a pair of raffle tickets, prize unclaimed and a photograph of him with another crew member.

'We're democratic... in some ways,' purrs Number 2 at one point. Though this is the dreamiest episode in the series, Skene is still keen to make political observations too. McGoohan would certainly have approved of the suggestion that democracy was in some ways an illusion that the higher-ups wheel out when it's convenient, then retract when it isn't.

In an episode where the disposability of the Villagers is made brutally clear, we're given a little clue as to why Number 6, uniquely, is exempt from this policy. 'This man has a future with us,' Number 2 insists. Really?

Someone who *doesn't* have a future and clearly knows it is Roland Dutton, a former ally of Number 6 from the pre-Village days, played by the excellent Australian actor Alan White. 'Such noble thoughts are long dead,' he intones grimly. 'Soon, Roland Walter Dutton will cease to exist.' Unlike some of the other former "friends" of Number 6, like the treacherous Cobb, used by the Village to play tricks on him, Dutton is the real thing.

There's an unusual scene when Number 6 tries to get into the Town Hall, but is stopped by a force field and an intriguing line of dialogue from a random villager with a chin-strap beard 'It's fussy who it lets in.'

CHRIS: There's a suggestion of sentience there. Arguably, Rover has that sentience as well. Or are they controlled? Is there an illusion of sentience or artificial intelligence? Is this where McGoohan was going with this? A satirical comment on our dangerous habit of allowing technology to think for itself?

CAI: If you're talking about prescience, you're not going to get a more on-target prediction than the Covid-style face shield that one of the Villagers wears behind Number 2 while she makes an announcement about the Carnival! I did spot a reference on the copy of the *Tally Ho!* from 'Many Happy Returns'. The headline reads 'What's Behind The Town Hall?' Presumably, it remains a mystery because no one can get in!

Like 'Arrival' and 'Free For All', 'Dance of the Dead' benefits greatly from the extensive location shooting at Portmeirion. It's all the more wondrous following episodes like 'The General' where studio versions of Portmeirion were used, largely by way of a painted backcloth. Being there on the ground freed Chaffey's camera crew to move in a way that created something truly cinematic.

The scenes on the beach look like something out of *Ryan's Daughter* compared to some of the artificial sand scenes they were sometimes forced to use. The lighting, eschewing studio lights to make the most of Magic Hour dusks and dawns, is particularly effective.
It seems to have its own specific cinematography, though Brendan J Stafford was the DP throughout the series. It all contributes to the atmosphere of magic realism that Skene was alluding to.

Finally, it's Carnival time. Honoured guests include Julius Caesar, Cleopatra, Elizabeth I and, inevitably, Napoleon. Number 6 appears in his own dinner jacket looking very much like 007. Quite how he still has his own tux remains a mystery. Perhaps Mrs Butterworth brought it back with her from 1 Buckingham Place? Number 2 offers an alternative theory when he asks why he doesn't have a costume. 'Perhaps because you don't exist.'

One can drink at the Carnival, and not just the moonshine cooked up in a cave for the likes of Eric Portman. Here, it's Champagne, a '58, no less. However, despite this rare opportunity for Village-sponsored drunkenness, things take a sudden turn for the sober. Number 6 sneaks out into the Town Hall and finds, among other things, the body he had launched into the sea. Yet another plan has failed. Number 2 discovers him, led there by Tammy the black cat, in a refreshingly untrained performance. 'Never trust a woman. Even the four-legged variety,' says Number 6, rather sourly.

Tammy exemplifies a specifically feline element to the show. Number 2's treatment of Number 6 is playful and cat-like, something that is emphasised occasionally by the deliberately mewing violins in Ron Grainer's score. For all her trouble, poor Tammy appears to get trapped in the morgue as Numbers 6 and 2 leave.

The 'body in the morgue' plot point suits the episode's position in many fan lists as their preferred Episode 2, putting to bed the question of what Number 6's friends, family and work colleagues are thinking. Are they looking for him? Are questions being asked at the highest level? Is there a search party? Well, they are about to receive, as Number 2 says, a 'confirmation of a known fact.' Any loved ones will soon get the news that he is as dead as the outside world is to him.

To compound his failure, he is brought back to the Carnival where a kangaroo court of his 'peers' (including his 'Observer,' Number 240, who is dressed as Little Bo-Peep) has been assembled to try him for the illegal possession of the transistor radio. Number 6 is quick to dismiss this façade as the trussed-up French Revolution-style show trial that it is. Number 2 makes empty, meaningless gestures of balance and clemency, but it's all an act. Curiously, despite the Town Crier's insistence that no names be used, 'just numbers,' Roland Walter Dutton is summoned by his name; the same one on his telex-printed death sentence.

His fate is heartbreaking and genuinely chilling. In a scene reminiscent of the moment in *Planet of The Apes*, when Charlton Heston discovers that his friend and fellow astronaut has been lobotomised, Dutton is brought to the ball dressed humiliatingly as a jester, having evidently been given the same treatment. It is quite possibly the darkest moment of the entire series. Not only does it remove Number 6's one last shred of hope, but it reveals just how remorseless the Village can be.

The 'jurors' pronounce a similar sentence for Number 6, who calmly walks away from the scene, before wisely breaking into a sprint.

CAI: It's called 'Dance of the Dead', and this is a genuine horror movie moment. The sound of the Villagers' scream, rising up as they are galvanised as one to chase after Number 6, put the fear of God into me when I first saw this scene. It's utterly chilling.

CHRIS: It's a collective scream, the Villagers as a gestalt entity, and that made it even more terrifying.

CAI: It's quite remorseless about the Villagers themselves. In allegorical terms, the Villagers are 'us.' And it doesn't go easy on 'us.' *The Prisoner* is often very happy to accuse its own audience of complicity; of being unquestioning, conforming sheep.

Number 6 escapes into a conveniently helpful underground passage which leads him into a room where he discovers a 1960s teleprinter behind a modesty screen. What is it printing? Is this Number 1? Number 2 doesn't let on when she appears. She merely stresses what she has been repeating all the way through the episode. He's dead to the outside world. Conform, or else. When the broken teleprinter starts mysteriously working again, she laughs us into the end credits.

CAI: This is the only weak link for me: the ending. It doesn't even really have an ending. He's sentenced to death. When the Villagers find him, they will kill him... but won't. The idea that the teleprinter was Number 1 was something that Anthony Skene was quite keen on, but it isn't made clear at all that it isn't. It's maddeningly vague, rather than challengingly enigmatic.

Who's the Two?

There is a wonderful meta-reference when Number 2 appears on the beach at sundown, dressed as Peter Pan, the stand-out scene in the episode. Around 1946-47, Morris played Peter Pan on stage in a much-celebrated performance, playing against Alistair Sim as Captain Hook with Donald Pleasance as Gentleman Starkey, can you imagine?! There is a famous photo of Morris practising her lines next to a statue of Peter Pan and at the time, her performance was thought to be definitive.

Initially, Number 2 was to have been dressed as Jack the Ripper but the costume was changed when Mary Morris was cast. Anthony Skene had been told that Number 2 would most likely be played by someone like Trevor Howard or Alec Guinness.

Born in 1915 in Fiji, she was a RADA-trained theatrical powerhouse from a ridiculously early age, Mary Morris was a deliciously androgynous, diminutive actress with a powerful and mischievous presence. Her career off-stage was largely television-based, including a Chris-pleasing appearance in a *Doctor Who* serial called 'Kinda' in 1982. She passed away at the age of 72 in 1988 in Switzerland.

CHRIS: To me, she was as iconic a Number 2 as Leo McKern. There's a richness to her voice. There's a playfulness, almost a flirtatiousness between her and Number 6 which he reacts to brilliantly.

Scores

CAI: I gave it 5 and a half. I docked half a point for the weak ending, but otherwise, I thought it was a unique, strong, vivid and intriguing episode and I loved it.

CHRIS: It just never landed with me. I watched each episode twice, once to enjoy them and again to make notes, and I found myself just tuning out. I'm not even sure why, but I could happily skip this one. Mary Morris is the only reason I'd watch it again so I gave it 3 and a half.

Cai: 5.5 out of 6
Chris: 3.5 out of 6

episode nine
Checkmate

Number 6 discovers that he is not the only 'rebel' in the Village. Carefully trying to work out who the prisoners are and who are the wardens, he assembles a group of like-minds and plots with them to overthrow Number 2.

Another early entry, filmed mainly on location at Portmeirion by Don Chaffey, might just lay claim to being the most iconic episode of the entire series. Put 'The Prisoner 1967' into your search engine and likely as not, the first image you see will be Number 6 holding The Queen's Pawn on a pole with a cape over his shoulder, it's even an action figure (as of 2023).

Gerald Kelsey's script was one of the earliest to be commissioned. He had been on holiday in Germany and visited a castle with a large chess-board carved into the garden. He was told of a local legend, that the Baron who once lived there would force underlings to play as human chess pieces, and once they were taken they were beheaded. 'Don't worry, that's not allowed here,' Number 6 is reliably assured.

Kelsey showed this episode to Markstein, who was especially tickled by the way one of the 'pieces' claims to have really enjoyed the game, even though he was simply a human statue being manoeuvred around the board by someone else, a delight one might have expected from McGoohan rather than his producer.

CHRIS: There's something sinister about the repetition of the loudspeakers, often talking over themselves 'Pawn to Queen's 4!' the repetition building urgently and threateningly. There's also a sort of pin-hole wipe effect that starts this episode (uniquely), which helps start things off at the heart of the action. Feels almost subconsciously like the opening of a James Bond movie.

If one were so inclined, one could view the entire episode as a chess match, with Number 6 playing Number 2. So interpreted, one has to finally conclude that Number 2 has been about seven moves ahead of his quarry from the very first play.

'Checkmate' features a very eminent guest star in George Coulouris whose character, it is suggested, was once a Count, but who is credited rather prosaically as 'Man with the Stick', something that will give UK fans of Vic & Bob something to snigger about.

Rosalie Crutchley plays the Queen with an adorable, childish innocence, conjuring up memories of the little kid who would follow you around the playground at primary school, asking questions all the time and trying to fit in. She is hypnotised by this week's sinister Village quacks (Patricia Jessel and the wonderfully-fringed Bee Duffell) into falling in love with Number 6 and unwittingly transforming herself into a human tracking device.

CAI: In those scenes, when Number 6 is rude or curt with her and even shouts at her, he took an almighty dip in my estimations because she is so charmingly naive and vulnerable. Her performance, bursting with a passion she doesn't know what to do with, channelled through a sort of awkward Joan Grenfell persona is so adorable, it's one of the stand-out supporting roles of the series.

She also makes a lovely cup of hot chocolate. The charming scene of domesticity as she brews them both a cuppa in his house was filmed as an afterthought and apparently the camera crew, not given enough time to set everything up properly, had to tiptoe around the actors while wearing slippers to hide any noise. Number 6's conciliatory tone after he scolds The Queen and upsets her is sublimely sweet.

As mentioned, Peter Swanwick's temporary replacement as this week's Supervisor is Basil Dignam. Ronald Radd makes his only appearance as erstwhile troublemaker Number 58, aka 'The Rook.' An omnipresent ITC stalwart, Radd was a scarcely believable 37 years old when he shot 'Checkmate'. He was noted for being very delightful company off-screen; a disproportionate number of 'wonderful' stories about making *The Prisoner* from the cast members involve Ronald Radd and his antics.

Denis Shaw returns as the jovial shopkeeper. We had huge fun researching this famous *Colditz Story* actor. Apparently, he had a reputation of being the rudest man in Soho, as well as being forever in debt and an all-around roustabout. According to Christopher Lee, Shaw started the bar brawl that led to Oliver Reed getting slashed in the face and receiving a permanent scar.

We found a lovely tale about a woman who once asked him, 'Are you... Denis Shaw?' 'Yes,' he replied, 'But why the hesitation?' 'Because it's such an awful thing to ask anybody.' It was said that his capacity for conflict led to his early dismissal from the series (in 'Hammer into Anvil', the shop is noticeably under new management).

Filmed back to back with 'Dance of the Dead', Checkmate is similarly blessed with widespread access to Portmeirion in all its glory. There is a constant theme of pursuit in the episode: everyone is being followed, and the location allows Chaffey the chance to stalk his characters without the fear of running out of scenery. You get to see the drive into Portmeirion which is rare. Even the beach is real.

CAI: It's another reason why this is such a famous episode. In fact, this would make the perfect first episode to show an uninitiated friend and get them into *The Prisoner*. It's all here.

The cult of the individual is discussed here. Chess, it is said, satisfies the need for power, but that satiates only two people (or sides), the people playing, who want to win at any cost. The pieces, or the people are irrelevant and disposable.

Number 6 and the ex-Count talk a stroll around the Village (spot the off-edit where they clearly start walking from their marks after the director calls 'Action.') During their chat, they discuss the ability to judge sheep from a sheepdog. 'How do I know black from white?' muses the Count, 'By their dispositions. By the moves they make. You soon know who's for or against you.' However, the Count's advice comes with the warning that all plans fail, including his own. 'In time, most of us join the enemy against ourselves.' Number 6, somewhat foolishly, fails to see that the seeds of his own failure in this episode are sown into his own plan.

CAI: It's to McGoohan's great credit that the way he plays Number 6 in each episode varies *just* a little bit. In his 'Checkmate' performance, he is aloof. The way he talks to the Rook, 'By your manner, I knew you were a prisoner: subservient.' That's charming, isn't it?! I'd have told him to get stuffed. Yet Number 6 *has* to be a little aloof for the mechanics of the plot to work. His aloofness is ultimately his undoing.

CHRIS: There's also a power dynamic going on within the group of rebels he assembles. Number 6 is clearly the alpha male, and he doesn't understand that by being the alpha male, he's scuttling his own ship.

Having disobeyed the loudspeakers and made his own independent chess move, The Rook is dispatched to the hospital to undergo a psychological test. Number 6 is invited to watch by Number 2. Apparently, Radd went full method in this scene and denied himself water so as to appear genuinely thirsty.

CHRIS: I enjoy the doctor's hubris in thinking that the Rook is 'cured.' She's an expert who has got it completely wrong, and she's blinded by her confidence in the validity of her own information. Ego gets the better of people sometimes and ego often replaces research, fact or empirical evidence. Sometimes, like the doctor here, people just want to save face. Happens a lot!

Psychology plays a complex role in this episode and it's front-and-centre in these hospital-set scenes. The Rook is subjected to an experiment in which he is parched and only rewarded with water if he obeys certain commands. Number 6 is also subjected to a word-association test that he rubbishes with his answers. 'Hope?' 'Anchor. It's a pub I used to drink in.'

Nonetheless, this probing does result in a telling exchange between Number 2 and the Psychiatrist, who says that Number 6 has a negative reaction to pain and that the ability to hide that 'would require superhuman willpower.' It's a little throwaway line but it does sum up what sets Number 6 apart from everyone else.

Number 6 patrols the Village seeking out fellow rebels, filling the chess section from his newspaper with coded messages to himself. Closer inspection reveals that the chess puzzle has been stuck rather carelessly onto an actual newspaper featuring a story about flooding in Kidderminster.

The rebels set about assembling their escape kit by scavenging the parts they need from the Village's own surveillance equipment, including a video camera, an actual camera for once, not a ret-conned granite bust, and a public phone. Quite what you need a public phone for when absolutely everyone is within a short walk away remains an unanswered question.

CHRIS: Number 6 says, 'Everybody's near in this place. Far too near.' I wonder if the public phone isn't an intentional comment by McGoohan on the laziness that too much 'helpful' technology engenders in us. Yes, you can walk across the street to chat to someone in about sixty seconds, but then again, why bother when I can just phone? I've had emails sent to me from people in the same office as me! There's a post box in the next episode. A post box! How lazy can you possibly be to send a letter in the Village rather than just posting it yourself?

Number 6 may be a pawn throughout this episode, but he sees himself as a knight. Even the mirror he looks into at one point is shaped like a knight's shield. This informs his behaviour: he thinks of himself as an heroic knight on a crusade. The theme of self-image, or how people view themselves, often with delusions of grandeur is something that is more relevant today than at any time, in a world of social media when one can effectively curate a distorted avatar alternative of themselves for public consumption.

The Rook too sports a heraldic shield on his beach towel. Look out too for the use of chessboard-style black and white contrasts which are used whenever possible.

With all the pieces of the transmitter assembled by the Rook, and all the rebels ready in their positions, the escape plan finally gets the green light. A distress signal is sent out to a passing ship, the MS Polotska is actually the gunrunners' boat from 'Many Happy Returns' given the briefest of makeovers. This results in the Supervisor making a surprisingly generous offer of help:

thinking that it's a downed plane, he asks Number 2 if they should send assistance.

Clad in a natty judoka tunic, Number 2 declines, suggesting that the Polotska will pick up any survivors. His mind is elsewhere; concentrating his body and his mind on the very thin piece of wood before him which he eventually judo-chops in half. Peter Wyngarde claimed to have rehearsed this martial arts move meticulously. A shame then, that the full spectacle of the chop is edited out. It does at least show that this Number 2 is a man in control of his own anger.

Like a scene from Denis Shaw's old TV show, the rebels scale the watchtower Colditz-style and take out the guards manning the spotlight in a brilliantly choreographed bit of violence. For all the futuristic, science-fiction elements of *The Prisoner,* the break-out attempt in 'Checkmate' feels very hands-on and *Great Escapey* in tactical terms. It keeps things effectively grounded and tense.

CHRIS: We're only talking just over 20 years since the end of World War II, so it would still have been fresh in the minds of the audience, and a lot of the cast and crew too. Think of 9/11. That's as long ago to us as the war was to everyone watching and making *The Prisoner*. God, how depressing!

The rebels now march on the Green Dome and take Number 2 hostage. None of them seem as suspicious as they perhaps ought to by Number 2's diffidence, calmly offering his wrists for the rebels to bind with rope. 'How disappointing,' he purrs, half-smiling.

When the distress signal suddenly stops broadcasting, Number 6 leaves the group to investigate. It's a shifty move. It gets even shiftier when he gets down to the beach and makes the decision to abandon his teammates and swim out to the Polotska alone. Once aboard he is greeted by British actor Terence Donovan (who would soon emigrate to Australia where he would eventually become Doug Willis in *Neighbours*, starring alongside his son, Jason).

For about 15 seconds, Number 6 thinks that he is on his way home to London, but he is quickly disabused by the sight of Number 2 on the ship's TV screen. 'I hate to disappoint you, but the Polotska is *our* ship.'

The full extent of Number 6's failure is now made clear.

Who's the Two?

Peter Paul Wyngarde, aka Cyril Goldbert. Possibly. A truly fascinating and unique actor if ever there was one. His biography is something of a mystery since huge swathes of it, possibly even all of it, is a fabrication of his own design. He claimed to have been born in Marseilles, though other reports, including his death certificate, state that he was born in Singapore. Even his birthday in 1927 is up for debate.

Assuming that this isn't apocryphal, he was raised in Shanghai and was close friends with J.G. Ballard with whom he spent time in a Japanese prison camp. He may have arrived in the UK in 1947, and ten years later had scored a lead in the excellent horror movie *Night of The Eagle* (co-starring fellow Number 2 Colin Gordon). He also made an impact with very little screen time as the ghostly Quint in the classic *The Innocents*, and was one of The Avengers' most memorable adversaries in the wonderful and notorious episode, 'A Touch of Brimstone'.

An old acting and drinking buddy of McGoohan's, Wyngarde claims that he was originally slated to play Number 2 throughout the entire series (a claim Derren Nesbitt also made). His high cheekbones, long features and velvet cello voice saw him playing many 'exotic' - read 'foreign' - characters in dozens of TV shows including several ITC programmes. It was for ITC that he played possibly his most famous part, Jason King in *Department S*.

King was supposed to be a rather tweedy Oxford don-type character who would act as a consultant to the main characters. Wyngarde transformed him into a cross between Charles II and Marc Bolan; an outrageous open-shirted playboy with a taste for the high life. Such was his impact that Jason King eclipsed the other characters in *Department S* and was given his own eponymous spin-off show in 1971, the only character in ITC's history to be granted such an upgrade.

For about two years, he was just about the most famous person in England, a fashion icon whose extraordinary sartorial excesses were copied wholesale by millions. He even released a self-titled album (re-released brilliantly as *When Sex Raises Its Inquisitive Head*).

He suffered from the same problems with alcohol that would bedevil Patrick McGoohan, problems that were compounded and intensified by a gross indecency charge in 1975 which drastically hampered his career. An entire generation rediscovered him five years later as the villainous Klytus in *Flash Gordon*. Despite the fact that he was acting through a gold mask, his voice was unmistakable.

He also has the singular honour of being a Marvel Comics character: an X-Man called Master-Mind, aka 'Jason Wyngarde.'

The world was a better place for having Peter Wyngarde in it. A remarkable actor, a singular presence, and an extraordinary life, which drew to a close in January 2018, at the age of 90… possibly.

Scores

CHRIS: Five solid stars. Great performances from Rosaline Crutchley, Ronald Radd and Peter Wyngarde of course, who doesn't actually have that much to do, but is possibly all the more powerful for his restraint.

CAI: I gave it five too. It's absolutely buzzing with ideas, all of which are well realised. I enjoy the cynicism; the delight that Peter Wyngarde is barely concealing, knowing from the beginning that Number 6 is not just creating his own trap but walking into it too.

Cai: 5 out of 6
Chris: 5 out of 6

Hammer into Anvil

Number 2 tortures the widow of a dead agent so sadistically that she leaps to her death. Number 6 is too late to save her and vows to take revenge on Number 2. Mounting a campaign of baffling gestures and behaviour, Number 6 convinces his quarry that it is he who is being spied upon by his displeased employers.

Listen to some of the quotes about Number 6 from some of his former adversaries: 'He's very single-minded; I sometimes think he's not human.' 'You'll never force it out of this man; he's not like the others.' 'He can make even the act of putting on his dressing gown appear as an act of defiance.' Etc. He has revealed a skill set that would make any screen secret agent feel second-rate, and to date, he has used these skills to try and outwit his captors and escape. In this episode, we witness the frightening prospect of what happens when someone with all those talents… turns them on you.

The twelfth episode to be shot, 'Hammer into Anvil' was written by Roger Woddis. His name might be familiar to anyone who used to read Punch magazine, which regularly published Woddis' poetry. A highly literate author, Woddis' episode is peppered with references to beloved writers like Goethe and Cervantes. He was originally headed towards a career in medicine but left to write for the left-wing Unity Theatre, before serving in North Africa and Italy in World War II.

He continued to write during the war and by the early 1960s was contributing to That Was The Week That Was and also The New Statesman. His play, World on Edge was first staged in 1965. Woddis is therefore an uncommon element in The Prisoner. Unlike most of the other writers hired by Markstein, he had very few television scripts to his name. 'Hammer into Anvil' is one of only four TV credits on his CV.

CHRIS: It was quite a rare outlet for his writing, but then he was able to embed his political and satirical writing style into a strong idea which is psychologically complex.

CAI: I think it represents, possibly more successfully than another other episode, what McGoohan's view of authority was. It's a naked, aggressive attack, delivered in a wonderfully passive-aggressive manner.

Possibly the safest pair of hands in the business, director Pat Jackson returns for his second episode. It begins away from the usual pursuit of Number 6 and his well-concealed information; Number 2 has other business. He is interrogating the traumatised wife of an agent (played by the hauntingly beautiful Hilary Dwyer, star of the 1968 horror classic, Matthew Hopkins: Witchfinder General) and is decidedly unpleasant to boot. His patience finally snaps and he switches to even more savage tactics. We are kept away from the details of this development by the TV watershed people, but Dwyer's screams suggest nothing less than torture.

Her screams are overheard by Number 6 who runs to her aid. Anyone familiar with Portmeirion will be astonished that he manages to run the full mile and a half from just outside the Hotel on the front, all the way to Castell Deudraeth, in less than ten seconds.

He arrives a moment too late, as Dwyer throws herself out of the window to her death. 'You'll pay for that,' threatens Number 2, but it's a threat without teeth, unlike Number 6's response. 'No. You will.'

Not for the first time, Number 6 is goaded into action by the mistreatment of a woman. Once again, his 'weak spot' is revealed to be a damsel in distress. Contemporary viewers might be critical and suggest that it's one of a million examples of 'fridging.' This is a trope named after a *Green Lantern* comic which showed the girlfriend of the hero murdered and stuffed into a fridge. You'll be seeing fridges now every time a female character is killed off so that the male hero can avenge her and learn something about life.

Giving him the benefit of the doubt, his failure to save Dwyer fires up his inner knight of honour. In the background, very subtly, funereal bells ring out, signifying death. It isn't long before he is summoned to see Number 2, an invitation he refuses, leading to the first fight scene of the episode and a game of 'Spot the Stunt Double' for the viewer.

CAI: Frank Maher once again really earned his money in this episode. He must have lost so much weight, not just scrapping but constantly walking around Portmeirion being followed by a camera crew; he's in this one almost as much as McGoohan.

Dragged to the Green Dome by a gang of sure-fisted stuntmen, Number 6 is seated before Number 2 for questioning. For extra emphasis, Number 2 draws an epée from his shooting stick and brandishes it threateningly at Number 6, even pressing the tip into his forehead. Number 6 remains unperturbed by his dealings with this, as he calls him, 'professional sadist.'

Number 2 is interrupted by a call via Colin Gordon's memorably impractical red phone. It seems that there is no such thing as pleasant chit-chat on this particular phone. Like Gordon before him, this Number 2 is visibly uncomfortable while making his report. Something that Number 6 latches onto with great interest.

CAI: This is the moment when he spots Number 2's blind spot. He instantly realises that for all his sadistic bravura, Number 2 is a weak and paranoid man. When he calls after Number 6, 'I'll break you!' Number 6 responds with a contemptible, 'Yes.' You can see that a plan has already formed in his mind.

He puts this plan into action with immediate effect, heading down to the Village Shop, now under new management since the deportation of Denis Shaw from the supporting cast. It's now being run by Village sneak and all-around Bizet enthusiast Victor Woolf 'There's no one to touch Davier. It takes a Frenchman.' It is here that we are treated to our first leitmotif: Bizet's *Prelude to Farandole*, from *L'Arlésienne*. It follows Number 6 around as part of the score, but it also features on a vinyl album in the Village Shop music section. Number 6 asks to listen to six copies in the booth, checking his watch each time before returning them un-purchased.

CHRIS: The 'Davier' reference is, I think, deliberate. Davier is a French word for dentist's forceps. I don't think it's a coincidence that Woddis chose what might be a torture device to name his fictional conductor. A throwaway touch, but a lovely one. I also found the choice of the *Farandole* telling, in that it's a chain dance. Like the Conga, when everyone holds hips and dances around (as they do in the Christmas episode of *Duty Free*), a chain dance is when people link arms or hold hands and dance around each other, but it's the connotation of the word 'chain' that stands out. It might be a tenuous link (no pun intended) but it's an appropriate choice.

A glance around the Village Shop is quite revealing. We can deduce that the photographic equipment promotion from 'Many Happy Returns' has now finished, replaced by a push on ornate cuckoo-clocks. These range from 35 to 50 work units. The *Tally Ho!*, by contrast, is 2 work units, which seems an extortionate amount for what is essentially a sheet of paper. We also see that the Village have their own record label, plus a journal called 'Village Now' in the magazine racks, perhaps as an upmarket competitor to the more tabloid journalism of the *Tally Ho!* It might also be a Village TV listings magazine. Imagine that!

SATURDAY

★
**Top Shows
For
Saturday
Night**
★

WORLD OF SPORT
From 12.45

Introduced by
No. 8
featuring Kosho,
Chess, Kosho, Virtual
Shooting, Kosho

2.0 KOSHO

No. 78 takes on No. 435 in the third round
of the No. 3 Memorial Competition.

3.0 CHESS

From the Village Square. The Man With
The Stick retuns to take on No. 301 in a
rematch following last week's thrilling
eighteen move checkmate. Will he prevail?

4.30 KOSHO

Highlights from the third round.
Commentary by the Butler.

5.0 VIRTUAL SHOOTING

The final of the Town Hall Cup. No. 45 will
be taking on No. 97 in the winner-takes-all
conclusion to this annual tradition of
silhouette targeting marksmanship.

5.45 KOSHO

Highlights from the third round.
Commentary by the Butler.

Be seeing you!

SATURDAY 20

VILLAGE NETWORK ON CHANNEL SIX   OCTOBER

It's the Arts, 9.30

• • •

Number 6 watches on in
disbelief as Number 47 films
an expensive tinned peaches
commercial for the Village Shop

See 7.55

6.0   **THE VILLAGE'S FUNNIEST SURVEILLANCE VIDEO BLOOPERS**

Settle in for the evening as
cheeky prankster No. 69
presents a cavalcade of
hilarious gaffes that
surveillance has picked up
this week. Expect a gaggle
of unfortunate run-ins with
Rover, a botched lobotomy
and a repeat of the popular
video showing No. 235
accidentally running herself
over with her own taxi!

6.30   **GARDENING CLUB**

No. 7 shows you how to
utilise seasonal sea mist to
get the very best out of your
hydrangeas. Also featuring
helpful tips about keeping
knotweed at bay from
No. 19 and his twin brother.

7.30   **THE GREAT BUTTERWORTH BAKE-OFF**

Former No. 2 Mrs.
Butterworth produces yet
another marvellous
celebration cake. Cut out the
recipe from today's Tally
Ho! and you can follow her
as she prepares and bakes a
Battenberg cake with her
own special marzipan icing.

7.55   **ELECTION ADDRESS**

Number 2 entreats you to
use your vote to elect the
Village's 'citizen of
character', No. 6.

8.0   **SPEED LEARN WITH THE GENERAL**

Hosted by the Professor.
Tonight, you will learn about
the complex history of
Colonel Charles Gordon,
from his service in the
Crimean War through to the
siege of Khartoum via his
time as Governor General of
The Sudan and his command
in China of the Ever
Victorious Army.

8.02   **WHO WANTS TO WIN 100 UNITS?**

Hosted by No. 78. Another
citizen dares to take a turn in
the famous black Aarnio
chair for a chance to answer
questions about Village
history and public policy.

8.35   **FILM PREMIERE 'THE GREAT ESCAPE'**
village edit

Hannes Messemer leads an
all-star cast as the brave
Kommandant Von Luger,
who uses all the powers at
his disposal to prevent a
treacherous band of guests at
his luxury recreation retreat
from escaping and wreaking
havoc in wartime Europe.
His patience is especially
tested by a troublesome
American 'individual' who is
repeatedly and easily
recaptured. Cast: Hannes
Messemer as Von Luger,
Hans Reiser as Herr Kuhn
and Steve McQueen
as Unmutual.

9.30   **IT'S THE ARTS**

with No. 89 MBE. Our genial
host is joined by shopkeeper
No. 112 to discuss Davier's
seminal recording of Bizet's
l'Arlésienne suite, and to
announce a sale on
Village-brand tinned peaches.
No. 88 also previews this
year's Arts Festival and enjoys
a rare interview with reclusive
tapestry artist No. 38.

10.30   **MUSIC TO END YOUR DAY**

The Supervisor hands the
great responsibility of 24 hour
surveillance to his underlings
for one hour, while he selects
his choice of relaxing tunes to
lull you to sleep after another
beautiful day.

11.30   **WEATHER**

Showers later.

CLOSEDOWN

Feel free.

Number 2 demands that special surveillance is placed on Number 6 and that all suspicious activity be reported to him directly, something Number 6 uses fully to his advantage. Assisting Number 2 is his sidekick / henchman, Number 14, played by Basil Hoskins. Hoskins, we learned, was the live-in lover of the magnificent character actor Harry Andrews (*The Hill, Ice Cold in Alex*) and they are buried together, which is terribly sweet.

An aggressive adversary from the off, Number 14 becomes the first person to challenge Number 6 to Kosho, the 'National Sport' of the Village. It's a rather odd sport which involves two players bouncing on trampolines with the aim of throwing one's opponent into a dangerously small paddling pool set in the middle.

CAI: This would never get past health and safety regulations these days. If you fell from the platform into that tiny pool, you would either snap your spine or break your neck. Those cheap motorcycle helmets wouldn't help at all. And why the heavy tunics? It's a silly game.

There's another scene that is so utterly pointless that it seems to have been added purely to pad the episode out to the required length. Number 2 uses an oscilloscope to prove to a bewildered psychiatrist that he has been speaking to Number 6. Of course, he has. It sounds precisely like Number 6. Then again, such demented time-wasting does show where Number 2's fragile mind is at this point.

Number 6 posts a letter to the Supervisor's radio requests show 'To Number 6. Warmest greetings. May the sun shine on you today and every day.' from Number 113. Number 2 demands an explanation, given that Number 113 is a deceased old lady. Number 6 is well aware of this, seeing her tombstone in the graveyard. To confuse matters even further, Number 113 is not just one, but two characters from 'Free For All'[37] (the two journalists). A little carelessness there from the production department.

CHRIS: Swanwick is back! He's back, he means business… and then he gets sacked. He's also a DJ. Maybe that's where he's been for the past few weeks? On a Village roadshow, or DJing at a wedding? It's like hospital radio, piped into your house whether you want it or not; a Village version of Simon Bates' schmaltzy *Our Tune* show…

---

[37] Number 113 and his counterpart Number 113B.

543
Hospital Lane
The Village
VI G32

Tel: (OOOI) 543

Dear Superviser,

I would be very grateful if you could play my request on the Village Radio show. It would make such a lovely tribute to my late fiance.

We were due to be married in September. My fiance, Number 877, had spent the night at his stag party in The Cat & Mouse along with his friends. It turned into a party for the ages - Number 487 was his best man and we all know what he's like after a few.

Suffice it to say, my fiance spent the night sleeping on the beach along with the landlord and Number 36 - who apparently had been kicked out for playing Kosho on the bar.

When he woke up, he made his way back to The Village at the same time that Number 2 was showing a new man around - 6, I think. Number 2 ordered everyone to stop suddenly, but my fiance panicked and started to runaway. As a result, Rover was summonned and smothered him to death.

I'm sure that despite his crime, he was a good, kind man and I was looking forward to many years with him. I would also like to thank the caterers for being so understanding about the last-minute cancellation.

I would like to request the Village Brass Band's beautiful version of The Tornados classic 'Telstar' in memory of a good man.

Yours sincerely,

Number 543.

Swanwick is humiliated by Number 2 and fired (there's a lot of firing in this episode and slapping too). Swanwick is replaced there and then by Derek Aylward, an actor famed for alternating roles in prestige productions with appearances in saucy 'erotic' British comedies like *School For Sex* and *I Like Birds*. His obituary in The Independent memorably began, 'The curious career of Derek Aylward encompassed the sophisticated, long-vanished world of

129

pre-Osborne West End theatre, the formative years of television drama in Britain and hard-core pornography...'

The ubiquitous Victor Maddern, star of pretty much every British comedy made in the 1950s also makes an appearance. He desperately wanted to work with McGoohan and signed up for this as soon as he heard about it.

Number 6's destabilising campaign continues relentlessly. He purchases one of Victor Woolf's reasonably-priced cuckoo clocks and leaves it as a 'gift' for Number 2, who immediately thinks that it's a bomb.

CAI: I did find the Village bomb disposal unit rather hilarious, especially having seen *The Hurt Locker* when the bomb diffusers are clad in inches-thick Kevlar hazmat suits with blast plates. The Village equivalent is two chaps with tin helmets and a bucket of sand.

CHRIS: The use of the cuckoo clock is, I think, a deliberate and cheeky reference to Number 2's state of mind: cuckoo.

Knowing that everything he does will be reported back to his nemesis, Number 6 leaves blank papers on the stone boat. He traps and uses a pigeon to send cryptic messages to 'someone.' He sends the nursery rhyme 'Pat-a-Cake, Pat-a-Cake, Baker's Man...' via Morse code to 'someone.' He places a Spanish quote from *Don Quixote* in the *Tally Ho!* 'There is more danger in the Village than is dreamt of.' Finally, he buddies up to Number 2's own Sancho Panza, Number 14, in full view of a snitching waiter.

All of these antics convince Number 2 that Number 6 is a spy (called D6) sent by the authorities (or 'X04') to report back on him. By the time Number 6 arrives at the Green Dome to visit him, Number 2 is demented, broken and alone. In a call-back to the chain dance of Farandole, Number 6 tells him that he is a weak link in the chain of command, waiting to be broken.'

Thumb-screwed by Number 6 into admitting that he is finished, Number 2 eventually picks up the dreaded red telephone and resigns his position. A victorious Number 6 leaves his enemy utterly destroyed, weeping like a child in his Aarnio chair.

Who's the Two?

Patrick Cargill returning... or preceding his appearance in 'Many Happy Returns'.

CAI: I rather like the idea that he *is* Thorpe. It would make Number 6's contempt for him make even more sense knowing that he was most likely responsible for having him parachuted back into the Village after his escape.

CHRIS: I think they're two separate characters. ITC did reuse actors all the time, but it's nice that it's an unspoken, unanswered question. It works either way.

Cargill and McGoohan's friendship went back many years. Cargill had even directed McGoohan in several plays, including *Ring For Catty* in 1957, which co-starred McGoohan's wife Joan Drummond. He initially had a career in the military, stationed in India during the war. He was also good friends with Patrick Macnee. He was in a truly wonderful episode of *The Avengers* called 'The Murder Market' (directed by 'The General's Peter Graham Scott) where he plays an officious wedding organiser who takes Steed on a cake-tasting test. 'I'll be quite frank with you, Mr Steed,' he mews tartly, 'Some of our clients would make even Cupid lose hope.'

In fact, his comic abilities (especially a talent for farce) are what most viewers will remember him for, which makes his sadistic Number 2 so surprising. He appeared in two *Carry On…* films, played a bumbling policeman in The Beatles' second film, *Help!* and also played the doctor in one of the most famous sketches in British comedy history, 'The Blood Donor' from *Hancock's Half Hour*. His slightly forgotten sitcom *Father Dear Father* was an immense success in the late 60s and 70s.

CHRIS: There's a very funny story about Cargill, who was gay, having dinner with playwright Ray Cooney, and taking a fancy to a rather handsome waiter. The waiter mistakenly took Cargill's soup spoon away, leading to him saying, 'Oh look Ray, the dish has run away with the spoon!'

His last performance, sadly, was playing Neville Chamberlain in the woefully misconceived Adolf Hitler sit-com *Heil Honey I'm Home!* which was cancelled after just one episode to the astonishment of no one.

CAI: I think his Number 2 is one of the great strengths of the episode because he's playing the sort of mid-management dimwit that anyone who has ever served in a workplace has had to put up with at some point; the classic bully. Someone right in the middle who has power over some of the workforce but still has to suck up to the people above him. What Number 6 spots in him is his awareness, however, buried and kept private, that he isn't that good.

CHRIS: He's also a narcissist. He blames everyone for his mistakes and never himself, which is another trait in bad middle managers.

Scores

CAI: 5. It does its job with ruthless efficiency. Perhaps one of the most purely enjoyable episodes of them all. Because of the nature of the series conceit, Number 6 essentially has to lose at the end of each episode. Sometimes he gets little wins, but ultimately, he ends up where he started. All escape plans fail. This one though is a 100% victory and it's immensely satisfying.

CHRIS: 5. It's one of my favourite episodes because it's so clever. It has a very well-constructed narrative. Number 6 has a purpose and he stops at nothing until he succeeds. He doesn't need guns or fistfights (although he's contractually obliged to have one), just his ingenuity, intelligence and cunning. It's like a chess match, only by now he knows the rules of the game.

Cai: 5 out of 6

Chris: 5 out of 6

P.S. In a very touching tribute to the Network Distribution founder Tim Beddows, who died unexpectedly in 2022, Network put 'Hammer into Anvil' out online for free in 2023, digitally scanned from a 35mm film broadcast by ATV in 1976, including the original bumpers, period commercials, and a new introduction from Catherine McGoohan. Network has since gone into administration which is a huge loss to fans of classic films and television. Their Blu-ray restoration of *The Prisoner* is without doubt the finest ever released.

episode eleven
It's Your Funeral

An initially cynical Number 6 teams up with the daughter of a rebellious watch-maker to prevent an assassination plot against the outgoing Number 2.

'It's Your Funeral' was directed by Robert Asher; an unusual choice since he was really a comedy man. Possibly his most famous film was *The Intelligence Men* (1965) starring Morecambe & Wise, which has a pretty poor reputation but is a perfectly charming if slight spy caper. As cinematic ventures starring TV double-acts go, it's a lot better than *The Boys in Blue* with Cannon & Ball.

CAI: I nearly saw that at the cinema. We went all the way to Rhyl to watch *The Empire Strikes Back* and we got there after a long journey and they'd sold out! I have never stranked so much in my life. I could not have folded my arms any closer to my rib cage if I had tried. In the end, we saw *Tron* which I deliberately didn't enjoy as an act of rebellion, but the only alternative was *The Boys in Blue*, which no one was prepared to countenance, even as an act of defiance. Val Guest directed it, a fine director (*The Quatermass Xperiment* and *The Day The Earth Caught Fire* spring to mind), and he ends up having to make that. The ignominy!

This was production order number eight, so we're halfway through. It seems that by this stage McGoohan's temper was fraying with the pressure building up and amassing upon his shoulders to such an extent that he was constantly losing his temper. This was shot before episodes like 'A Change of Mind', 'A. B. and C.', 'The General' and 'Many Happy Returns'. It gives you some indication of how long it took to knock this episode into shape that the previous episode they shot was 'The Schizoid Man'.

A lot of what happened *behind* the scenes turned out to be far more interesting than what happened on the screen. Things got so bad that Robert Asher was sacked by McGoohan midway through the production.

Perhaps this was the episode when McGoohan realised his dream of creating a miniseries with its wonderful allegory and its tight construction was starting to become a bit of a standard ITC product which had been taken off him to some extent. He had taken on too much. He was directing, he was producing, he was writing, he was responsible for paying out the money and everything ultimately came down to him. Markstein was by this point starting to see his influence ebb.

Taking most of the flak on this episode was the unsuitably genial Robert Asher, who fled in tears having been given a 'hairdryer moment' by McGoohan. According to Annette Andre this verbal bashing took place in the middle of the studio in front of everybody. Film librarian Tony Sloman commented that he'd never seen a more unhappy person than Robert Asher on the set of 'It's Your Funeral'.

Derren Nesbitt has said that he thought McGoohan was on the verge of a nervous breakdown. Nesbitt invoked McGoohan's ire by playing his Number 2 like someone who didn't know what was going on. Nesbitt countered that it was the only way to play him since nobody on the set, including the director, had any idea what was going on either. Mark Eden also commented that 'Pat was going through a very bad time and teetering on the edge of a nervous breakdown because of the pressure on him.'

Eden said, 'I seem to remember that he had a big row with the director, fired him and directed the rest of the episode himself. It didn't make for a happy time.' It's impossible to tell who directed what and how much of this was directed by McGoohan, but Asher does still get full credit, whether he wanted it or not.

The acrimony is there for all to see in Mark Eden's fight scene with McGoohan, rolling around together on an embankment. Eden is a bit of a unit, intimidating even in a light pink jacket. Of the two he's the heavyweight to McGoohan's welterweight. Interestingly, while Frank Maher normally stepped in to perform McGoohan's fight sequences, this time McGoohan did it all himself (maybe it was to avoid having to use close-ups). Apparently, McGoohan had his hands around Eden's neck and Eden was terrified because, by the look on McGoohan's face, it seemed like he'd lost it. 'He was actually throttling me.'

CAI: He'd reverted to his *Hell Drivers* character. Very 'Method.'

CHRIS: Well yes, but there's Method acting and then there's attempted murder!

Annette Andre also stated that she tried to get out of doing the programme because McGoohan was so rude to her; very dismissive of her takes and always correcting her. At this point, Annette Andre was fairly new on the scene, a delicate flower in need of a bit of nurturing and attention. It's even said that he tried to edit as many of her scenes out as possible. 'I tried to talk to him at one point and all he would do would be to put you down.' This of course is only one person's side of the story (well, actually it seems to be about eight people's side of the story).

'Your pupils are contracted.' It's a memorably dry bit of McGoohan delivery, but there are some, well, *unique* line readings going on here too. He stretches the word 'Phoney' into six high-pitched syllables and one wonders if he's directing at that point or if Robert Asher was there, already on the wrong foot with him, being dared by McGoohan to restrict his performance.

All this enmity was possibly a lancing of the boil because it was really only in this episode that McGoohan let loose such a level of unfettered rage. It wasn't the last time he'd fall out with a director or even fire one, but it would never again be done in such a humiliating public way. Perhaps Tomblin had a word in his ear? McGoohan was a good man at heart and above all, he was a professional and it would have not sat well with him to have acted so unprofessionally in front of so many people.

CAI: I hero-worship McGoohan and he is an idol of ours but I think his treatment of Annette Andre was rotten. He does not come out of this episode very well and it's there in his performance as well. He's like a taut knuckle. He's clearly in a bad mood.

There's a wonderful book called *Inside The Prisoner* by Ian Rakoff (a series editor who would later co-write 'Living In Harmony') and this is what he said about 'It's Your Funeral'. 'The commissioned writer, Michael Cramoy, was given a limiting brief. He was to write a story around existing stock material. This was the least original script in the series, a fabricated uninspired storyline implanted in material already shot, like the cut-out games for children where heads can be switched to different bodies.'

So that is how it started 'We have some footage. Can you please put a plot in there somewhere?' Truly, there is a veritable surfeit of reused footage in this episode. There was a little bit of new Portmeirion exterior footage shot, when the villagers are holding up the Number 2 placards of Derren Nesbitt, and the shot of Number 6 and Monique walking over to the bell tower, which features stand-ins.

CAI: I think we have established by this point that if they're being shot from behind or from a distance, it isn't the real actors!

This is essentially a bottle episode. In many ways, it doesn't feel like a *Prisoner* episode at all. There's no allegory. There isn't even an escape attempt, even though he ends up with basically a 'gun to their head' moment where he suddenly has a bit of leverage, and he doesn't use it at all. He lets someone else escape instead.

It's a plot that could easily have fit into an American drama serial, which makes sense when you consider US writer Michael Cramoy's history. He wrote several episodes of *The Saint* and *The Baron* but he also wrote for *Dragnet*. He also wrote for *Rin Tin Tin*, the rather cut-price *Lassie*, or possibly the upmarket *The Littlest Hobo*.

Cramoy's writing career ended shortly afterwards, in 1969, aged 54. (He died in 2001, so he enjoyed a lengthy retirement.) In fairness, Cramoy did a fairly creditable job within a very restrictive brief, but rather like the computer in 'The General', once one starts asking 'Why?' the episode blows up. It really does not stand up to any kind of scrutiny. For example, at the end when Number 2 is wearing the Great Seal of Office with the bomb inside it, Derren Nesbitt's Number 2 is waiting for it to go off, but standing about two feet away from him!

It's the only episode where you have an 'acting' Number Two. After the election episode in 'Free For All', this makes absolutely no sense. It's the kind of set-up that is necessitated by the plot, rather than sense or logic. The outgoing Number 2 says that he's been away on holiday and is only returning to hand over power. Is this gardening leave? And who is trying to kill him? And why?

CHRIS: Why wasn't the outgoing Number 2 introduced earlier in the episode?

CAI: Because they needed to introduce him later for the plot to work, but that's not how plots work. Normally, when something like that doesn't make sense (which it doesn't) they take it out, but they need to have the scene where he meets Van Gyseghem *after* warning Nesbitt. But how can you meet the old Number 2 when you've already met the new Number 2?

They're writing around a problem, rather than solving it. It is interesting though that for once, there is a Number 2 who is essentially on Number 6's side.

Nesbitt does a lot of his acting on the phone, presumably to Number 1, but who's to say, and also with his glasses.

CHRIS: I've read that there is a *Prisoner* drinking game where you have to take a drink every time Derren Nesbitt takes off his glasses[38]. You'll be under the table in no time.

Actors love props. Peter Cushing, famously, was a masterly prop handler. Noël Coward loved cigarettes and cigarette cases. There's a lovely story about Donald Pleasance who Coral Browne described as a 'handkerchief actor,' forever playing with little props, which made it impossible to cut around him and edit him out of a scene.

Number 2's foppish front is a mask covering up something far more passive-aggressive and calculating. When Number 6 comes in to warn him about the attempted coup, he puts on the standard, 'Ah, my dear chap…' routine, which is completely at odds with the devious plotter we've been watching thus far. There is a lovely louche touch though when he lazily presses a button with his foot rather than getting up from his Aarnio chair.

CAI: I remember watching this episode when I was 17 and thinking that Nesbitt was an incredibly young actor for such a part, a charismatic dynamic popstar-looking guy. Watching it again he's a lot nastier than I recall. He's nasty to his subordinates as well, and everybody knows someone who has spoken down to them in that condescending, snipey way. He's very ruthless. More formidable than I remembered.

It's refreshing to see a young Number 2 after all these older men, all the better to reflect the mood of the times. There was something undeniably 'Swinging Sixties' about Derren Nesbitt with his striking blonde hair (which was a hold-over from a film he'd just made with Frank Sinatra, *The Naked Runner*).

---

[38] In an interview with Derren Nesbitt, he confirmed that the glasses acting was all his idea.

There's a line that Number 2 says when Annette Andre's character faints or collapses, 'She's become a lady in distress.' This goes back yet again to Number 6's 'weakness.' However, this is about the eighth time it's been targeted and by now it's becoming something of a cliché.

His habit of standing up for women is a little ironic considering how shabbily he treats his female co-star on this occasion. Then again, he got on like a house on fire with Jane Merrow and Angela Browne. He just reserved a baffling contempt for Annette Andre. It's not like one can see his point: Andre is excellent in the part: charming, vulnerable, strong and challenging. There's nothing there for a director or co-star to get upset about.

The episode is not without some genuinely interesting ideas, whether by accident or design, not least the concept of 'Jammers' though one automatically imagines a tent full of Women's Institute volunteers selling their splendid preserves.

CHRIS: Made me think of Bob Marley!

Radio jamming, a wartime interference technique does, with *Prisoner*-like prescience foreshadow fake news and misinformation though most likely by accident. Another future grab comes in the form of Number 2's colossal glasses, which have an intercom built into the arm, and his watch through which Number 2 can chat and collude with Mark Eden. The first Apple watch? Yet again, what was science-fiction in *The Prisoner* became science fact in the future; another explanation for *The Prisoner*'s time-defying agelessness.

There is one element of 'It's Your Funeral' however that was extremely 'of-the-moment.' If there was one thing that became popular in the 1960s besides lava lamps and the Merseybeat sound, it was assassinating people. JFK and Malcolm X had already met their makers and the murders of Robert Kennedy and Dr Martin Luther King would be committed within a year of the episode being broadcast. There are traceable elements of *The Manchurian Candidate* (1962) here too; both share the plot pulse of someone trying to prevent an assassination. The brainwashing element of John Frankenheimer's classic is absent here but is spread widely across the rest of the series.

139

Giving it the benefit of the doubt, one can apply a little Marxist film theory here too. There are echoes of the Kuleshov Effect, which centred around the manipulation of emotions in cinema by the use of contrasting images. This was demonstrated by filmmaker Lev Kuleshov by prefixing three very different images with the same single image of a man's face: a dead girl in a coffin to show sadness, a bowl of soup to convey hunger, and a rather pretty girl reclining suggestively on a *chaise-lounge* to indicate lust. The man's face doesn't change, but the audience's perception of him is shaped entirely by the image that precedes him.

There's something similar going on here when the footage of Number 6's interview with Derren Nesbitt is cut together to falsely suggest that he is a perpetual wolf-crier. There's a Marxist slant to the depiction of the Villagers here too, which is something that shifts from episode to episode. In some episodes, the Villagers are sheep-like and even hostile, in others ('Checkmate' being the best example), they are capable, as in this case, of resistance and rebellion. It isn't just Number 6 here, it's him and his team.

At one point, we are given a blow-by-blow account of Number 6's daily routine. So insistent is he to commit to a regular timetable of events that a computer can work out what he'll be doing next with pinpoint accuracy.

CHRIS: It's Robert Rietty doing the voice of the computer but who is the voice supposed to be? There's this disembodied voice, but there are shots of the computer as he is speaking, so is this the computer speaking? At the time computers didn't speak like that. If anything they sounded like Robbie The Robot or the weird voice from *Billion Dollar Brain* (1967). He goes to his homemade gym and lets Frank Maher practice on the bars. He then goes water skiing! This is all before 9 am, for crying out loud!

By the time he goes for a daily game of chess and wins, always in an eleven-move checkmate, one starts to reflect on the algorithms that dictate social media today, and how these algorithms build up a profile of you. They've built up a profile of Number 6 which is so accurate that it can even predict the future, stretching credibility somewhat, when Number 6 buys the old lady a bag of candy.

The use of 'candy' instead of 'sweets' is curious. There's a lot of coffee drinking going on too, rather than the classic English tea. Americanisms are not uncommon in *The Prisoner*. In 'Free For All', for instance, Number 6 refers to 'Autumn' as 'Fall.' Little concessions to the US market, perhaps?

Ultimately, this is all sheer padding. Clear evidence of what Ian Rakoff described, largely cut together from stock footage. It doesn't further the plot. It doesn't benefit Number 2 to know what Number 6's daily routine is. If anything, it undermines the episode's logic since if Number 6's habits were so utterly predictable, they would have known what he would do at the end and prevented him from preventing the assassination. It's all very fun but completely pointless.

CHRIS: It reminds me of one of the great 'Scenes that should never have been shot,' namely the flower-shop scene from *The Room* (2003), where Tommy Wiseau turns up at a flower shop and says, 'Hi! I'd like a dozen red roses please!' and she says, 'Oh hi, Johnny. I didn't know it was you. You're my favourite customer!' Then he says, 'Oh thanks a lot. Bye!' and leaves, petting a dog on the way out. You're just thinking, 'Why did you bother to go to all the trouble to shoot that scene?'

CAI: Every scene in *The Room* makes you think that.

CHRIS: Something else that tickled me was the next scene when the computer engineer hands the print-out of Number 6's routine to a woman, who then hands it to Wanda Ventham's computer attendant who is only about six feet away! He doesn't get up and put it on the desk, instead, he hands it to a pointless intermediary who then hands it to Ventham. Is this a subtle way of just saying that sometimes within companies or businesses; within the workplace in general, roles are created that have absolutely no value and can easily be done by other people? A generous reading, though it certainly chimes with McGoohan's distaste for bureaucracy.

CAI: I reckon they accidentally cast the role twice and both of them showed up on the set. Wanda Ventham is sat there thinking, 'I thought I was playing Person Who Is Handed Computer Read-Out.' Robert Asher had to say, 'Look, you're both getting paid. Wanda, you sit there and you, love, you take the paper off him and hand it to Wanda, and then let's get some lunch.

Don't tell Pat we double-booked you. He already seems a bit miffed about something...'

Ultimately, after weeks of trying to work out how to fulfil the brief, they just came up a little short. The creative process doesn't follow the standard journey from a great idea, to a script, to shoot. Instead, it's a haphazard process. Perhaps knowing this from the off, McGoohan's irritability (to put it mildly) is understandable. This is, eventually, the best that they could do.

The Kosho game is a case in point, going on for far too long, probably with an eye on extending the running time. Originally this was to be a judo match but was switched to Kosho, which meant that they were able to pad it out with footage of Basil Hoskins' match from 'Hammer into Anvil'.

CAI: The rules of Kosho make no more sense the second time around. I think we should find a gym that would let us play Kosho, but I suspect that at least one of us would die.

It's not an un-enjoyable episode, but up to now the run has been pretty consistent and it comes after an especially strong episode. It just feels like a misstep. Conversely, this is one of the very best episodes for guest stars, positively spilling over with acting talent. Of course, we have the wonderful Annette Andre as Number 50, or Monique (a bit like Alison in 'The Schizoid Man' she gets an actual name).

CAI: She has a black badge. I've given up looking for significance when it comes to the black badge thing.

CHRIS: No, I think that when you get your badge you get them in different colours so you can match them with your outfits.

Andre would go on to become an ITC staple, appearing across their whole roster of shows but made her most indelible impression as Marty Hopkirk's widow, Jeannie in *Randall & Hopkirk (Deceased)*. Then there's Mark Eden, who was probably most famous in Britain for playing Alan Bradley in *Coronation Street*, in which he was killed by a tram in Blackpool[39].

---

[39] The character of Alan Bradley was killed, not Mark Eden who sadly died in 2021.

He was also in one of the first episodes of *Doctor Who* in a serial called 'Marco Polo', playing Marco Polo (the merchant-explorer, not the game) which also starred Derren Nesbitt. And let's not forget Martin Miller as the watchmaker, a great stage actor who also became an ITC regular. Peter Swanwick's also back, in old footage and new, with a bit more hair it seems, having been fired by Patrick Cargill in 'Hammer into Anvil'.

CHRIS: 'I think he's been to HR and they've reversed the decision on his firing.

CAI: I reckon everyone on that set, apart from McGoohan, was like a pack of giggling school-kids, having a great time until McGoohan walked into the room like a stern headmaster, then they all suddenly shut up and went back to reading their scripts.

CHRIS: We have *three* famous parents in this episode. We have Wanda Ventham, Benedict Cumberbatch's mum. We also have Charles Lloyd Pack aka Roger[40]'s dad and Emily Lloyd's grandad, but most importantly there's Andre Van Gyseghem, father of Joanna Van Gyseghem from... *Duty Free!*

Who's the Two?

Derren Nesbitt was a familiar face on television but he also had by this point a thriving career in films. He was fantastic in *Victim* (1961) with Dirk Bogarde, as a vicious blackmailer in leather motorbike trousers. He was possibly too good as his sinister performance led to him largely playing baddies for several years. Perhaps his most famous cinema role was in *Where Eagles Dare* (1968), with Richard Burton and Clint Eastwood, where he played the villainous SS Officer Major Von Hapen.

A unique actor who always stood out, especially after he dyed his hair bright blonde. He'd worked with McGoohan before, firstly on *The Adventures of Sir Lancelot* and then in two episodes of *Danger Man*, so they knew how the other worked.

---

[40] Trigger from the classic BBC sitcom *Only Fools and Horses.*

In 1969, he worked again with his friend, George Markstein on the groundbreaking ITV police drama *Special Branch*. He played DCI Elliot Jordan in the first two series of a show that would greatly influence other hard-bitten procedural dramas like *The Sweeney* and *Juliet Bravo*.

Six of One's Ant Brierley did tell us a lovely story about the time Derren went to their convention in Portmeirion, and he was being driven on a Mini Moke surrounded by fans in costume, and he shouted out to them, 'The last time I was here I had a fucking bomb around my neck!'

Scores

CAI: It's enjoyable, but it was a barely-salvaged mess. I gave it a three.

CHRIS: Despite some wonderful performances I didn't think you could give it much more than despite the wonderful guest stars. It's not perfect, it's not great but it's not a total loss of an episode. There are moments to enjoy within it. I gave it a three too.

Cai: 3 out of 6
Chris: 3 out of 6

A Change of Mind

Number 6 incurs the wrath of the Village when he is declared 'Unmutual' and ostracised by his fellow citizens. His Unmutual status comes with the threat of re-education in the form of a lobotomy.

'A Change of Mind' was written by Roger Parkes and directed by Roy Rossotti... for about fifteen minutes, until Patrick McGoohan had, well, a change of mind. This was one of the first scripts Parkes had ever written, but it became a springboard for several ITC shows to come. He had originally worked in farming and agriculture before becoming a journalist for the *Daily Express*, then moving to the BBC to work as a story editor and eventually finding himself in the same orbit as George Markstein.

Parkes was fascinated by the classic *The Manchurian Candidate*, both the film and Richard Condon's book, and the themes of brainwashing and paranoia fed directly into his *Prisoner* script. Handily, his brother Colin was a psychiatrist and was often called upon by Roger to provide ideas and advice regarding the script's neurological themes. Despite this, McGoohan wasn't always convinced by some of the ideas in the script, in particular the mechanics of the lobotomy operations. He was taken by recent research about ultrasonic brain penetration techniques, which sounded pleasingly futuristic and were incorporated into the story.

Markstein was a fan of this episode and remained so, later saying in the early 1980s, 'I think it's a cracking story with a sinister theme which 16 years later has become even more relevant.'

Roy Rossotti was charged with direction duties, having just helmed a very enjoyable episode of *The Avengers* called 'The Bird Who Knew Too Much', co-starring John Wood and Ron Moody who both play their parts as though they were tropical parrots. According to the cast and crew, Rossotti spent his first morning walking around the set searching for innovative shots and interesting camera angles. By the time everyone had finished their lunch and headed back to their marks, Rossotti was gone and McGoohan was calling the shots. Angela Browne later said that Rossotti 'Was talking a great deal of care and because he was taking care, he was taking a great deal of time and Patrick was very much, "Let's get on with it!" Patrick was getting more and more twitchy.'

The 2nd Assistant Director, John O'Connor recalled, 'I remember Patrick coming onto the floor and saying "The director's not very well and won't be coming back after lunch. Will you arrange for a car to take him back to London?" Tony Sloman said that he found Rossotti in tears in the car park after lunch.

CAI: Perhaps the problem with Rossotti was that he'd been a Second Unit director on *Doctor Zhivago* (1965), and if there's one person you do *not* want to pick up tips about 'just getting on with it' on a television series, it's David Lean.

The themes of 'A Change of Mind' are certainly full of interest and intrigue. Brainwashing, coercion, and even criticism of torture as a means to extract reliable information. More than anything though, it's about 'fitting in' and the price society makes the individual pay for going it alone.

CAI: It reminded me of an episode of *The Twilight Zone* called 'To See the Invisible Man' from 1986, where a criminal is forced to wear an implant on his forehead which means that no one is allowed to interact with him or even acknowledge his existence. He thinks it'll be a cakewalk but it isn't long before he's begging people to talk to him or even just look at him.

Even as proud a social outcast as Number 6 seems somewhat put out when, having been declared an 'Unmutual,' his greetings of 'good morning' are purposefully ignored. He's spent the whole series not wanting to be a part of this charade until he's told he's not *allowed* to play with the other kids, and suddenly he has a more nuanced perspective on the matter.

The episode begins with some reused footage from 'It's Your Funeral', padding out some rather obvious set-work, as Number 6 goes about his routine on his home-made gymnasium, periodically turning into Frank Maher, then air-punching the camera. He is approached by a couple of giggling thugs, one of whom is played by *UFO's* Michael Billington, who was famously up for the part of James Bond twice, before having to make do with being shot dead in the pre-credits scene in *The Spy Who Loved Me* (1977).

CAI: This scene, and the sinister guitar twanging over it, had me thinking about *Anchorman* (2004), when Wes Mantooth and his co-presenters accost Ron Burgundy and his news-team, all overblown threats and intimidation. 'What are you doing on our station's turf, Burgundy? You're about to get a serious beat-down!'

Having been filled in by Number 6, Billington, a 'last word' type, clearly scarpers, telling him that he'll face 'The Committee' for this.

CHRIS: The first thing that came to my mind after all this talk of The Committee, was the viral video of The Handforth Parish Council Zoom meeting (in which a petty, trumped-up councillor famously bellowed, 'You have no authority, Jackie Weaver!!!'). The committee in this episode symbolises this perfectly. It's in their costumes. There are the top hats, which represent the upper echelons, but also the standard Breton tops of the Village denizens. I wonder if that's a conscious decision: to indicate that these are just common people... who think they're of a higher status. Anyone who has ever dealt with an obstructive local parish council over an easily solvable issue might arrive at the same conclusion!

The committee represents bureaucracy at its most infuriating, petty and ineffective and it's something that was very much a bugbear of Patrick McGoohan, directing under his 'Many Happy Returns' alias, Joseph Serf. Frank Maher later credited McGoohan's decision to abandon the UK along with his family to a nonsensical dispute with the local council about a fence on his property. Reflecting the times somewhat, the committee is made up entirely of men, but the appeals sub-committee that later pays a threatening visit to Number 6 are all women.

Not only are they completely useless, but they applaud themselves at the end of their session. Number 6 however, is more than happy to prick their balloon of pomposity by casually tearing up the questionnaire of confession that they've made him write. However, he's already witnessed a taste of what's in store for him when villager Number 93, Michael Miller, he of the immaculately squared-off beard, is made to stand by a rostrum and repeat that 'they're right.' He is inadequate. His pleas of 'Believe me' build into a demented scream, before he walks off to the warm applause of the others.

CHRIS: I felt that this was a very prescient foreshadowing of what's happening today with social media, a towing of the line out of fear. One might not agree wholesale with a certain sentiment, but still feel the necessity to publicly state that they do, to defer the possibility of being attacked by one side or the other. Fitting in, essentially.

The parallels with 21st century social media and its effects do make this an especially relevant episode. Anyone coming fresh to *The Prisoner* today would almost certainly read all sorts of inferences to 'cancel culture,' which is essentially what is happening to Number 6.

Number 6 greets Number 61 politely but is completely ignored, now that his anti-social attitude is under investigation (keep your eyes peeled for the passing car at the top of the lane, an awful lot of 'business' takes place on the mocked-up version of this path). In Portmeirion, it leads to the statue of Hercules. They clearly wanted to get their money's worth after all the work that went into replicating it). Number 6 spies the news about his investigation in the brand-new *Tally Ho!* Upon closer inspection, one can see that the rest of the paper is filled, literally, with gibberish (an unintentional bit of satire about the media, perhaps?).

Echoing the role of his observer in 'Dance of the Dead', the beautiful but stern Number 86 is assigned by Number 2 to teach Number 6 the error of his ways. She too was once, as she says, 'disharmonious,' but was eventually made to see sense. She was played by Angela Browne, a fine actress whose husband was the voice of Gerry Anderson's *Captain Scarlet*, Francis Matthews.

In complete contrast to poor Annette Andre, Angela Browne had a marvellous time working with McGoohan, they'd played opposite each other before in *Danger Man*[41]. Asked by McGoohan if she needed anything, she quipped that a glass of Champagne would be nice. When she got back to her dressing room, there was a chilled bottle of Champers waiting for her. Number 2 actor John Sharp was equally effusive about his *Prisoner* experience.

Later on, Number 6 attends a meeting of The Social Group; mainly young student types - what on earth *they* are doing in the Village is another matter - and maintains his policy of non-participation. Despite their age, these young folk are every bit as conformist as their elders and chide Number 6 for his attitude. 'You're trying to undermine my rehabilitation; disrupt my social progress!' yells one. 'Rebel! Reactionary!' they chant hatefully. *Citizen Smith* this is not.

A trip to the hospital to have his knee reflexes tested allows Number 6 to glimpse a poor patient being subjected to some aversion therapy not dissimilar to the eyelid-immobilising Ludovico technique that Malcolm McDowell is put through in Stanley Kubrick's *A Clockwork Orange* (1971). It's a chilling scene and gives Number 6 an inkling of what to expect if his Unmutual status is given the green stamp.

---

[41] *Danger Man* Season 1, episode 6 - 'The Girl in Pink Pajamas'.

CHRIS: The patient he meets who claims to have once been Unmutual but is now 'cured' has clearly had a lobotomy. The whole issue of lobotomies was contentious from the off, but thematically it's the stuff of Cronenbergian body horror. They've taken something away from you, a facet of your being. In this case, it's anger and inhibition. In a way, you're being lessened; it's horrific.

His resolve not to fit in remains undiminished. For his intransigence and refusal to conform, Number 6 is officially declared to be an Unmutual. This, to use an old expression, means that he is 'sent to Coventry[42].' In more modern parlance, he is 'blocked' by the rest of the Village, even to the extent that his phone is cut off.

Number 2 takes great delight in seeing his quarry gradually capitulate to the pressures of absolute ostracisation. At one point, he finds himself alone in the woods, solemnly gazing at a flock of geese in flight.

CAI: I always loved that shot. Number 6's features soften a little as he looks at the birds flying away. You could argue that it's emphasising his solitude but I think the geese represent the possibility of escape, which seems more impossible to him now than ever.

Number 2 calls him to gloat and to warn him that his social conversion is behind schedule, after which, 'You just won't care.' A baying mob arrives, led by the formidable ladies of the appeals sub-committee who had previously bragged about their 'considerable moral courage.' Little of that is in evidence when they beat the shit out of Number 6 with their rolled-up umbrellas and supervise his dragging up to the hospital for 'treatment.'

CHRIS: One thing that I find very troubling, and it's something you see a lot of these days, is that the Villagers watch Number 6's medical procedure on TV. On colour TV, no less. It could be that it's being staged for the benefit of the Village to create plausible deniability. Then again, it's like they are producing this to pacify the Villagers who have now been riled into becoming

---

[42] An English idiom that many historians believe dates back to the English Civil War in the 1640s where captured Royalist soldiers were sent to and imprisoned in the city of Coventry.

a vicious mob. Even so, what could be more horrific than broadcasting a lobotomy on live television? Well, apart from *The Jeremy Kyle Show*[43].

This sequence may well be predicting the worst excesses of TV to come, but it is equally prescient in its use of wireless headsets that the doctors use here, but won't be using in real life until the 21st century. The eerily accurate foreshadowing in this scene makes up for the rather scattergun attitude to the editing which is all over the place.

Harking back to his transformation into a brainwashed political shill in 'Free For All', Number 6 is 'cured' and leaves the hospital to a hero's welcome from the crowd. Though his demeanour is now far sunnier, he does retain a trace of the old Number 6, particularly when he spots Number 86 spiking his tea. Note the Portmeirion pottery range getting a little plug via Number 6's tea set.

CAI: This is what I remember most vividly from this episode and I think about it every time I make a proper pot of tea, which is becoming a far more frequent occurrence as I get older. Whenever I spoon in the loose leaves, I use the 'Number 6 Technique:' Warm the pot first. Always rinse it out. One for me, one for thee, one for the pot and one for luck.

Number 6 does the old switcheroo with Number 86's doped-up tea and she ends up drinking it by mistake. Her taciturn demeanour soon dissolves into something far more flirty. In fact, in Roger Parkes' script, she was initially written as a far more romantic character with designs upon Number 6, but McGoohan predictably objected.

CHRIS: If there was such a thing as Village Tinder, Number 6 would definitely swipe right on Number 86. She's perfect for him. She's a doctor, she's intelligent, and she's beautiful. She has a lot of characteristics that Number 6 would certainly have found attractive. And I love her line, 'I'm higher than Number 2,' which would have been quite censor-baiting in 1967.

In another allusion to *A Clockwork Orange*, Number 6 returns to his homemade gymnasium and finds himself up against the same pair of thugs that

---

[43] A British Tabloid TV talk show that ran from 2005 to 2019. It was eventually taken off the air after a guest committed suicide following an appearance on the show.

started this whole mess in the first place. Like Alex being assaulted by his former friends after the Ludovico treatment, Number 6 is unable to fight back, initially. Unlike the former Droog, Number 6 eventually summons up his former self and gives his assailants a good pasting again.

By now Number 6 has worked out that his lobotomy was a sham, and that they're trying to keep him drugged to make him think that it was genuine. He decides to turn the tables on Number 2, using a hypnotised Number 86 as part of his plan.

He calls the Villagers together, ostensibly to thank Number 2 publicly for converting him. 'The butcher with the sharpest knife,' he tells the crowd, 'has the warmest heart.' According to Roger Parkes, this was an actual Chinese saying which he tweaked slightly. It's an aphorism-friendly episode. 'The slowest mule is closest to the whip' is another; also 'He who digs a pit will one day lie in it.' They all seem to hark back to Parkes' previous life in the world of agriculture.

The conclusion of the episode is desperately weak, made frankly embarrassing by deploying someone who looked nothing like John Sharp as his body double. The scene where the Villagers pursue him to the Green Dome is rendered comic by this astonishing bit of miscasting.

Number 6 unveils his hitherto unseen talents as a hypnotist, lulling Number 6 into a trance by swinging his watch in front of her face as if this were a children's cartoon. Chris did successfully identify the watch as a rather beautiful vintage Tissot PRS 516. Number 86 is convinced to call out Number 2 as an Unmutual in front of the Villagers. This is enough to send Number 2 (or his tall, thin stand-in) to leg it to the Green Dome for safety.

Surely we have seen that the process of being declared Unmutual is something that requires stages of discussion by the committee and a decision by its members. You can't just shout it on a whim. And this is Number 2, who is in charge of the entire Village. Why didn't he just order an Orange Alert and have Number 86 detained?

Who's the Two?

John Sharp had become a familiar face on British TV by 1967, more often than not playing avuncular landlords. He played such a fellow in the excellent *Avengers* episode, 'Murdersville', albeit a villainous one. He also appeared in *Coronation Street*, as well as Kubrick's *Barry Lyndon* (1975) and Terry Gilliam's *Jabberwocky* (1977). He made a memorable appearance as an uptight German *maître d'* in the gloriously funny 1984 spoof *Top Secret!* and his final role was in the BBC Sunday evening classic *Lovejoy*.

We found a wonderful quote from him. 'I've also had some very off-beat parts, like the man who was eaten by his lawn-mower in *The Liars*.' Surely a TV show worth seeing!

For whatever reason, Sharp makes perhaps the weakest impression as Number 2. It could be that his natural charms (he was by all accounts an incredibly pleasant chap) were such that he wasn't able to pull off the innate sinister authority or dominance required to play a genuinely formidable authority figure. He rather over-does his villainy here, with a laboured head-tapping tic and a gratuitous tendency to repeat himself for emphasis.

His Number 2 is also a terrible sexist. 'Stuuuuuupid woman!' he bellows, when he sees that Number 86 has fallen for the old switched-cup routine. 'Females!' he scoffs, earlier. 'If that woman makes one mistake, we could lose him.' He does at least manage to give his character one memorable trait: biscuit nibbling.

CHRIS: We've already had the likes of Patrick Cargill, Mary Morris, Guy Doleman, Leo McKern, and Peter Wyngarde, who all had a certain gravitas, and Sharp didn't quite have it. Perhaps that was intentional? Maybe they wanted to lessen his authority and impact in this episode. He's not intimidating or scary, just nasty, like a sort of racist uncle.

Scores

CAI: I gave it 3. It's full of fascinating, intriguing, potentially extraordinary ideas. As such it could well have been one of the key episodes. For whatever reason though the execution is flawed and it simply doesn't hold together;

perhaps because the director didn't realise he was the director until halfway through the first day of shooting. It's... OK, but it should have been brilliant.

CHRIS: It's an episode that didn't grab me the first time around and I haven't revisited it that much. I watched the DVD with Roger Parkes' really interesting commentary. To be fair to him, his script was pulled apart by others for various reasons. There are good points: it's the first time Number 6 meets Peter Swanwick, which is a bit of a moment, albeit brief but it remains my least favourite episode, so I gave it a 2.

Cai: 3 out of 6
Chris: 2 out of 6

Do Not Forsake Me Oh My Darling

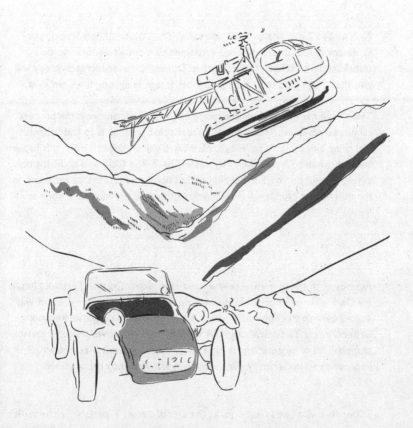

Number 6's mind is transplanted into another man's body so that he can leave the Village and seek out Professor Seltzman, the only man capable of reversing the process. While he's away, he reconnects with his fiancée, Janet.

This is very much the joker in the pack. From the opening few seconds, something is awry. For a start, it's a cold open (for the first time in the series, the title sequence is preceded by a scene, set in a darkened room where service agents watch a slide show and discuss a mysterious professor). In the Village, we are swiftly introduced to something brand new: helmeted guards, reminiscent of Bond villain henchmen, who barge into Number 6's house and drag him to see Number 2, making sure his face isn't visible to any cameras as they do.

As Number 2 explains to someone called The Colonel (Nigel Stock), one Professor Seltzman has invented a machine that can allow minds to be transferred into other people's bodies. Dominance over this technology will give the Village (and their side) a huge advantage in fighting the Cold War.

The Village has one such device, but it can only work one way; the process cannot be reversed. The only way to make that possible is to find Seltzman and bring him back to the Village. Number 6 will be keen to make this happen because when he leaves the Village, it will be in The Colonel's body. It's only when he wakes up back in his old London home and catches his reflection in the mirror that Number 6 realises what those Village swine have done to him.

Famous as the main musical theme from *High Noon*, 'Do Not Forsake Me Oh My Darling' was the original title lined up for 'Living in Harmony', but it was shifted over to this episode where it makes absolutely no sense. Returning writer Vincent Tilsley had originally titled it 'Face Unknown', which is much snappier. All of its iterations re-titled over different territories, are an improvement. In Germany, for example, it was brilliantly rechristened '2+2=2.'

Tilsley throws a line in early on, as the agents discuss Professor Seltzman. 'It's just possible that there is no clue to be found,' which one suspects is Tilsley letting the *Prisoner* fans feverishly try to decode everything, that this one is just a straight espionage thriller being written around a missing lead actor. That's precisely what it is, and it's a rather enjoyable one too.

Directed by the ever-reliable Pat Jackson, this has often been assumed to be the first episode of a second series, which isn't the case. However, it does mark the start of a change of circumstances within the production. By this point, Lew Grade had gone cold on the project. The hoped-for 26-episode production had by now been whittled down to a mere seventeen and, according to some sources, the money had stopped flowing as freely as before. McGoohan, it is said, accepted his role in John Sturges' *Ice Station Zebra* (1968) in part to raise money to finish the series.

George Markstein had upped sticks and left, though ironically, this is precisely the kind of action-packed, allegory-free episode he would have championed. The new look opening and slightly altered theme music also suggest that the producers were looking for ways to break free of the restrictive Village setting.

Without Markstein though, the production lost his impressive collection of writers' phone numbers. Consequently, crew members were now being asked to submit scripts and ideas. Sound editor Eric Mival pitched two ideas, unsuccessfully, but editor Ian Rakoff's script about a Western version of the Village would be green lit. Two very intriguing scripts, 'Don't Get Yourself Killed' by 'Checkmate's Gerald Kelsey and 'The Outsider' by Moris Farhi had already been nixed by McGoohan.

CHRIS: According to Robert Fairclough's companion book, had the series been renewed for a second series, the format would have followed the one presented in this episode, so there was an idea that they would have sent him out on missions, spying for the Village. Whether he had his original face or not is unclear. It might have been a *Doctor Who*-style thing where Saltzman's machine meant that instead of a new Number 2 each week, you could have had a new Number 6, but that's just me speculating!

There is so much reused footage in this episode that it sometimes feels like a 'Clip Show.' Patrick McGoohan must have gone through at least two tanks of petrol the day they filmed him driving his Lotus around London (and it is quite clearly McGoohan driving even though it's meant to be the considerably thicker-set Nigel Stock behind the wheel). The library footage of France and Austria back-projected behind Stock as he pretends to drive across Europe convinces nobody, despite the French bistro soundtrack piped over it.

Number 6 appears to have completely forgotten what's happened to him since he was abducted. Walking up to his own house, we hear his thoughts as he pads about the room, reminding himself to take the car in, do some shopping and buy a present for Janet.

In a montage cleverly referencing the original title sequence, 'Number 6' hops into the Lotus 7 and drives to work. Markstein's character of 'Man Behind Desk' has been recast in his absence. Now it's Danvers who gets to have his tea spilled by an aggressive Number 6. Danvers has retained Markstein's print of Philips' Mercantile Map of the World which hangs in the office, a reused prop, we suspect from the key *Danger Man* episode 'Colony Three'. There's a nice little bit of character building with Danvers, whom Number 6 patronisingly remembers was born in Bootle and took elocution lessons to get rid of his Scouse accent.

We see him take a trip up to the top floor in a once-popular Paternoster lift, the continually elevating doorless lifts onto which one would step on and off. Any contemporary Health & Safety Executive officer would faint at the very sight of one (there are now only three left in the UK). Number 6 is given an unusual code name, ZM-73, though we get to hear his many other European aliases, including his German codename, 'Schmidt,' which is a translation of Smith, the name he gives to Mrs Butterworth in 'Many Happy Returns'.

There's a pleasingly analogue feel to the subsequent cloak-and-dagger action as he tracks Seltzman down. Seltzman eventually buys Number 6's story after looking at his handwriting on an envelope that famously gives Portmeirion its first mention of the series and he is tracked down via a hidden address secreted with some photo slides which must be lined up in a certain order. It's an enjoyable, old-school spy-show moment, slightly undone by the sight of the greatest secret agent in the country having to use his fingers to count to ten.

CAI: As soon as I saw that, it reminded me of a scene from *Dracula AD 1972* (1972), when Peter Cushing works out who 'with-it' teen tearaway Johnny Alucard is working for by carefully writing his surname backwards. No one with half a brain would have to use a pen to work that out, but it's the same sort of performative deduction that Nigel Stock has to go through here for the audience's benefit.

Having been gassed by William Lyon Brown's undertaker who has been following Number 6 for the entire episode, Number 6 and Professor Seltzman are brought back to the Village to face Number 2. Number 2's knowing use of 'Heil' when he meets him does throw up the uneasy implication that Seltzman might have been a Nazi, much like the rocket scientists who were secreted out of Germany to help NASA in the 1950s.

Seltzman deploys a variation on Number 6's teacup switch from 'A Change of Mind'. He agrees to perform the reversal procedure on the condition that he is alone. He then swaps Number 6's mind back into his own body but underneath Number 2's nose, he swaps his mind into the Colonel's body and the Colonel's into his own.

Only when 'Seltzman' tremblingly asks Number 2 to 'Tell... Number 1... that I did my... duty...' does Number 2 realise he's been hoodwinked. Suddenly, Patrick McGoohan sits up, possibly still wearing make-up from the *Ice Station Zebra* set, and claims that the Professor is now 'Free to continue his experiments in peace.'

Number 2 watches in horror as he observes a reused clip of a helicopter taking off, telling us that Professor Seltzman has escaped. Quite why Number 2 doesn't pick up the yellow telephone and calmly say to the Supervisor, 'Bring the helicopter back please,' is a complete mystery. We know from the end of 'Arrival' and 'The Schizoid Man' that helicopters taking off in the Village rarely carry on to their intended destination.

As so often happened in *The Prisoner*, Hugo Schuster gave his final performance playing Professor Seltzman. The beautiful Zena Walker plays Number 6's fiancée, Janet Portland. One has to admire Tilsley's mischief in giving Number 6 a love interest to handle passionately... as soon as the actor playing him wasn't Patrick McGoohan! Convincing her of his identity by kissing her, he asks,' Who else could have given you that message?'

CAI: I can imagine that scene if McGoohan had played it. 'Who else could shake hands with you and keep you at arm's length like that? I hope you're not planning on staying the night, there's only one bedroom.'

Thematically, the whole body-swapping gimmick was quite ubiquitous in the 1960s. The ultimate play on 'double-agent,' it led to Steed and Mrs Peel swapping their minds with Freddie Jones and Patricia Haines in the *Avengers* episode 'Who's Who???' The final episode of the original *Star Trek*, 'Turnabout Intruder' has Kirk and an unhinged ex-lover switching minds to the bemusement of the crew.

As an acting challenge, it's an interesting conceit and it's an idea that has resurfaced periodically ever since, from the body-swap comedies of the '80s like *Vice Versa* and *Like Father, Like Son*, to the high-concept megastar-swap carry-on that was 1997's *Face/Off*. Fans of *Red Dwarf* will fondly recall the episode 'Body Swap' when Rimmer and Lister exchange minds to hilarious effect.

Despite the potentially fascinating sight of Number 6's personality housed in another man's body, Nigel Stock is unable to conjure up even a vague sense of McGoohan lurking inside him. Perhaps though, that was intentional. It's possible that an attempt by Stock to impersonate McGoohan might have led to an exaggerated, heightened version and reduced him to a caricature.

CAI: I've always loved Stock as an actor, especially as the eccentric inventor in *Young Sherlock Holmes*, which I used to watch repeatedly as a young lad. (On television, Stock was also one of the great Dr Watsons to Peter Cushing's Holmes.) Ultimately, he's undone by his innate kindliness. He has a sort of teddy bearish gait to him, quite unlike McGoohan's sharp, strident bearing. It's worth pointing out though that Alex Cox, when we interviewed him, was a big fan of Stock and his work here, so that can't be discounted.

It's also an early example of an eponymous show without its title star, which is something Markstein might have had in mind when he was trying to extend the concept to 26 episodes.

CHRIS: *Doctor Who* managed this by having the lead actor regenerate into a different one, but there are more recent examples of so-called 'Holiday Episodes' like the *Doctor Who* episode 'Blink', *in* which the Doctor barely appeared and Carey Mulligan played the lead. There was an *Incredible Hulk* episode too, 'Proof Positive', which was all about the reporter, Jack McGee, and doesn't even feature Bill Bixby.

It's another 'Celebrities' Relatives Episode!' The photographer who can't promise him a flattering portrait is the brilliantly named Lockwood West, father of Timothy, grandfather of Samuel and father-in-law to Prunella Scales. Furthermore, a famous uncle is attending the party: John Nolan, whose nephew Christopher is now one of the most famous directors in the world.

Interview with
Rick Davy of 'The Unmutual'

At this point, Rick Davy from The Unmutual Website (www.theunmutual. co.uk) was asked to defend this much-maligned episode. Here are some of his comments from our interview with him:

"Do Not Forsake Me Oh My Darling' always ends up at the bottom of fan polls but I love it, mainly for four reasons. I love the music, which is among the best in the series except perhaps the jaunty French music we hear when he's driving through the Alps! I love the reworking of the theme tune and Albert Elms' version of *My Bonnie* is superb.

'The second thing: I really like the stock footage, no pun intended. Nigel Stock couldn't drive so the only time we see him in the car and not McGoohan is when he's arriving at the port, and they've pushed the car past the cameras (It wasn't the original Lotus 7 from 'Arrival'. That one had been sold so a new model was hastily sought out and rented from the owner.) What I love about the footage is that they didn't just reuse old footage from 'Arrival', they used off-cuts from 'Arrival' so you see shots that you wouldn't otherwise see. I'm a real devotee of the production of *The Prisoner* and trying to match up which episodes things were filmed for.

'I enjoy the scenes in the MGM backlot, which is used extensively when he's supposed to be in Austria. There's a nostalgia factor too. It reminds me of the first time I saw it. For a ten-year-old, this is great kids' sci-fi stuff mind-swapping! I vividly remember seeing this when I was kid, and turning to my brother at the end and saying, 'That was good, wasn't it?!'

'There's a tendency as adult *Prisoner* fans, to go into the minutiae and try to analyse what everything means, but we sometimes lose sight of how much fun it is. Same with 'The Girl Who Was Death'. You can say we don't need them and they're just filler. Maybe, but they're still great fun! They don't make much sense, but they don't have to.

'Most importantly, this episode adds to the discussion. We find out so much about Number 6 from this episode. It adds to the 'Who's side are they on?' debate. Are his bosses in on it or not? We can't have that conversation without this episode. They're *not* fully in on it, because the Village are going after their guy as well as Number 6. If the Intelligence Service were in on it, the undertaker wouldn't need to gas them both at the end. Potter could have abducted them himself. (The fact that he's called Potter and so is Christopher Benjamin's character in *Danger Man*, 'The Girl Who Was Death' suggests something far more intriguing than anyone intended.)

'Yes, the plot has more holes in it than a fishing net. Yes, the writing leaves a bit to be desired. Yes, Nigel Stock's dialogue as Number 6 is pretty appalling and un-McGoohan-like. I think Stock was miscast, though he is a fine actor.

'Originally, the way they were going to get around McGoohan not being there was to have a travelling circus come to town and make Number 6 disappear! The rather more pragmatic David Tomblin, who knew they were up against it, said we haven't got time for these shenanigans. Let's do a straightforward 50-minute spy episode. The same thing happened with Tomblin's 'The Girl Who Was Death', which was based on one of his unused storylines from *Danger Man*.

'Then there's the vexed issue of Number 6's fiancée, Janet, hitherto unmentioned for the past twelve episodes. Well.. no one's ever *asked* him about her before so why would he tell anybody? He's famously quite clammy about giving out personal information. The only time his wife has come up is in 'The Chimes of Big Ben' when Nadia asks him if he's engaged and he tells her to go to sleep. He could have just said no. And who wrote that episode? Vincent Tilsley. It all ties in.

'We also know that Janet's father runs the Intelligence Service that Number 6 works for. This raises a bit of a dilemma. You'd think that it was proof that Number 6's side doesn't run the Village. Surely the easiest ploy for the Village would be to say to him, 'We have Janet. Talk, or she gets it,' and they don't. Then again, maybe that's because the boss is her dad. Therefore they *must* be in on it, otherwise, the Village would have just abducted her and threatened to torture her in front of him.

'Alternatively, in this episode, it's pretty clear that they don't know where he's been since he disappeared. They know that he's looking for Seltzman, but they don't know that there's someone else tailing both of them. So, for an episode with not much to decipher, it actually gives us the most information to chew on about one of the key questions of the series: what side are they on?'

Who's the Two?

Clifford Evans, a little late in the day, became the first Welsh Number 2 in the Wales-shot series. Evans would have been familiar to television audiences at the time from the acclaimed TV drama *The Power Game*, but he had several movie credits to his name going back to the 1930s. He was very effective in a couple of Hammer movies, playing lycanthropic Oliver Reed's aristocratic father in *The Curse of The Werewolf* (1961) and a memorably drunk Van Helsing proxy in Don Sharp's superb *Kiss of The Vampire* (1963).

He made regular appearances in action-adventure TV. You name it, he was almost certainly in it. He was especially good in one of the very best *Avengers* episodes, 'Dial a Deadly Number', in which he and John Steed go *mano e mano* in a wine-tasting challenge. When Steed successfully deduces that his glass of rouge is a 'Château Lafitte-Rothschild, 1909… from the northern end of the vineyard,' Evans lets the monocle fall from his eye with immaculate timing.

Born in Caerphilly, he started working in the film industry as a very young man. He was the second unit director on a film called *The Silver Darlings* (1947) and produced several others before stepping out in front of the cameras. Age suited him though. He developed interesting craggy features as he got older that could radiate kindliness or equally stern officiousness. It was a very 20th century face: he wouldn't have looked out of place in either of Harold Wilson's governments.

It's a pity that he didn't get a chance to shine more as a Number 2, appearing as he does merely in the bookend scenes. Nonetheless, he does become the only Number 2 to wear his badge on his right collar rather than his left. Were this any other episode, we might have gone digging for significance but as it's this one, we're assuming it was someone in wardrobe getting up to mischief.

Scores

CHRIS: I just found it very hard to analyse this episode. There simply isn't enough substance. The biggest point of interest for me is the existence of the Amnesia-Machine. Why don't they just wipe his memory every day if they've got one of those? Rick's interview did awaken in me some feelings of nostalgia though. It's admirably experimental, but if this had been the first episode of a new series, I don't think it would have been strong enough as an opener. I much preferred it to 'A Change of Mind' though, so I gave it 2.6.

CAI: I enjoyed it a lot more than I remember and I admire the way they cooked this all up having been forced into a corner by not having McGoohan. It's a bit like 'It's Your Funeral', in that it's an episode built around an external problem that they have to write around, only it's a lot more fun. I gave 'A Change of Mind' 3, so I had to bump this one up a little. 3.6.

Cai: 2.6 out of 6
Chris: 3.6 out of 6

Living in Harmony

An unnamed cowboy who looks a lot like Number 6, finds himself in a western town called Harmony. He quickly becomes embroiled in the machinations of the corrupt Judge who wants the stranger to become the town sheriff. Refusing to pick up a gun, he is drawn into conflict with the Judge's psychotic henchman. However, all is not what it seems…

Yes, it's the Cowboy one.

By now, the production had caught up with itself and episodes were no longer being broadcast in bizarre sequences. This was the fourteenth episode to be shot and the fourteenth to be screened (in the UK at least).

The question we have to ask ourselves is this: are they now coming up with brilliant ideas, rebelling against the constraints that they have created for themselves and developing the potential for a *Prisoner* universe without borders… or have they just run out of ideas?
There's a famous story that it was Frank Maher, having a drink with McGoohan after a game of squash, who suggested that they make a Western episode. 'There's an idea,' thought McGoohan…

CHRIS: It would have been a union's nightmare! The editor turns into the writer while the executive producer becomes the director. One can imagine the demarcation officer being locked in a cupboard until the shooting ended.

David Tomblin, for so long the steadying hand on the tiller, made his directorial debut here and took a writing credit too. The other credited writer was Ian Rakoff, who we talked about in the chapter on 'It's Your Funeral'. Rakoff, a South African now working in the UK was an assistant editor on three episodes of *The Prisoner*. Rakoff wrote about his first tense meeting with McGoohan: 'Pat paced round the room. Thus far, there seemed to be nothing at all good about his demeanour. He was pacing about as fast as when he was the thoughtful Number Six on camera, alone in his room and agitated.'

McGoohan had, it seems, been in a meeting with Lew Grade which had not gone well. McGoohan told Rakoff he should base his script on Grade. 'The power, the politics, the money behind it all. He's the one that's in control. He's the one that says stop and go.' After what seemed like an eternity, Rakoff was finally dismissed and was about to leave and presumably hit the nearest bar to console himself when McGoohan asked, 'Do you want to write a western with me?'

Their relationship got off to a fine start. Rakoff closely associated McGoohan with another mentor and 'gentleman rebel,' Lindsay Anderson. Alas, McGoohan was spirited away to film *Ice Station Zebra* and Rakoff had a less fruitful relationship with Tomblin, who had now taken charge of the episode and had already started rewriting his script.

The wordless opening was filmed on Dunstable Downs in Bedfordshire. Number 6 appears, dressed in cowboy duds and soundtracked by a Morricone-style guitar, only without a horse, saving the production the cost of an animal wrangler (McGoohan would get a horse later in the episode; a splendid beast called Viking). Some TV stations were worried that audiences might not have realised that they were watching *The Prisoner* and so added the title sequence, denying viewers a deliciously bold bit of blindsiding. There's an equally lovely touch when the title 'Living in Harmony', in the tell-tale Albertus font, emerges over the following scene of brutal violence as McGoohan's gunslinger is filled in by a posse of cowboys.

Very cleverly, the essential set-up of *The Prisoner* is replicated in an entirely new milieu. Rather than resigning, Cowboy Number 6 hands in his tin star. Instead of Number 2, we have the Judge. Instead of Number 2 wanting to know why he resigned, here the Judge wants to know why he won't carry a gun. The newcomer remains tight-lipped about his past and refuses to join in, just as he does in the Village, and the reaction of the townsfolk / villagers is equally hostile. Leaving Harmony is every bit as impossible as it is in the Village, only instead of inflatable balloons, there are deputised cowboys dragging him back every time he escapes.

The Judge is keen to recruit this newcomer to the Village of Harmony, but this man cannot be bought. The Judge submits him to all manner of intimidation but he cannot be pushed into picking up a gun, even when confronted with the Judge's in-house silent psychotic, The Kid (Alexis Kanner). The only ally he appears to have is the saloon's beautiful barmaid, Cathy (Valerie French), whose brother is currently languishing in jail. Cathy aids Number 6 in breaking out of his own cell, but he is soon brought back by the Judge's posse.

He is persuaded to take on the role of Sheriff but still refuses to pick up a weapon. His anti-gun stance repeatedly gets him into skirmishes. Another failed escape attempt this time ends with Cathy being accidentally killed by the Kid. This proves too much for Number 6, who finally straps on his gun belt, tosses aside his sheriff badge and goes looking for the Kid with vengeance on his mind.

McGoohan would cable Tomblin from the set of *Ice Station Zebra*, telling him that he was receiving lessons on how to draw a gun, Western-style, from none other than Steve McQueen and Sammy Davis Jr. Alexis Kanner meanwhile was practising his quick-draw at home with a Colt Peacemaker. The duel between Number 6 and the Kid is all the more frustrating for being edited to make the outcome a little vague. Number 6 gets the fatal shot in, though a frame-by-frame analysis shows that the Kid drew first. Kanner claimed that he picked up the rather nice touch of holstering his gun before falling dead from a Gregory Peck western.

With Cathy's murder avenged, the episode lurches into a sudden twist straight out of *The Twilight Zone*. It turns out Number 6 is in a Western set, wired up and wearing a headset. The cowboys he's been living in Harmony with are all cardboard cut-outs, their conversations spoken into his ears via microphones. It's all been a proto-virtual reality tour; it's a narrative directed by the Village. Rather elaborately, it seems that the western set has been constructed not too far from the Green Dome[44].

When he pops in, he finds the Judge, Cathy and the Kid, all looking very 1960s. Kanner looks very *Substitute*-era Roger Daltrey, with all of them revealed to be working for the Village. There follows something of a coda, as Number 22 (Cathy) wanders back into the Western set to question her actions, and is subsequently murdered by Number 8 who has taken his fantasy too far and still thinks he's the Kid. As Number 6 races back to try and save her, Number 8, in a fit of pique, takes a swan dive from the top of the stairs.

CAI: It's all a bit melodramatic, this. Kanner's death is particularly odd. Why does he leap to his death? I say leap, he falls about six feet. At worst, he'd have put his back out or maybe twisted his ankle. All this screaming and fainting might have been a way to give Number 6 something of a victory, but after the impact of the big reveal in the saloon, it feels gratuitous.

---

[44] The Mini Moke in this scene accidentally displays its real number plate rather than 'Taxi.' This particular Mini Moke was rediscovered fairly recently rusting away in Holland by *Prisoner* fans Phil Caunt and Jeremy Guy, who lovingly restored it and now show it at conventions.

The episode was shot on the set of MGM Borehamwood where much of 'The Chimes of Big Ben' and 'A. B. and C.' had been filmed. The costumes were from Bermans & Nathans, film costumiers, which might explain why, if one were to be a little unkind, a lot of the actors look like they're wearing fancy dress. Then again, how many Westerns were being filmed in Britain at the time? We could only think of *Carry On Cowboy*, but our research led us to the surprising fact that the first ever Western, *Kidnapping By Indians*, was actually filmed in Blackburn, Lancashire in 1899.

'Fearless' Frank Maher was a Western obsessive, so this episode was a highlight of the series for him. 'Westerns are my thing,' he said. 'I love 'em.' It was heavily influenced by Sergio Leone's 'Dollars' films, certainly the first one, *A Fistful of Dollars* (1964), which had recently been released in the UK. Like that film, there were more facial close-ups than dialogue. Not only did Maher advise on the set dressing and such elements based on his encyclopaedic knowledge of the genre, but after thirteen episodes of playing Patrick McGoohan at a distance, he finally got to play his own character, Third Gunman no less.

Maher's children also appear in the background, as does the son of assistant director Gino Marotta, who wanders into shot at one point the poor lad was originally given some dialogue but it was cut.

The discordant juxtaposition of the Village's futurism alongside classic Western tropes immediately calls to mind Michael Crichton's sci-fi classic *Westworld* (1973). Perhaps more tenuously, there is a similarity to *Vanilla Sky* (2002), in so much as the main character is constructing a false reality from remembered cultural artefacts. The deluge of Western archetypes on display here suggests an alternative reality crafted from the memories of a thousand Saturday morning trips to watch Republic serials at the Roxy cinema.

There's Mexican Stan, played by the toothsome Larry Taylor who was actually from Peterborough, which might explain why Robert Rietty plays his accent. There are saloons full of card-playing heavies, whores with hearts of gold and piano players ready to stop playing whenever the wrong person walks through the swing doors.

CHRIS: Something about those saloon doors always bothered me. The swing doors were there to obscure anything illicit going on inside and to act as ventilation for a room filled with cigar smoke. At night though, there'd have been proper lockable doors too, otherwise, anyone could wander in and take what they want, but you hardly ever see them in westerns, just those swingin' saloon doors. The impracticality is maddening!

There's also a *Hang 'Em High*-style lynching. Tomblin creatively shoots this scene from the victim's point of view, eliciting a sense of genuine horror and panic. Though the act itself was never going to be allowed on prime-time TV, the scream from Cathy is painful enough to chill the blood.

Even so, it was a contentious scene that was cut from the broadcast in several territories. There was even a tragic story that became attached to the episode: a 14-year-old boy had accidentally hanged himself and his bereaved father attributed it to him having just watched 'Living in Harmony'. In France and America, the entire episode vanished. No one has ever truly explained why. Some say it was the sad tale of the young boy, others that it was deemed too critical of The Vietnam War, another that it was the use of hallucinogenic drugs that did it (had they not seen 'A. B. and C.'?).

It is certainly a thrillingly violent episode. In one especially good brawl, Number 6 bests three gunmen with his bare hands as they try to goad him into using a firearm. In one such scene, Frank Maher's Third Gunman was launched through a window but missed the safety mattress on the other side. Apparently, his subsequent stream of profanity was enough to shock even the saltiest of crew members.

That wasn't the only onset mishap. When the Kid stubs out his cigar on the back of Michael Balfour's neck in the saloon, there was supposed to be a protective patch there but Kanner missed it. Balfour's look of sudden agony is more than just first-rate acting!

One contemporary reviewer has suggested that this was the episode when *The Prisoner*, to borrow a phrase from the internet, 'jumped the shark.' This is pretty unfair, though it's quite possible that this was the episode when a sizable chunk of the audience decided that enough was enough and abandoned the series, leaving a faithful core behind to gloat about their sophistication. It does at least dare to do something different.

CAI: There was an acceptance by this point that they weren't going to get to 26 episodes, and McGoohan never thought the concept would stretch that far in the first place. Nevertheless, this episode does suggest that they really could have gone anywhere with it. If, as Maher suggested, it is all in the mind, there are no boundaries.

CHRIS: If McGoohan had gone on to make another series, the possibilities would have been endless. Space, alternative realities, time travel, back to the first iteration of the Village (when we'd see who inspired the stone busts). So long as they could pull it back to the Village by the end of it and link the action to their machinations, it could work. That's how *Doctor Who's* survived this long.

CAI: I'm glad that they didn't, ultimately. I also like the fact that it's seventeen episodes; I like the oddness of that. I can't think of any other shows that only have seventeen episodes. It's a contributing factor to its uniqueness.

David Tomblin would go on to become perhaps the greatest assistant director in modern film history, with credits like *Barry Lyndon* (1975), *The Omen* (1976), *Superman* (1978), *The Empire Strikes Back* (1980), *Raiders of The Lost Ark* (1981) and *Gandhi* (1982) to his name, and *Braveheart* in 1995, which reunited him with Patrick McGoohan. He makes a pretty good fist of his first crack as a director, revealing a natural talent for blocking and keeping the story moving forward apace, elevating an hour's worth of television into something genuinely cinematic.

CAI: The shot at the climax when Cathy, aka Number 22 collapses on the wooden staircase, and Alexis Kanner's face suddenly looms up at her from below is an absolutely fantastic bit of cinema. It's a superbly directed episode.

One person who agreed with that, perhaps unexpectedly, was Ian Rakoff. Dave Barrie told us, 'Ian went along to see it at MGM studios along with the rest of the crew. He sat there watching and couldn't remember what he'd written and what he hadn't, but said that Tomblin's direction was first class.'

Interview with Dave Barrie

Dave Barrie is one of the founding members of the Six of One Prisoner Appreciation Society which was so instrumental in keeping the flame of *The Prisoner's* influence burning. We asked Dave to share his experiences working with 'Living in Harmony' writer, Ian Rakoff.

'I was always keen on meeting the writers and Ian was on my hit list. I wrote to him and he agreed to see me. He was very wary of me because he'd already met a few dubious *Prisoner* fans, but he cottoned on that I went in on a deep level. He said, "Dave, I've been commissioned to write a book. Would you help me?" I said, "Ian, I'd love to."

'In those days I travelled widely and spent a lot of time in London. At the end of the day, I'd drive over to Ian's and I'd walk up five flights of stairs to his flat in this tall Georgian terrace. I'd usually get there just as he'd be serving a home-cooked meal, often homemade bread and hummus. I'd bring a bottle of Claret and we'd go through the manuscript for three hours. He'd ask me for comments, if the facts were correct, what else could I bring, etc. It was wonderful. I was there one day a week, three weeks out of four for about four months.

'By the end of the process, we'd be in one room discussing what he'd written, while his editor Steve was in another room trying to make sense of everything. To be involved in a project like that was wonderful.

'Ian was a man of substance, which is why Patrick McGoohan took to him. He was born in South Africa under apartheid, a system which he abhorred. He was a sickly child, but as he grew up, he started to associate with groups the ANC and at one point he was the only white member. He even carried a gun. However, he was warned that the authorities were on to him and that he'd better get out. Having worked in South Africa on a Richard Todd film called *The Hellions* (1961), which was a sort of variation on *The Gunfight at The OK Corral*, he used that to get into the film trade in London. He met John S Smith and followed him as an assistant on his latest project, *The Prisoner*.

'As such, he was there from the start pretty much and knew McGoohan well. McGoohan would come in at the end of the day, swigging a gin and tonic, and ask Ian to take a look at the rushes and make comments.

'Ian and I have been friends ever since our first meeting and I've invited him up to events at Portmeirion several times. I think his book is marvellous because it's about radical filmmaking and how he found a mentor in McGoohan's 'gentleman rebel.' In the book, he said that his association with McGoohan changed his direction. He was a thinking, caring egalitarian… Had he been a politician in his home country, he would have thrown his lot in with him.

'As a child, being confined to bed, he'd got hooked on American Western comics, so he really wanted to make a Western. He wrote a story outline and parallel to that, McGoohan, Tomblin and Frank Maher were propping up the bar at the Red Lion wondering what to do with the show. Maher said, "You know, this series is really all in the mind anyway. We can go anywhere. Why not do a Western?"

'It was fortuitous that shortly afterwards, McGoohan saw Ian's outline plot for what was then called 'Do Not Forsake Me Oh My Darling'. They got together and started writing it, and McGoohan was incredibly supportive. He told Rakoff, "Ian, you do know you're a writer, don't you?"

'What cut across all this was that they were running out of money. McGoohan had complete creative control, but that really made Lew Grade and his money men very nervous. There was a natural break in filming during which time McGoohan was signed up for *Ice Station Zebra*. He told Rakoff, "I'm awfully sorry but I've got to go, but I'll leave you in good hands: David Tomblin." Ian found that working with David Tomblin wasn't as easy as working with McGoohan. Although McGoohan was very demanding, he could see that Ian was on the right track. There came a point, unfortunately, when Ian and Tomblin were going in different directions.

'Ian lifted the idea of a town called Harmony from a Gene Autry comic. All the ingredients were there, but how do you get out? I thought that was done wonderfully, the cardboard cut-outs and everything. It's all very clever and I'd never seen anything like it before. You could pick fault in the theatrical deaths of the antagonists at the end, but I liked it because you could argue that they had been fed the same drugs and had immersed themselves too much in the reality that *The Prisoner* was experiencing. So yes, 'Living in Harmony' liberated the series even further. One of my favourites.'

'Living in Harmony' marked the Prisoner debut of an actor who would become synonymous with the increasingly surreal final act of the series, Alexis Kanner. The French-Canadian actor had been making waves throughout the 1960s, proving especially popular in the role of DC Matt Stone in *Softly, Softly*, the *Z-Cars* spin-off. He and Dave Barrie became close pals in later years, as he told us:

'Alexis! What a guy. I've had nothing but admiration for Alexis since I was tasked with being his minder at a convention we put on. When I interviewed him in 2003 at Portmeirion, it emerged that he'd worked with Tomblin before. He and McGoohan liked his acting. They thought he'd be just right for the part of The Kid. He had this charisma. The camera loved him.

'Tomblin called him and asked if he wanted to do a western. Alexis called back and said, "Do you know, I could make this a lot better if I didn't speak." Normally actors want more lines but not in his case. I got him to read out the original lines and gave a long-standing Six of One member, Glenys McCairns the part of Cathy, and when you hear the two of them in conversation, despite whatever gravitas that Alexis could bring to it, the dialogue isn't terribly good; a bit pedestrian. By dismissing it, it became so much more.

'He and Tomblin got on really well. Tomblin told him to pick out his own costume but insisted on him wearing a top hat, like an undertaker. Alexis thought, "What can I wear that would make it look like I'd sourced everything from the victims that I'd killed?"

'He erupts off the screen. The casting director told Tomblin, "You don't want him, he'll eat up the scenery." He ended up in 'The Girl Who Was Death' too, on a whim. They used boot polish to colour his hair! He told us, "I didn't have a role but David was lonely and asked if I'd go along to a funfair with him."'

Who's the Two?

David Bauer was born in Chicago in 1917 but had more success in the UK (having been run out of town by Joe McCarthy and his HUAC pals). For fans of films and TV from this vintage, Bauer is a very familiar face and voice.

Something of a cut-price George C Scott, he had granite-like features and a chest like a wardrobe. In fact, he starred alongside Scott in *Patton* (1970) and it's a mystery that he wasn't typecast into playing more cigar-chomping US generals.

Like William Hootkins and Shane Rimmer, he was a UK-based American accent-on-demand. He was more prevalent on TV than in the movies (including several ITC shows, naturally), but he made an impression in films like the Amicus portmanteau *Torture Garden* (1967) playing an American movie mogul in a very cheap-looking 'posh' restaurant.

Possibly his most recognisable part was the ridiculously yet gloriously named Las Vegas funeral director Morton Slumber in the 1971 Bond movie, *Diamonds Are Forever*.

We couldn't work out whether or not his hair had been dyed for this part. As Number 2 at the end, his hair almost appears to have shades of lilac to it. There's also a trace of a British accent, or an attempt at one, perhaps to distinguish between his twin roles as Number 2 and the Judge.

Scores

CAI: I wasn't able to reconcile the conundrum of whether this was an ingenious new direction for the series or the start of a new phase in desperate barrel-scraping. It's a much better episode than I remember; as an allegory upon an allegory, it works very well. As much as anything, it's a rollicking wheeze so I gave it a four.

CHRIS: When I first saw it I didn't like it, but that's probably because I didn't like Westerns when I was younger. Watching it with fresh eyes, it deserves more credit than it gets. It does set up the potential for a whole new direction for the series, which is no small thing. There's a reason Dave Barrie is such a fan. I gave it four as well.

Cai: 4 out of 6
Chris: 4 out of 6

episode fifteen
The Girl Who Was Death

A secret agent known only as Mr X pursues a deadly quarry, a beautiful girl called Sonia who seems determined to kill him in an increasingly ingenious manner. Sonia's father is a Napoleon-obsessed madman who wants to destroy London with a lighthouse-sized rocket.

In 1992, Channel 4 were coming to the end of a nostalgia series called *TV Heaven*, a compilation of various episodes of vintage television shows all broadcast in a certain year. The series concluded with 1968 and on the 2nd of May, genial bow-tie-wearing host Frank Muir introduced episodes of *Please Sir!*, *The World of Whicker*, Monty Python antecedent *Do Not Adjust Your Set*, and finally, an episode of *The Prisoner* called 'The Girl Who Was Death'. Watching in their respective homes, both still school-aged, were Chris Bainbridge and Cai Ross. They were completely transfixed.

As a choice of an episode that typifies everything that *The Prisoner* represents, 'The Girl Who Was Death' is perhaps the least representative option of the seventeen available. It seems that this was something of a screw-up in the film library and not for the first time. For a 1982 ITV compendium called *Best of British*, someone was tasked with choosing the most iconic *Prisoner* episode and selected 'Dance of the Dead'. Whomever was sent to fetch the tape had a desultory shimmy through the options, saw the word 'Death,' grabbed it with unearned confidence and handed this episode to the line manager instead. *TV Heaven* made the same mistake 10 years later.

However, what they broadcast and what we saw that night was quite an extraordinary hour of television that was unlike anything we'd seen before. Hallucinatory, comic, absurd, thrilling, ingenious and immensely enjoyable, it infected us both with the *Prisoner* bug and our obsession with it started that night. Plus, it primed us with magical serendipity for Channel 4's re-run of the entire series in September of that year to mark its 25th anniversary.

David Tomblin based the episode on the idea of a book being read to children, which would enable him to take the action out of the Village. 'The Schizoid Man' author Terence Feely was tasked with writing it. 'I went away and wrote a lunatic plot which could have come from a child's storybook but which did move in a parabola back to the Village, so that we could get out of the Village.'

There was some talk of this episode being extended to a film length or a two-parter. So enthused were Tomblin and McGoohan by the episode that they flew to Cannes where Feely was on holiday, and asked him to write a two-hour version. Ultimately, the plan was nixed by Lew Grade.

The genesis of the plot dates back to the final days of *Danger Man*. The episode is teeming with *Danger Man* references, intentional or not, and anyone keen to prove that Number 6 and John Drake are the same person will invariably invoke 'The Girl Who Was Death' as their smoking gun evidence. For a start, there's Christopher Benjamin as 'Potter,' whom he played in one of the final *Danger Man* episodes. Or is he? Christopher Benjamin certainly didn't think so and played the characters completely differently.

Plus, there's an episode of *Danger Man* called 'The Paper Chase' (co-starring Peter Swanwick) in which John Drake dresses just like McGoohan does here when he walks into the pub and drinks a poisoned pint. Also, utterly delightfully, the fast-bowler at the cricket matches was an actor called John Drake. Drake was hired on the spot when McGoohan found out what his name was, and this is emblematic of the playful spirit of wink-winkery that runs through the whole episode.

We hosted a Twitter debate about 'The Drake Debate,' asking followers to choose between 'Yes he is,' 'No he isn't,' and 'It's irrelevant.' The winner by a considerable margin was 'It's irrelevant.' Surprisingly, the 'yes' camp came in second. Then again, George Markstein is on record saying, 'There was no mystery. Six was a secret agent called Drake.' Tony Sloman, the *Prisoner*'s film librarian also claimed that the name Drake was on continuity sheets when he first joined the series. McGoohan, though, was absolutely adamant that Number 6 was NOT John Drake.

Even with that in mind, the question cannot be answered conclusively, and that, ultimately, is how it should be.

CHRIS: A lot of people dismiss 'The Girl Who Was Death' but I think it's one of the pivotal episodes. It is doing something different. It's taking the mickey out of the spy genre. At the end of the episode, Number 6 places a clown in front of the Village's cameras. To me, this looks very similar to the clown on Test Card F, which older viewers might remember (the girl, the clown and the blackboard, remember?). You can take this in two ways. Perhaps it's just Number 6 saying that the Village are clowns, but I choose to see this as a sly dig at television and the shows that have been mercilessly mocked in the previous hour.

The episode may well be having fun at the expense of other spy shows and especially *The Avengers,* this could easily have fitted into the fifth season when the Mrs Peel episodes became colourful in more ways than one but it certainly has its cake and eats it too. They're having an enormous amount of fun making this, almost as much as we are watching it.

CAI: You could fall in love with the 1960s just by watching 'The Girl Who Was Death'. I did. 1992 was the 25th anniversary of both *The Prisoner* and *Sgt. Pepper's Lonely Hearts Club Band,* so the '60s were everywhere and I fell for them hook, line and sinker. I didn't listen to anything that wasn't from the '60s for a whole year. It certainly didn't hurt that I was completely in love with Justine Lord (who plays Sonia). I even went out with a girl back then simply because she looked like her. She is so specifically '60s-glamorous, it's astonishing that she didn't become a world-famous icon. Dressed top to toe in white (all her own clothes) she was every bit the Carnaby Street icon as Twiggy or Jean Shrimpton. A little bit like Annette Andre, Justine Lord managed to ruffle Patrick McGoohan's feathers somewhat and he was not especially kind to her. Lord, though, simply laughed it off.

A high-ranking officer, the Colonel, is murdered by an exploding cricket ball, one run short of his century too. The bomb was set by a beautiful and mysterious girl dressed in white. Number 6, or at least a secret agent who looks just like Number 6 but is known if anything as Mr X, is called into action by Potter, cunningly disguised as a shoe polisher. Mr X takes The Colonel's place and spends the episode pursuing the girl and avoiding her deadly traps (she is permanently one step ahead of him).

These delightfully eccentric opening scenes take square aim at all the spy tropes that had been delighting young TV fans since James Bond ushered in secret agent mania. Potter has a radio transmitter hidden in his shoe brush, straight out of Q Branch or *The Man From U.N.C.L.E.* 'Ridiculous,' McGoohan mutters and he is given his marching orders in a record shop listening booth by a side of vinyl, *Mission: Impossible*-style (though Jim Phelps' tapes never spoke back to him. Oh by the way, that's Alexis Kanner's voice on the record!).

CHRIS: It is all a little bit silly. Let's face it, if you're a proper secret agent, dressing up as Sherlock Holmes complete with deer-stalker and detachable lamb chop sideburns isn't going to fool anyone. He's even sat in the Turkish baths getting steamed away, wearing the Holmes moustache!

CAI: Undercover spies making themselves as visible as possible are the target of the satire here, James Bond in particular. The bad puns 'It certainly wasn't cricket' are especially Bondian. Roger Moore would often talk about the absurdity of this ultimate secret agent who was so secret that every bartender in the known world knew what his favourite tipple was. It's tempting to see this as McGoohan's disdain for a role that he turned down, perhaps aware of the inherent nonsense that the part would have entailed.

Another spy trope is the car which, ideally, would be something that the good people at Dinky could package as merchandise / advertising. For this episode, our hero drives a snazzy Lotus Elan S3. This might itself be an insider joke since the Elan was all set to be Number 6's car from the very beginning. McGoohan went to the Lotus manufacturers to inspect his option but noticed something much more suitable in the background.

The Lotus 7 looked at him. He looked at the Lotus 7. It was love at first sight. Of this super-sleek speed machine, McGoohan said, 'We needed a car for our hero. Something out of the ordinary. A vehicle fit for his personality... This was it. A symbol of all *The Prisoner* represented: standing out from the crowd, quickness and agility, independence and a touch of the rebel.'

CHRIS: That's what it needed. It's all well and good *Randall & Hopkirk (Deceased)* and *Department S* using the same cars to save ITC some money. *The Prisoner* needed something unique. Something that reflected the personality of its title star. Of course, for a spy, it does rather draw quite a lot of attention, but then that seems par for the course in 1960s TV spycraft!

Directed to the Thatched Barn pub by his beautiful nemesis, Mr X takes a moment to enjoy a quick pint. As he downs it, he becomes aware of some writing on the bottom of the glass. Only when he drains the lot does he see the complete message 'You have just been poisoned,' written in the famous Village Albertus variant font... possibly.

CHRIS: I noticed something for the first time: the font they use here is NOT the Albertus variant font. With Albertus, the 'e' is closed and rounded, as in here. In the Village variant the 'e' is a modified capital 'e' like a reversed 3. I like this because they've gone to the trouble of NOT using the Village variant to show that this story is happening outside the Village.

CAI: The first time I went to The Prisoner Shop in Portmeirion, they used to sell 'You have just been poisoned' stickers that you could stick on the bottom of pint glasses. I bought about ten. I gave Chris one of my last ones and I've just got the one left now. I have no idea why they don't make them anymore, outside of the potential for terrifying non-*Prisoner* fans who won't get the reference.

Having survived an attempt to steam him alive in a Turkish bath, a ploy lifted directly from *Thunderball* (1965), Mr X is called into a fairground boxing booth where he meets Harold Berens (who had previously played the journalist Number 113 in 'Free For All'). Here he plays the referee and in a short role, gets a lovely bit of comic mileage from the pause in his line, 'No biting or kicking... except in moderation.' McGoohan adored Berens and relished any opportunity to have him in a scene.

So why *is* McGoohan running around dressed as Sherlock Holmes? Frank Muir asked just that when he introduced the episode on *TV Heaven*. It was all to do with McGoohan being called back to finish reshoots on *Ice Station Zebra*, which suddenly took him away from production for as long as six weeks. Location work continued, with the dependable Frank Maher trussed up in a Sherlock Holmes outfit, shot from behind whilst capering around a pair of funfairs in Battersea and Southend. McGoohan would film his scenes wearing the same Sherlockian get-up in front of a screen months later. Alexis Kanner cameos here as a David Baileyesque photographer, his badly dubbed wide-boy epithets gleaned from his chauffeur, who was by Kanner's account, a bit rum.

There was to have been another bit of elaborate silliness here, with Number 6 being led into a maze which eventually becomes a tropical jungle and being attacked by a New Guinean head-hunter before being led towards a marauding clown on stilts by a talking parrot. Mercifully, perhaps, the scene was never shot.

CAI: One of the first things I ever took from this was how effective the editing was, and it's still dazzling. One cut from the slap he gets in the fairground to him lifting his cap stands out. Editor Eric Boyd-Perkins was a late arrival to the *Prisoner* team and had cut his teeth on films as varied as *Bridge on the River Kwai* (1957) and Hammer's *The Gorgon* (1964) (he'd go on to edit the seminal *The Wicker Man* in 1973). There are all sorts of tales of chaos and uncertainty about this episode but Boyd-Perkins doesn't just salvage the footage, he cuts it together like an orchestra conductor. It was so much more ingenious and cinematic than anything else being made on TV at the time.

Mr X pursues Sonia in his Lotus. There ensues a wonderfully surreal car chase, in which Sonia, by dint of the merest twist of her finger, sends Mr X's world spinning, literally as the back-projection behind the car starts turning upside down as a sitar plays on the soundtrack. Very 1968!

CAI: I thought that this might have been another gentle little dig at one of the evergreen dependables of the spy show, or film, the rather unconvincing back projection that never bears any relation to the direction the actor is steering. It's terribly effective. By this point, the episode has established that it has no great desire to stick to any rules and that nothing is really off the table, not even gravity.

The chase takes them to the deserted set-like village of Witchwood, home to a chain of shops linked by their nominative determinism. In a very *Avengers*y touch, the butcher is Mr Bull, the baker is David Dough, and let's not forget the candlestick maker, Leonard Snuffit.

CHRIS: Let's be thankful there was no gynaecology surgery! It's another touch that harkens back to childhood, not unlike Windy Miller from *Camberwick Green*; providing context that a child would understand. It's a very childish episode, not in a detrimental way. Even the violence is comedic. The traps that Number 6 is subjected to in Witchwood are straight out of the Adam West *Batman* series.

All of Sonia's elaborate plans are rather dazzling but (like so much of this), they don't make a great deal of sense. She sets up a sequence of continually devilish plots to kill him, yet always leaves little notes for him to find *after* he inevitably survives them. Knowing in advance that she'll fail, one has to wonder why she's bothering at all. The Witchwood traps alone must have taken weeks to set up.

CHRIS: It's just a waste of time! But then again, it's not *The Prisoner* that's crumbling here, it's the story; logic is being lampooned.

The traps are memorably staged, as are Mr X's often-inspired means of escape: it's almost a PG certificate, proto-*Saw*! Finally, having tired of the chase, Sonia whips out a bazooka and destroys the bulldozer that Mr X is steering towards her. Naturally, he dodges the explosion by hiding under a manhole. How? Honestly, do you care about that at this stage? There's no time to ponder in any case because seconds later, he is clinging to the landing gear of Sonia's helicopter as she unwittingly flies him to her secret lair.

He discovers an underground cavern which turns out to be the headquarters of the diabolical villain, Professor Schnipps, a Napoleon fan and Sonia's father. He has surrounded himself with a small platoon of devoted Napoleons to serve as his henchmen.

CHRIS: One of them is Joe Gladwin, who you might remember from the British sit-com *Last of The Summer Wine*[45], which ran for seemingly 300 years. It was a dependable final act for comic actors facing their dotage with no one else willing to hire them. In a way, you could say that it was a Village for actors. There was no escape for them, not even by hurtling down a Yorkshire hillside in a bathtub.

Schnipps' plan is to fire a lighthouse-shaped rocket which will destroy London. Mr X is temporarily captured and tied up. He escapes his bonds and turns the tables on his captors, tricking themselves into blowing up the lighthouse while they're still in it.

CAI: Once Kenneth Griffith shows up, every twenty seconds there's a bit of 'business,' all of which works. Genuinely comedic with pin-sharp timing. It's still funny now, watching it for the millionth time. The gags all land.

Griffith's Napoleon costume was an in-joke along the same lines as Mary Morris' Peter Pan costume, as he had only very recently played Napoleon. Once the dust from the explosion has faded, we are suddenly back in the Village. The whole thing was 'a blessed fairy tale.' Number 2 (Griffith) and his

---

[45] As of 2023, *Last of the Summer Wine* is credited by The Guinness Book of Records as the longest running sitcom in the world, running for a total of 37 years and 31 seasons / series.

assistant (Lord) thought that he might let something slip if he was reading a bedtime story to a group of children. However, as the man says, 'That one wouldn't drop his guard with his own grandmother!'

Why on earth are there children in the Village? Was it the case that their parents were both spies so they had to kidnap the whole family? Intriguingly, it does suggest that captured spies, once brainwashed into a wholesale acceptance of conformity might meet, say at the Cat & Mouse, fall in love, settle down and have kids. That said, it would lead to pressure on the Village's resources. Perhaps that's why we haven't seen any until now?

CHRIS: A lot of people seem to miss the point of the storybook, that this is a fictional representation… of a fictional representation. A play within a play. He's reading a story to children but there are no words in the book, just pictures. He's making it up, constructing a narrative from the images that are already in the book. It also reminds me a little bit of *The Wizard of Oz* (1939) and how one perceives the events that take place in that story. Dorothy lives in a sepia-tinted world, and after she's dropped into this vivid Technicolor land, the people she knows from back home are transposed onto these new characters. It becomes part of her coping mechanism. She's telling a story in her head but she's having to cast it mentally. Likewise here, the children are listening to this story being read to them by Number 6 and are casting him as the hero. He in turn is casting Number 2 and his assistant as the villains.

Who's the Two?

Kenneth Griffith… or Kenneth Griffiths as he was, before Mr Griffith, his headmaster at school advised him to drop the 's' as a way to stand out from the crowd.

Born in Tenby on the beautiful South Wales coast, he served in the RAF before becoming an actor. He became a regular presence in British comedies from the late 1950s and '60s like *Private's Progress* and *I'm All Right Jack*. As well as an actor with an unmistakable, inimitable eccentric style, he was also a writer, script editor, most notably on the acclaimed 1986 mini-series *Shaka Zulu* and a keen stamp collector.

He was a documentary maker too, of great renown. Something of a political firebrand, his uncompromising documentaries were often controversial; none more so than his 1973 television film about IRA revolutionary Michael

Collins, *Hang Up Your Brightest Colours*. Griffith was a passionate supporter of Irish republicanism which the Independent Broadcasting Authority banned. It wasn't broadcast for another twenty years. The successful court case that ensued awarded him enough money to buy his house in London.

He and McGoohan were very much simpatico in their worldview and both men respected each other greatly. Griffith contributed a delightful foreword to Robert Fairclough's superb Official Companion book, which is well worth reading. Fairclough told us a wonderful story about this. 'Halfway through the interview, his phone rang. He answered it. "Yes? No. No, still here..." then hung up and said, "Sorry about that. It was O'Toole. We ring each other up to make sure we're still alive."'

Scores

CAI: This one could either have been a one or a six! As a countermeasure to the episode's unfair 'filler' reputation, and as an indicator of its importance in our history of discovering *The Prisoner*, I went above and beyond a little and gave it a 5.

CHRIS: I gave it a 4.5, and the reason is the nostalgia factor. Without this episode, we might not ever have made the podcast in the first place.

CAI: I watched this with my eight-year-old son. He's watched a few *Prisoner* episodes with me and always got bored and left, but he was enraptured by this one.

CHRIS: It's designed for children. Even the final line of the episode was a lift from Derek McCulloch's sign-off at the end of *Children's Hour* on the BBC. 'Goodnight children... everywhere.'

Cai: 5 out of 6
Chris: 4.5 out of 6

episode sixteen
Once upon a Time

Number 2 seeks and receives approval for Degree Absolute: the ultimate test in which he will drag Number 6 psychologically through his entire life in one final attempt to discover why he resigned. One week locked in a room together, and only one of them will walk out alive.

Unbelievably this was the sixth episode to be filmed. This is an extraordinary fact. The idea that the production bounced from this to the audience-pleasing 'The Schizoid Man' is so discombobulating that one can scarcely get one's head around it. For the actors, it would be like finishing a seven-month run in *Equus* on Friday then curtains up on *Run For Your Wife* on Monday evening.

CAI: 9.2 million people watched this. Imagine the kids playing with their dinky Mini Mokes by the TV watching *this!* I wasn't a huge fan of this episode when I first saw it, largely, I suspect, because I just didn't know what was going on. I still found myself a little lost this time but now I was excited and challenged to be lost within it, desperate to work it out and get to the bottom of everything.

The shooting of a TV series in non-sequential order was nothing new and was certainly par for the course in *The Prisoner*, but tonally, thematically and certainly in terms of the content, this bore almost no similarity to the previous five episodes, Markstein, as we will see later, was completely dumbfounded. Just to get into the headspace to act and direct it must have been a dizzying experience for McGoohan.

CHRIS: I think that because this is only episode six (in production order), McGoohan wanted to shoot as much of his vision earlier rather than later. I've heard it argued that it was designed to be the last episode of a planned first season but that makes no sense because it's just too short a first season even for a UK-based show, especially for an ITC show which were all designed for syndication.

For all the feverish speculation about the timing of this episode, it might well be boiled down to as mundane a factor as availability. Leo McKern was performing at the time at the Garrick Theatre in *Volpone* so there's a good chance his schedule alone might have accounted for the seemingly insane idea to shoot this so early on.

It was originally titled 'Degree Absolute', after the process Number 6 and Number 2 endure in the episode. Of course, it is a punning reference to *decree absolute*, which will be a familiar expression to anyone who has ever been through a divorce.

CHRIS: Imagine the surprise when my own decree absolute arrived in the post after my own divorce and I was able to glean some delight from the slightly opaque *Prisoner* reference. Every cloud etc.

An extraordinarily sparse, Beckettian two-hander, this has echoes of Pinter's *The Dumb Waiter*, in which two hit men sit in a basement waiting for a 'job' unaware that one of them is the intended victim. In its shifting hierarchy of authority between two adversaries, it shares its DNA with Anthony Shaffer's 1970 play, *Sleuth*.

It is also laced with references to McGoohan's days in the theatre, some more obvious than others. This theatrical aspect provides an apt moment to bring up Henrik Ibsen's *Brand*, the play that brought McGoohan to nationwide attention. This was McGoohan's *other* great passion, even after *The Prisoner*. His daughter, Catherine has said that if there was one part that was tailor-made for her father, it was Brand: the lone wolf, the isolationist, enraged at the world in which people are constantly failing to live up to his expectations.

McGoohan had been gathering good notices in theatrical productions, a bit of 'telly' and some walk-on parts in the movies, most famously in *The Dambusters* (1955). He'd impressed Orson Welles enough to get cast in the great man's production of *Moby Dick*, playing Starbuck. Then, in 1959, he played the title role in Henrik Ibsen's bleak tragedy *Brand*. Such was the immense power that he conjured up and radiated that people were quickly talking about him in the same breath as Olivier and Burton.

CAI: It was a bit like the first run of Jez Butterworth's *Jerusalem*. I hadn't heard of Mark Rylance at that point but I'd met people who had seen it and they didn't even have the words to describe what they'd experienced. It was the kind of elemental God-touched performance that doesn't seem humanly possible. That was the kind of reaction that McGoohan was getting when *Brand* was at the theatre.

The BBC filmed the play in all its stark monochromatic glory, and was available on DVD. McGoohan spent years of his life trying to get a *Brand* film off the ground. It was even part of a post *Prisoner* deal with ITC, which eventually came to nothing.

CHRIS: His obsession with this character of Brand says a lot about McGoohan as a person, especially his morality. Brand has exacting moral standards and looks down with scorn on those who don't meet them. McGoohan too had a highly moral streak that was likely a result of his Catholic upbringing, not just at home but at school.

His schooling turns up as one of the first chapters of Degree Absolute, as Number 2 takes on the position of his teacher. It is the first of several autobiographical elements in this episode. Many of the stages here are taken directly from McGoohan's own life. Some are fictionalised, some are just plain made up, but essentially this episode follows McGoohan's path rather than *The Prisoner's*.

It was written and directed by Patrick McGoohan (no pseudonym required). It was written, he claimed, in a 36-hour writing binge, which might account for the unique and quite demented nature of the script. Aware that it would be viewed with incredulity by many, he credited the screenplay to one Archibald Schwartz. A famous tale has props master Mickey O'Toole taking McGoohan to one side to ask, 'What idiot wrote this?'

It was the first draft. The words and directions spilled out of McGoohan's feverish mind straight onto the page unedited. He took the famous adage that writers should write about what they know and applied it to this episode: part autobiography, part psychological analysis. Interestingly, in the script itself, the characters were called ANGELO, LEO, and PAT. Not P for Prisoner, but PAT. Had this been the case all along? Was P short for Pat rather than Prisoner?

CAI: It reminded me of the primal scream therapy phenomenon. Not the excellent band, but the Arthur Janov-inspired therapy concerned with the repressed pain of childhood trauma. Janov encouraged patients to re-engage with it to overcome it. John Lennon was the most famous fan of this technique, and he cited it as an influence on his first, painfully autobiographical solo work, *Plastic Ono Band* (1970). I thought that was all very hippy-sixties stuff, but Janov's book didn't come out until 1970, so 'Once upon a Time' predates it.

What follows is a struggle for supremacy, from the cradle to the grave, through the seven ages of man. Infancy, schoolboy, teenager, young man, middle age, old age and dotage and death.

The action starts outside of the Embryo Room, in one of the final Portmeirion-set scenes of the series. It's a very odd scene, as Number 6 accosts a villager (former cave-dwelling chemist John Cazabon) and starts barking random words at him. The Villager is not unreasonably puzzled by this, looking uncomfortable just being near Number 6. Perhaps by this late stage, Number 6's antisocial behaviour is such that he's become *persona non grata* with absolutely everyone.

He's still of keen interest to Number 2, who is flicking through his files. Past images of Number 6 from the series flash up on the screen to remind us of the battles of old. This Number 2, though very familiar, is a very different Leo McKern to the one who was once so complementary about his abstract art. For one, he is a prisoner himself: watched over by Rover who sits bulging cheekily in a chair…

CHRIS: …disappointed that he can't ever become Number 2 as the badge would burst him.

Making the theatrical allusions crystal clear from the start, the screen on which Number 6's footage is played, is revealed from behind a retractable set of curtains. There's then an outstanding shot of McKern, standing in front of the screen, inserting himself into the action like an oddly protective, omnipotent spirit. It echoes a shot from Peter Weir's 1998 *The Truman Show*, where Ed Harris' 'Creator' Christof stands in front of a big screen and strokes the image of a sleeping Jim Carrey.

The Butler cops an earful for not removing Number 2's unwanted breakfast fast enough. Perhaps the Butler too has taken on a little of Number 6's intransigence and is himself starting to rebel?

Number 2 sets in motion the ultimate challenge, Degree Absolute. A two-way fight with only one winner. 'I require approval,' says Number 2, then intriguingly he states, 'I am a good man. I *was* a good man, but he will be better.' This builds upon the implication put forth by Mary Morris' Number 2 that 'This man has a future here.' Is the Village looking for a leader? Has that been the game all along?

CHRIS: To run the place, he has to accept his place, which he never does. Most people do accept the situation that they're presented with, but he doesn't want to live in their bubble. The whole conceit of the Village is to make him appreciate it, adapt, accept it, and make the best of it all, but he rebels at every turn.

CAI: He probably wouldn't mind living in a bubble so long as it was his bubble.

McKern famously struggled in this episode. He was already facing a touch of burnout from multiple performances of *Volpone*, and the extreme demands of this episode (physically and mentally) led him to suffer a genuine nervous breakdown. McGoohan walked into his dressing room and found McKern curled up in a foetal position. Given what McGoohan was going through at the time, struggling to cope with the huge pressures of making this show and taking on too much responsibility himself, you realise that you are witnessing two actors struggling at the very edge of sanity.

It was Stanislavskian method acting taken to the extreme. This was McGoohan reaching into himself, pulling it all out and displaying it, warts and all. When asked about this, McGoohan very understatedly quipped, 'It's good to get a few things off your chest, isn't it?' It's catharsis and it's so autobiographical that the only way to analyse the episode is to view it as such. This is McGoohan putting himself through the shredder.

The residual staff are let go. 'Timesheets as normal; double night time.' Bureaucracy never rests! Then again, it also implies that with Number 6 holed up in The Embryo Room for a week, the rest of the Village doesn't matter. The Supervisor remains in attendance, but he essentially has a week off to practise his DJing.

With the assistance of the throbbing Pulsator, lowered once again onto Number 6's face while he sleeps, Number 2 approaches him singing children's nursery rhymes in one of the least soothing baritones imaginable. Number 6 is now hypnotised and remains so, a childlike figure led by Number 2 into the arena of conflict.

The stage is set, the curtains are open, the house lights are dimmed, and down we descend towards The Embryo Room. It's dressed exactly like a studio stage, right down to the black drapes. Like many plays, especially more abstract productions, the depiction relies not on sets but on props. A rocking horse, a blackboard, a wonderful lawn-mower / mini-tractor, and what was supposed to be some kind of brain-washing device but which was more likely an upstanding 1960s hair dryer; Mickey O' Toole on fine form here.

CHRIS: As someone who has worked in theatre, I see this very much as a deliberate stage performance. The allusions here are all theatrical. This episode could easily be transferred to the theatre. It actually was staged, in 1990, at the Edinburgh Fringe, with Samuel Beckett's *Endgame*, fittingly, put on afterwards.

The childhood stage of Degree Absolute feeds off something that was very much in the air, culturally, in the late 1960s. Artists were returning to the artefacts of their childhood. Jonathan Miller's TV version of *Alice In Wonderland* was a major event, starring just about everyone (including Leo McKern who played The Ugly Duchess).

Lewis Carroll's work in general became immensely popular once again, as did Kenneth Grahame and Edward Lear: you can hear Lear's voice in John Lennon's nonsense book, *A Spaniard in The Works* and his song, *I Am The Walrus*, and in the music and lyrics of Syd Barrett-era Pink Floyd. *Bike* from their *Wind in The Willows*-referencing first album, *The Piper at the Gates of Dawn* (1967), is a delightful childish melody that develops into something unnerving.

Likewise, most of the Edwardian-era toys that crop up in *The Avengers* take on a sinister edge, often a murderous one. The use of childhood iconography to unsettle had been a running theme throughout *The Prisoner*, the use of nursery rhymes in particular and it's ratcheted right up as Degree Absolute begins.

CHRIS: As we might put it these days, Number 2 is trying to 'Retcon' Number 6's psyche, delving into his past to find out why he's so rebellious and perhaps rewrite his history so that he might become more cooperative.

It's only when he goes to school that the challenging nature starts to appear. Up until then, he had been largely silent, licking an ice cream, a sublime bit of acting from McGoohan. Acting 'childlike' is so often an irritatingly over-baked over-reach for many performers.

Young Number 6 also has a great affinity with mathematics. He is 'very good with numbers.' Good enough to work in a bank as a clerk, which he does here (and did in real life). Even within his trance though, he refuses to accept *his* number. His brain refuses to allow him even to count past the number six. The same thing happens later on when Number 2 essentially goads him into counting to six but Number 6 just looks confused and maddened. It's as if they're trying to trick him into first denying the identity they've forced upon him and then having to reach out for it like a harness to pull himself out of this insanity.

During World War II, McGoohan moved from Sheffield to Leicestershire where he attended Ratcliffe College, a Catholic boarding school. One of his classmates there was his future *Braveheart* co-star Ian Bannen. At school he excelled at boxing, which resurfaces here. His skills as a boxer have been evident throughout the series, in his gait and in every fight scene.

CAI: I remember a documentary about Peter O'Toole who talked about T.E. Lawrence being a middleweight boxer and that nugget of information informed his entire performance; the way he stood and lowered his head, looking upwards, the whole thing. You see that with McGoohan through *The Prisoner*. Even unconsciously, he often seems to be on the front foot, ready to take a swing.

In 'school,' sporting an Eton-style straw boater, he refuses to snitch on a fellow pupil and is summarily caned for his impudence. 'You're a fool,' bellows headmaster Number 2. 'Yes, not a rat.' It is the Butler who does the caning, roped in to do another man's dirty work. Number 2 also tells him, 'You mustn't grow up to be a lone wolf.' This might well have been a little in-joke between McGoohan and himself as 'Lone Wolf' was the original title for *Danger Man*.

Lewis Greifer had already said that McGoohan was 'A one-man band' and Number 2 uses this as an insult during a fencing match. Fencing was something many actors would have been taught at drama school back then, as it required balance, movement and poise, as well as the sword-fighting skills needed to get through the third act of most Shakespeare plays without fatally stabbing another actor. This match does end with Number 2 goading Number 6 into skewering him in the shoulder with an un-tipped epee. Number 6 looks devastated, and Number 2 has to spend the rest of the episode confounding the continuity people with his sling.

He is arrested for speeding and sentenced to spend time behind bars, the first time we see actual bars in *The Prisoner*. It's a telling if rather unsubtle semiotic; behind those bars is a domestic living space. Not only are these comfortable, well-equipped quarters, but as Number 2 says, it's detachable. You can go anywhere: the inference is that no matter where you go, you will always be a prisoner.

Trapped inside this prison his anger reaches fever pitch and he rails against his jailor, gripping the bars tightly, fobbing off Number 2's repeated questions about why he resigned. He declares at one point that he resigned, 'For peace of mind... Too many people know too much!'

CAI: I think that line is really important. I think it's a summation of McGoohan's core belief that we are all evolving too quickly and being manipulated into accepting these enormous technological developments into our lives without ever questioning them. We know too much, so much so that we might as well know nothing. It also works as a Cold War spy trope, so it's a lovely twofer.

His date of birth, right down to the precise time 4:31 am, 19th of March, 1928 rules out any chance of him being old enough to have fought in the war. Number 6's history fudges this rather inconvenient fact by airbrushing away a few years. He goes on a bombing run and is eventually captured. Number 2 takes on the role of a commandant barking in German 'You're 19 years old! You're thirsty for glory! You kill without thinking!'

CHRIS: There's a lovely theatrical parallel with the RAF scene. If you're a DSM (Deputy Stage Manager) as McGoohan once was or a technician, you're backstage, getting a cue 'Standing by...' and then initiating the cue by pressing a button. It's something of a leap but it works in the context of this episode's theatricality. It does also tip a wink to the war films that McGoohan starred in when he was starting out, like *The Dambusters* and *Sgt. Musgrave's Dance*.

194

There's a lovely moment when it is revealed that the organ music scoring the scene is actually being played, diegetically, so to speak, by the Butler.

CHRIS: I love that! It's a wonderful breakdown between the world of fiction and reality. The autobiographical aspects of the episode create a performative element. The stage-set emphasis of everything makes this on some level a little love-letter to the theatre. Room is provided for the actors to occasionally improvise, like the way Angelo Muscat fans Number 2 down during the boxing match, which he made up on the spot.

The last grace note of theatrical allusion comes in the final stages when we suddenly become aware that the actors are being lit by followspots[46]. These are moveable stage spotlights, usually.

The seventh day soon arrives. Seven days does seem like a long time to stretch this out. We couldn't help but wonder what happened when they clocked off at five-thirty. A civilised dinner for two each night, perhaps a crossword puzzle or a board game? We know there's enough food on board for six months. They have a butler at their disposal who has repeatedly displayed a mastery at cooking breakfasts; one can only imagine what culinary magic he could have conjured up.

Eventually, the tables start to turn. Perhaps, Number 2 is letting this happen? Sometimes in psychoanalysis, suggests Number 6, the patient and the doctor switch places. 'It is essential in extreme cases,' replies Number 2. Having maintained his sanity and kept his secrets throughout his 'hypnosis,' with the effects now worn off, Number 6 finally locks Number 2 in his self-contained, detachable prison and watches, with a sense of horror as much as a triumph, as time runs out on Degree Absolute and Number 2 tumbles to the floor, dead.

CHRIS: If this is based on the seven ages of man, then death is the outcome and the only release from the Village.

---

[46] *Super Trouper* by ABBA is a song all about followspots ('*Super Trouper lights are gonna blind me... Oom-pa-pa. Oom pa-pa.*')

In the panic-stricken moments as time ticks away, Number 6 reinforces his position without giving anything away. Why did he resign? He didn't accept. He rejected. He may be a fool, but not a rat. He is himself, uncompromised.

'We'll need the body for evidence,' mutters Peter Swanwick's Supervisor. Why? Does the Village have its own crime unit and autopsy department? In response, Number 6 furiously smashes his glass to the floor. This denotes the amount of respect that he'd developed for McKern's Number 2 but also an anger directed at himself; that he has been involved in another man's death.

What do you desire?

Number 1.

I'll take you.

Scores

CHRIS: Without hesitation, I gave this a six. I didn't grasp the complexities of this episode when I first saw it, but now that I have experienced life to a certain degree, I now understand. It makes you appreciate what a singular talent McGoohan was.

CAI: I was the same the first time around. I had read that it was written in a mad hurry and that it was basically thrown together at the last minute and maybe that affected my appreciation of it. Now, I was staggered, not just by the episode but by the bravery to put this out as an action-adventure slot on a major TV network in prime time back in 1968. A brain-exploding, jaw-dropping six out of six.

Cai: 6 out of 6
Chris: 6 out of 6

episode seventeen
Fall Out

Having survived Degree Absolute, Number 6 is taken to meet Number 1 but must first play his part in a ceremony that lauds his successful challenge to retain his individuality while passing judgement on another pair of rebels. Will he join the Village, perhaps even lead them? And who or what is Number 1?

'*The Prisoner* is not a real piece of espionage like *Danger Man*.
It's an allegory, a fable, but I'm almost willing to bet
you see the point in the final episode.'
Patrick McGoohan

'I think it was an absurd pantomime.'
George Markstein

There is a popular opinion regarding the creation of 'Fall Out', that it was
written in a demented state of panic, made up on the spot, and was as a
consequence, an hour of meaningless gibberish. The baffled first reaction from
the TV-watching audience contributes to this legend and there is some truth
in the fact that McGoohan wrote the script, much as he had done with 'Once
upon a Time' the previous year, in a marathon four-day typing binge, fuelled
by regular deliveries of cheese sandwiches and scotch from Frank Maher.

However, the suggestion that this was pure nonsense is itself nonsensical.
McGoohan was the auteur of this episode and he poured into it parts of
himself often so subconscious that even he would not have been able to
identify them at the time. However, every second of the episode was
controlled and deliberate. *Everything* was there (or not there) for a reason.
Everything had meaning.

The Prisoner was now derailed from any links to the action-adventure spy
genre that birthed it. For its final hour, it became a unique work of abstract
art; the emptying of an artist's mind onto a celluloid canvas. There has never
been anything like it on television before or since.

The issue of whether McGoohan had his ending in mind from the off is
difficult to establish, mainly because McGoohan's versions of events are often
so contradictory. In the final stages of production, McGoohan had told Lew
Grade, 'We have no ending.' By complete contrast, in a 1968 interview with
Anthony Davies, McGoohan said, 'I envisaged it from the beginning. In a series
like this, you have to know at the outset what you're aiming at. You've got to
know the ending before you can begin, so I had the idea for the final episode
first of all, and took it from there.'

Speaking to Roger Goodman in 1979, McGoohan said, 'I hadn't got the specific ending that we finished up with but I certainly knew where it had to go and the way that it should finish, and the message it should put forth, but I didn't have that last script at the beginning. In fact, that last script was written by me very close to the end in 36 hours, just scribbling away and chiselling at it until everything I got, what we have, which as far as I'm concerned I think works. I wouldn't change it.'

CHRIS: I think a lot of people miss the point of this episode. They dive straight into the 1960s counterculture, especially the drug element. I think that in particular needs to be avoided. Outside of a love of scotch, the closest McGoohan came to a drug habit was the occasional paracetamol after a hard day playing squash.

The specific sixties elements of the episode *have* dated; things were dating faster than room-temperature milk back then. With-it fashions and fixations from January 1968 were already passed by August 1968. As an example, there's a famous *Star Trek* episode called 'The Way to Eden' which features 'space-hippies' which was barely contemporary while the episode was being filmed and was a joke by the time it was broadcast.

'Fall Out' though, has outlasted the unavoidable elements of the time in which it was shot. Kanner's 'Youth' is the only thing that betrays its period and it can still be watched and enjoyed now without fear of a cringe factor.

CHRIS: I would have hated to have been on that ITV switchboard that first night! You can imagine some poor operator clutching about twelve phones at the same time, trying to answer all of them, plugging jack cables in with bulbs flashing away. The people who had to field those calls are the unsung heroes of *The Prisoner*.

One has to wonder just how many calls from incensed viewers *were* made after the broadcast. It's become one of the legends of *The Prisoner*, along with the idea that it was those outraged audiences, like a pitchfork-waving mob, that led to McGoohan fleeing the country with his family like the embassy workers in Saigon in '75. It's a good story, but the reality was likely disappointingly prosaic in comparison.

It's tantalising to imagine the reaction, especially in the days of communal watching, when two or three generations of a family would watch television together, with no facility to tape it and watch later or wait for a repeat. One's first assumption would be that the mums and dads (and especially the grandparents) would have muttered 'Cobblers!' or something to that effect, while the youngsters thought it was amazing[47].

CHRIS: People were angry because they weren't aware of what television could do. It could challenge you and make you think. They were also angry because up until now, or perhaps 'The Girl Who Was Death', *The Prisoner* was an allegorical spy series. In 'Fall Out', the spy series element is gone and everything here was pure allegory. McGoohan actively sought this anger; anything but passive consumption. In an interview with The Observer in 1991, he said, 'If I gave all the answers, you would no longer have a role when watching it.'

McGoohan's education would have conferred upon him a great knowledge of, and indeed love for the classics; Latin and Greek mythology. One of the key texts that McGoohan would have read plays an enormous role in the understanding of 'Fall Out' is *The Republic* by Plato. In it, Plato describes the soul (or our psychology) as a tripartite, divided into three parts: appetitive, spirited, and rational. In 'Fall Out', all the characters in the Assembly Room, perhaps even the President, represent a facet of Number 6, in particular Alexis Kanner's youthful Number 48 and McKern's resurrected Number 2 like Freud's ego, id and superego.

Plato and Socrates (no less) discuss society and the ways and means of building a greater, fairer, and more efficient society, ideas which all surface throughout *The Prisoner*. Socrates suggests that they use the city as an image to see how justice comes to be in the soul of an individual, precisely how McGoohan uses the Village as the world in microcosm.

---

[47] The 'youngsters' as we imagine it look like a young Ray Brooks and *To Sir With Love*-era Lulu.

Socrates argues that psychological conflict points to a divided soul since a completely unified soul could not behave in opposite ways towards the same object and at the same time in the same respect.

Possibly the most famous passage from *The Republic* though is *The Allegory of the Cave*. It's worth seeking out to do it justice, but in summation, Plato presents a group of people chained up in a cave, only able to see the shadows cast against the wall by a fire, which they interpret through the context of their limited experience.

These people cannot see the life going on between them and the flames, only the shadows being cast, which they accept as reality. When they are unchained, many of them stay in the cave, content with the 'reality' of the shadows. Another leaves and is frightened and overwhelmed by what he discovers, but soon comes to realise what he has been missing: there is a sunlit life beyond the cave. However, when he returns to the cave to tell everyone, they refuse to believe him, preferring to accept the only 'reality' they've known, flickering away on the cave walls.

'Unlike me, many of you have accepted the situation of your imprisonment and will die here like rotten cabbages.'

This is the first episode to get a 'Previously on *The Prisoner*' style preamble, offering a succinct summary of the events of 'Once upon a Time'. Viewers are reminded that Leo McKern's Number 2 perished, that the Supervisor is taking him to Number 1, and that the living space where McKern meets his maker is moveable. All of these call-backs will pay off later.

The title sequence is absent. Instead, we get some aerial photography of the Village and the first acknowledgement of the location that had been enthralling viewers for the past year. 'In the grounds of The Hotel Portmeirion, Penrhyndeudraeth, North Wales. By courtesy of Mr Clough Williams-Ellis.'

The music score is different too, a variation that had already made an appearance during the London scenes in 'Do Not Forsake Me Oh My

Darling'. However, in league with the novelty of the location reveal, this punchy, dramatic new take on *The Prisoner* theme is hugely effective.

CAI: The hairs on my hand stand up just thinking about it. The first time I saw it, I was vibrating in my chair, I was so excited by this moment. The way the brass hits the title, 'Fall Out', is such an amazing portent of something incredibly exciting coming our way.

Number 6 is escorted by the Supervisor and taken down in a lift that drops them both into the sub-workings of the Village. The set of the subterranean tunnel system where the action takes place does have a rather hell-like quality to it, though McGoohan, always one to keep such things nicely vague and cryptic, was adamant that this did not represent some Dantean sub-text.

CHRIS: Something about this reminds me of H.G. Wells' *The Time Machine*. On the surface, they have the Eloi, docile, sheep-like people, always happy, a bit like the Villagers. Down below, you have the Morlocks, who are essentially using the Eloi as cattle, controlling their lives from beneath their feet. Very similar shades in *The Prisoner* and especially this episode. All the controlling is being done underground.

Number 6 is first taken to a changing room. In it, is a mannequin version of himself, wearing the suit he was wearing in 'Arrival'. To his left and right are coat stands hung with dozens of coat hangers. There is a wicker basket in the corner of the room. 'We thought you'd be happier… as yourself?'

CHRIS: Going back to the autobiographical analysis of 'Once upon a Time', this reminds me of a theatre dressing room. Actors and models have sometimes been referred to as 'coat-hangers' due to the variety of costumes they would wear throughout their careers. There's a scene at the end of Chris Rodley's *In My Mind,* where McGoohan is on a beach, scribbling something in the sand. Eventually, we see what it is, a coat-hanger. The other thing to note is the theatrical basket on the right in which costumes and curtains would be kept. I think that these are pointed, autobiographical references to his theatrical past, which plays into the theory that the Prisoner is Patrick McGoohan; he is playing himself.

There are so many autobiographical elements in *The Prisoner*, many of them hiding in plain sight: their shared birthday, right at the very beginning for example. The question should not be 'Where am I?' but 'Who am I?' McGoohan has spent his entire professional life playing other people, being a coat hanger. When he 'resigned' from *Danger Man*, he couldn't escape the cult of celebrity.

Curiously, when presented with his old suit, Number 6 reaches first for the shirt, and not his jacket; almost caressing it as he unbuttons it at the collar. As he does, we hear the unmistakable opening of *All You Need Is Love* by The Beatles. The Fab Four were all huge fans of the TV series by now, so that might have helped Everyman secure the right to use the song[48]. Sources vary but apparently, they paid between £48 and £65 for the rights, in perpetuity.

CAI: It's such a BIG deal, having a Beatles song in your show. That rarely happens. I remember when *Mad Men* was allowed to use *Tomorrow Never Knows* in an episode, it was such an extraordinary coup that it made the papers!

CHRIS: I read a quote recently from someone who said, 'I have come to the conclusion that 'Fall Out' was Part 2 of The Beatles' *Magical Mystery Tour*.' He had a point. They have quite a lot in common, certainly in terms of the way they were first received by a hostile audience.

What might have piqued McGoohan's interest in *All You Need is Love* was the fact that it was written for and played during the first live global satellite link-up, *Our World*, in 1967, tying it nicely to *The Prisoner's* ever-present global leitmotif.

Number 6 is led, past several jukeboxes (we don't know why), into the vast Assembly Room. It's an extraordinary set where a jury, wearing cloaks and masks, take their places while Bond villain-style henchmen prowl around steaming missile silos, all under the watchful mechanical eye of an enormous rocket, emblazoned with the number 1. In a single, 23-second-long take, Number 6 is taken to the centre of the room.

---

[48] Both George Harrison and Beatles manager Brian Epstein were regular visitors to Portmeirion. In the 1995 TV series *The Beatles Anthology*, many of George's interviews are shot in the Hotel Portmeirion with the bell tower looming in the background.

Eagle-eyed viewers might notice the establishment figure in a morning suit and top hat being flanked by guards as Number 6 makes his entrance. Background delights like this abound in 'Fall Out'. Why was he there? It's a deliberately choreographed action, so who or what does he represent? Is the establishment under siege or arrest, or is this the establishment protecting itself with its army?

The cavernous set was built on stages 1 and 2 at MGM Borehamwood, and borrowed from an already existing stalactite-heavy set from *Battle Beneath The Earth*, which had just shot there (an enjoyable if unremarkable post-apocalyptic adventure directed by Montgomery Tully. Co-star Earl Cameron is the film's other tenuous *Prisoner* link).

The cloaked Assembly members are a veritable UN of 'ists,' identified by their plaques as Activists, Pacifists, Nationalists, Reactionaries, Identification… and Youngsters, who also get their hooded representative. They all wear the same mask: a black and white variation on the Ancient Greek Drama mask, the smiling face of Thalia, the goddess of Comedy, juxtaposed against the tragic muse Melpomene. Light and dark. All very theatrical, another call-back from McGoohan to his repertory days. Or is this a reduction of the democratic process depicted here as nothing more than pure theatre?

All of the assembly members appear to be men, which is fitting if these are meant to represent the various facets of Number 6, specifically. This is an assumption though, as the masks prevent us from being able to gauge their gender. They remain anonymous, save for Michael Miller (from 'A Change of Mind' and 'The General') whose hedge-like beard is too formidable to be obscured by his mask. One of the Members is played by Mike Reid, who UK viewers will fondly remember as Cockney geezer *par excellence*, Frank Butcher from *EastEnders*. Peter Swanwick puts on his mask and hood and takes his seat, representing 'Identification.' Interestingly, behind him is a seat marked 'Security' which is empty.

CHRIS: Number 6 now has his sense of identity restored, but he still doesn't have his sense of security back. Either that or the actor playing 'Security' was late!

'Welcome!' announces Kenneth Griffith, draped in all the costumed regalia of a High Court judge. 'Well Come' is emblazoned upon the wall of the cavern.

CHRIS: It's one of the possible etymologies of the word 'welcome,' a portmanteau word essentially bidding someone 'arrive well.' Could this also be a nod to evolution and change? The way that language evolves? It echoes the separation into two words of Fallout too, as well as Peter Swanwick's strange delivery of that line, 'We thought you would be. Happier... As your... Self?' Things like that show that even language itself is being looked at by McGoohan with his critical, curious eyes.

Griffith may look like a judge but he is credited as The President (Griffith was asked at the time why he was dressed as a judge, and he replied, 'I haven't got a clue.') What does he represent though? The establishment? The law? The ultimate arbiter? Number 6's sense of responsibility? Judgement Day? Death, even? The final stage of the seven ages of man as referenced in 'Once upon a Time'? Perhaps: there is a palpable sense of death and rebirth in 'Fall Out'.

CAI: There's more of McGoohan's religious upbringing at work here than perhaps we first realise. There is a literal resurrection and then there's the use of the spiritual, *Dry Bones* later on. If this is McGoohan spilling his heart into everything, then his religious convictions, kept somewhat in check elsewhere in the series, would unavoidably play some part in proceedings.

Our hero listens silently as the President makes his speech, announcing that Number 6 has survived the ultimate test and as such, he is no longer to be referred to as Number 6, 'or any other number of any kind. He has gloriously vindicated the right of the individual to be individual, and this assembly rises to you... Sir.'

The speech is filled with memorable phrases, like 'The regrettable bullet.' Many people hold that this refers to the nuclear weapon, possibly represented here by the rocket. It's unlikely though that anyone building a rocket armed with a nuclear warhead, would think to include living quarters spacious enough to stockpile three dozen ornamental globes. Even so, it's difficult to see a colossal rocket in the middle of the set, in an episode called 'Fall Out' filmed during the Cold War, and not think that it's informed in some way by the ever-present threat of nuclear weapons.

Then again, the President's speech is not McGoohan's work but Griffith's. He stepped in at McGoohan's request to write it and give McGoohan a much-needed breather. They were very much on the same wavelength, and the

President's line about the individual's right to be an individual is the challenge of the entire series encapsulated in a single line of dialogue.

With the Butler stood loyally by his side, 'Sir' is seated on a raised dais in the chair of honour, to the tune of *For He's a Jolly Good Fellow* (given a slightly sinister discordant lilt as it finishes). It's not the first time we've heard this tune in the series. It's one of several Nursery Rhymes that pop up throughout. Catherine McGoohan has said that her father was very fond of such ditties.

There is talk of handing over the ultimate power, the payoff after all those cryptic asides from various Number 2s like Mary Morris' 'This man has a future with us.' However, there is some 'tedious ceremony' to get through first. This starts with the trailer from 'Once upon a Time' being lowered down into the Assembly Room, in a shot that seemingly takes forever. The trailer door also appears to have been altered: in the previous episode, it folds down from the roof. Now, it opens out onto the ground like the loading ramp of a cattle truck.

Inside is the body of Leo McKern's Number 2. It seems they didn't need it for evidence after all. Famously, McKern's return provided something of a continuity issue for the producers. Almost a year had passed since he'd filmed his death in 'Once upon a Time', sporting his famous thick beard and shoulder-length hair. He was now a much-cropped Leo McKern, trimmed back for his role in *Decline and Fall... of a Birdwatcher* (1968). A combination of repurposed footage from 'The General', unconvincing wig-work, some shaving foam and what looks like a vacuum cleaner / gas mask led to some rather clever sci-fi problem-solving.

We are about to get the complete set up of rebels, McGoohan's tripartite. We already have the individual, Number 6. We have the mutinous voice of authority in McKern's Number 2, and now we meet 'Youth' in all its 1968-style intransigence. Number 48 (Alexis Kanner) is the rebel by way of Carnaby Street, W1. (Kanner bought his own clothes, an irreverent spin on the Establishment-regulation top hat and tails.) Via Kanner's character, language is disseminated again, disconnected. He speaks almost exclusively in polysemous '60s slang. 'Trip, Dad, Hip.'

'Hip' sends Number 48 off into an impromptu version of *Dry Bones* which at first enjoys the baffled clap-along approval of the President, the room bound together briefly by the universality of music but which soon breaks down into an orgy of chaos, infuriating everyone and culminating in his chase and re-arrest by the guards.

CHRIS: I see the Assembly as like a gestalt entity; Number 48 is behaving like a child (he is Youth, after all). These are actions without consequences. He wants everything now and on his terms and revolts when he doesn't get it. Youth revolts, 'Because it must.' Sometimes it has no filter nor does it have the weight of experience or apathy. We were like Kanner at one point, when we first watched *The Prisoner* in fact but now we're more like McKern!

CAI: Kanner had an extraordinary, pantomimic quality to him. He could move like a ballerina. In fact, he reminds me of the spidery way Robert Helpmann (The Child Catcher) moved his body in *Chitty Chitty Bang Bang*. It's hard to picture him playing anything normal. He couldn't play 'Man in Room.'

Assuming that he is indeed playing a facet of the Prisoner, Kanner does make a rather effective young Patrick McGoohan. The two actors got on very well. McGoohan probably recognised that same fire within him.

CHRIS: I love the moment when Number 6 looks at Number 48 and says, 'Young… man.' When he says, 'Man,' Number 48 reacts, and I see that as confirmation of a man, not a child. He's been given respect and a title from his elders, and immediately makes a connection with 'Sir.' Number 48 has now received, as the President says, the 'recognition of a man.'

It's amazing how little Number 6 says and does in the first two-thirds of the episode. He has barely four lines and remains seated throughout, while the action whirls around him, but then if everyone here is a fact of his personality, they're doing the speaking for him. This begs the question, is the President a part of his psyche too or does he represent society? He's offering him power, asking him to take control, to lead the deluded masses out of the cave.

CAI: There's an echo of this in the penultimate track of Pink Floyd's *The Wall* when Pink goes on trial for all his misdeeds and the different facets of his own history, his mother, his teachers, his wife all testify against him, and has

207

built a wall around himself, is sentenced to be exposed to the world, warts and all, as the bricks are torn down around him.

Highlighting society's innate hypocrisy, Number 48's charges are read out in the sternest possible terms by Assembly Member 'Anarchist,' appalled at his 'most serious breach of social etiquette.' Number 48 tinkles his little bell in defiance before he is strapped back to his pole and lowered into a Perspex tube, out of sight.

'Sir. You approve the proceedings?' asks the President. 'I... note... them,' Sir replies.

It's time for the return of an old friend. 'I feel a new man!' roars the new-look Leo McKern before unleashing one of his trademark bellowing laughs. As soon as he sees Number 6, he greets him like a long-lost pal, even though he had only very recently played a large part in his untimely death. This only serves to establish that Number 2 is a 'new man' with a very different outlook than the one who just spent a week playing mind games with Number 6. Number 2 beckons the Butler over, but he remains instead by Number 6's side.

CHRIS: I think that the Butler is the body; the enabler. Everything he does helps make things happen. He makes breakfasts (magnificent ones) and drives the truck. Nothing works without him. Standing next to the seated Number 6, the pair of them are actually at the same level, body and mind.

In his speech to the Assembly, we find out more about Number 2's back-story. He was brought back. From where? The Houses of Parliament would be an informed guess given the final shot of him in the episode. He also claims that like Number 6, he too was abducted and woke up a prisoner in the Village. As he told Number 6 in 'The Chimes of Big Ben', 'We are both lifers.'

He once wielded great power. He had 'the ear of a statesman, kings and the prices of many a land.' If 'Fall Out' is McGoohan writing about himself, then his celebrity must play a part in the autobiographical elements. As the biggest TV star in the country, he too would have wielded great power and met some of the most famous people in the world.

CHRIS: This could very well link to the ego, as defined by Freud: the realistic part of one's psyche that balances the id and the superego. Like the man said, 'Ego is reason and balance like a man on horseback, who has to hold in check the superior strength of the horse. The poor ego has a still harder time of it. It has to serve three harsh masters and it has to do its best to reconcile the claims and demands of all three. The three tyrants are the external world, the superego and the id.' Then again, as Robin Williams said, 'Freud did enough cocaine to kill a small horse.'

The suggestion that Number 48 represents the id, Number 2 the ego and Number 6 the superego is not a new one, but one should note that the superego is the moral centre and Number 6's morality is, from 'Arrival' onwards, something that the Village was never able to corrupt.

Number 2 describes himself as a secure member of the establishment. 'What is deplorable is that I resisted for so short a time.' Once he leaves the podium, now that the ego has been restored to the balance, we note that the 'Security' Assembly member's empty seat has now been filled. A sense of security within himself, returning confidence, doubt assuaged?

For the first time, Number 1, the rocket-shaped elephant in the room, the ultimate variation on 'Chekhov's Gun[49],' is addressed. It communicates in a series of beeps, which fortunately the President speaks fluently.

CHRIS: I see this as a semiotic representation of the ultimate in human technological achievement, which will ultimately destroy us all, reflecting our limitless capacity for self-destruction. Narratively, it keeps the mystery going for longer. The President can engage with or react to it, but we still don't know who or what is behind that electronic eye.

Number 2 approaches the eye, staring it down with a combination of fear and fury in his gaze. 'Whoever you are, whatever you are, I'll die with my own mind.' The facets of Number 6 are coming together and the balance is beginning to be restored. Allies are preparing for revolt. As per Socrates' analogy, the soul is becoming unified.

---

[49] The 'Chekhov's Gun' rule is that "If you say in the first chapter that there is a rifle hanging on the wall, in the second or third chapter it absolutely must go off."

Number 48's rebellion was an anarchic foot chase, 'rebelling against nothing it could define.' Number 2's is a more visceral spitting into the eye of Number 1. For this outrage, he is manhandled and tied to his own pole and lowered into his own smoking silo like Number 48 before him. As he drops out of view he smiles at the audience and in a wonderfully meta-moment quips, 'Be seeing you!'

It's now time for Number 6 to address the members. He leaves his chair and makes his way to take the stand, accompanied by the very Beatle-y *Rag March* by Jack Arel and Jean Claude Petit. Film and music editor Eric Mival worked overtime in going through Chappell's Music Library to find just the right song for every occasion. Another memorable choice of his was the Mike Oldfieldesque *September Ballad* by Gary Bellington, which scores the lowering of the trailer and the removal of Number 2's body.

The President announces him as representing 'The right to be Person, Someone or Individual. He has survived intact and secure.' He hasn't buckled or been corrupted by the dominant ideology of the Village. Strange that it is the President himself lauding Number 6 for his steadfastness, but given his desire for Number 6 to lead them from the cave, it reflects the (sound) idea that an incorruptible person would make the best leader.

CHRIS: Like the people chained up in Plato's cave, understanding the sound of animals and carts through their narrow context, similarly today our worldview is shaped and limited by what we see on the news, on the internet, on social media etc. People think they've left the cave but they've just been led ever deeper into it. McGoohan may not have been able to have predicted algorithms and Facebook, but he was right in terms of where technology was ultimately taking us.

The President claims that Number 6 is 'magnificently equipped to lead us. Lead us, or go.' Number 6 will be given a million quid in traveller's cheques and a passport that will take him anywhere. His house is being readied for his return. There's a lovely inside joke when we see that Number 6's house in Buckingham Place is being prepared for his return. The estate agent Lageu & Sons is set-dresser John Lageu's little nod to himself. He's also given a purse of money, which Number 6 dutifully counts.

CAI: I think this is a bit like his per diem. I love the business of taking the money out of the purse to check how much he has, then pocketing it; money, a house, a passport. These are all the symbols of Western freedom and liberation. That's what's on the table for him.

Number 6 questions the President's certainty in his leadership skills. He repeatedly answers the President's every response with 'Why?' and much like the General, the President is unable to give him a satisfactory answer. It's only when he is told 'We need you,' that he replies, 'I see.'

CHRIS: This recognition of his leadership capabilities is another echo of Plato. He wrote about the Philosopher King who should be trained in everything from martial arts and gymnastics, as well as being taught mathematics and the classics until, at the age of 50, they are suitably educated and worldly to be able to lead. He has shown himself to be a leader. He builds his gymnasium and trains in martial arts, albeit in the strange form of Kosho. I think that this is all very Plato-led. Number 6 is trying to become the best human being he can using Plato's guidebook.

'All about you is yours,' the President tells him. 'You are the best of us … Keep us in mind, Sir. We are all yours.'

CAI: McGoohan said, 'Democracy is not a panacea, or a lesser evil, it's also an evil. Quite simply, this is where you live.' Perhaps that's what's going on here. He's reaping his rewards, rewards that he has earned, yet he will ultimately reject it.

Rather like an actor accepting an Academy Award, Number 6 steps up and addresses the Assembly. Or tries to. Despite repeated attempts to make his speech, he cannot get past the word 'I' without the Assembly repeating it in a deafening cacophony. Eventually, he is left screaming, almost dementedly, his words completely drowned out by the others.

CHRIS: The members are often described as 'interrupting' him, but I'd like to posit that this isn't an interruption. This is one person and he's being drowned out by his own voice. As facets of his personality, are the members all responding as one because they all have something to say? There's another reading though: everything is coming together now. Number 48, Number 2, the Butler, they're all onside, and now he's starting to get the Assembly onside in agreement with him. He's becoming more and more whole.

CAI: It could also be, again going back to the idea of McGoohan escaping his celebrity, a comment on the creative deadening that comes with so much uncritical adoration and worship. Regardless of whatever it is he's saying, everyone tells him it's wonderful and amazing because he's that Patrick McGoohan off the telly.

That we weren't supposed to hear what he is saying was part of the point, but keen viewers have been able to deduce that McGoohan's speech was based on a newspaper article about the devaluation of the pound. At one point, you can hear him shout 'Buzz off!' in frustration. The President looks on with a look of wisdom, silently and with an air that suggests that he anticipated all of this. 'And now I take it that you are prepared to meet Number 1? Follow me, if you would be so kind, Sir.'

Number 6 is led downstairs into a very Bondian, Ken Adam-style underground level. There, he is taken by the Butler past Number 2 and Number 48, both held in individual Perspex tubes inscribed with the words Orbit 2 and Orbit 48.

CHRIS: Orbit. The word derives from the Latin *orbis*, which means 'ring,' presenting us with another aspect of circularity; it ends as it begins. There is an insinuation that the rocket is heading into orbit, but it's just one of so many allusions to circles, orbs and globes in this episode; a final episode that will end with the first shot of 'Arrival'.

You want global iconography? Here's a room full of them. Beckoned forward by a bow from the Butler, Number 6 climbs a spiral staircase inside the rocket and arrives at a chamber filled with globes of all shapes and sizes and colours. There in the chamber, seated before a large television screen, cradling what appears to be a crystal ball, is a mysterious figure in a white cloak and hood. Number 6's infamous 'I will not be pushed, filed, stamped…' speech from 'Arrival' is playing on the screen. Once again, something strange happens at the mention of 'I.' It repeats, speeding up, getting louder and faster.

The figure stands up, emblazoned upon his cloak is a large Number 1. This is the moment a nation has been waiting for since the broadcast of the first episode. Who is Number 1? Number 6 approaches the figure and removes his black and white mask. Beneath it is the grunting face of an ape. Number 6 then pulls the ape's face away, revealing none other than... Patrick McGoohan. Number 6's wild-eyed alter-ego roars at him and runs away cackling. Number 6 chases him around the chamber, but Number 1 climbs up a ladder, disappearing through a hatch, looking down with a devilish giggle of delight, before slamming down the hatch. It's all over in barely a minute.

CHRIS: I noticed that when he meets Number 1, the imagery on the screen of him meeting Number 1 is actually a little bit ahead of reality, just by a second. I think that adds more weight to the idea that it's a comment on his own life as a TV star; the world he lives in. There's a falseness and a fakery to it.

CAI: Of all the globes in the room, the one that he is handed is completely transparent, I don't think it's a crystal ball. That to me seems like an acknowledgement that this word of fame and celebrity is empty. In fact, the only thing we see in it is the repeated slamming of the bars from the iconic end-of-episode sting. This is the prison. The bars are in here. And what does he do with it? He smashes it to pieces.

In a way, the ape mask is a middle finger to the hubris of the human race. In a famous Canadian interview with Warner Troyer from 1977[50], McGoohan said that the ape mask represented 'Progress. I don't think we've progressed much. But the monkey thing was, according to various theories extant today, that we all come from the original ape, so I just used that as a symbol, you know. The bestial thing and then the other bestial face behind it which was laughing, jeering and jabbering like a monkey.'

Alexis Kanner said, 'It couldn't be an anticlimax and we knew on the other hand that it couldn't be a climax. Well, one day I turned to Pat and said, 'I know. You pull the mask off and it's Lew Grade!' When McGoohan revealed the identity of Number 1 to David Tomblin, his creative partner replied with a shrug, 'I thought it'd be you.'

---

[50] This is available to watch on YouTube. Fascinating, and extraordinary for the staggering number of cigarettes smoked by both men.

Speaking to Six of One, McGoohan explained the final reveal by asking, 'What is the most evil thing on earth? Is it jealousy? Is it revenge? Is it "The Bomb?" What is it? When one really searches, it's only one thing. It's the evil part of oneself that one is constantly fighting with until the moment of our demise. So therefore, the most evil thing that I could put in there behind those masks was the grinning evil face of myself, just for a split second.'

Perhaps more than anything, the revelation that Number 1 was himself and not a Bond-style supervillain, or maybe Sean Connery, Roger Moore or Orson Welles in an audience-pleasing cameo, was what infuriated the general public.

CHRIS: I asked my step-daughter once, 'Who is your worst enemy?' and she replied, 'Myself.' We weren't even talking about *The Prisoner*! That is the message and I think it's actually a hopeful one. It is possible in life to achieve, to succeed and to be happy and secure and have a sense of self, but the only thing who can ruin that is not the government or society, but yourself. Obviously there are people suffering from mental issues and circumstances beyond their control, but as a general philosophy, it's a healthy, moral message.

CAI: I'm absolutely my worst enemy. You only have to look at how much I spend on cheese. I know lots of people who have never grasped this concept at all; literally everything that they've done wrong, every mistake they've ever made is someone else's fault, which is handy because they can blame someone else and never address their own self-sabotaging ways. It's a comfort blanket.

Once Number 1 has been removed and with the pieces already in place, Sir initiates the revolt. Returning back down the staircase, his eyes meet those of the Butler who, in his most expressive moment of the series, signals that the henchmen are just around the corner. Duly informed, Number 6 leaps off the staircase and attacks the guards, using a fire extinguisher for good measure. It was a stunt that raised the hackles of many in the production, as acclaimed writer and TV historian Robert Fairclough explained when we interviewed him for the podcast[51]...

---

[51] To hear our interview with the fascinating Robert Fairclough, listen to our episode 'Fall Out Part II'.

'Patrick didn't do the jump himself. He goes to jump and then it cuts and it's clearly Frank Maher. Maher said to him, "Patrick, we can't do it like this because if I land badly, I'm really going to hurt the guys, the stuntmen at the bottom of the stairs." Patrick said "No, I want it done like that." Frank said, "Well, I warned you." He did it like Patrick wanted the first time and of course he landed on a couple of the other stuntmen! No one was hurt seriously but it caused quite a bad atmosphere on the set (do bear in mind that stuntmen tend to exaggerate quite a bit). They were all in the bar later that day. Everyone was waiting for McGoohan to show up to see what would happen. McGoohan arrived, walked up to the bar and bought them all a bottle of whisky each.'

Having overpowered the guards, Number 6 peers out through the eye from inside the rocket. We see that the various Assembly members are milling about the room almost in a state of dazed bewilderment.

CAI: Without him there, everyone is just floating around aimlessly like blood cells.

CHRIS: I think that's definitely the intention. They have no sense of purpose at that point. It's not an accident; it was choreographed. McGoohan would have told them to just walk about in circles, not knowing what they were doing or where they were going.

The President alone sees that something is up. Billowing smoke alerts him to the fact that Number 6 has programmed the rocket to launch. The President orders the Village to evacuate. Suddenly, dressed in white robes, Numbers 6, 2 and 48 return to the Assembly Room armed with machine guns. As the Beatles return to the soundtrack to remind us that *All You Need Is Love*, our heroes gun down everyone and everything that moves.

CAI: This actually reminds me of another Beatles track, *Revolution 1*, where John Lennon sings 'If you talk about destruction. Don't you know that you can count me out... in.' Revolution was very much in the air in 1968 and McGoohan saw it coming. At the start of each episode, Number 6 asks, 'Whose side are you on?' and this is the moment when he picks a side, and he chooses violence.

The massacre was especially surprising, shocking even, given McGoohan's previous widely held revulsion at gun violence. John Drake rarely if ever carried a gun in *Danger Man*, nor had Number 6 in *The Prisoner*. Eric Mival was particularly upset about this scene. Writer and editor Ian Rakoff would next work on Lindsay Anderson's classic *if...* (1968) which ends similarly with a murderous machine gun battle.

CAI: I don't think that McGoohan is advocating violence, it's more of a catharsis now that the process is complete and He is Himself. The final seconds of the episode, which effectively sentence him to a life of permanent imprisonment, suggest to me that if anything he is being punished for having chosen violence. When he was talking to Warner Troyer, he described the gun violence in 'Fall Out' as 'sad.'

McGoohan told Alain Carrazé, 'There comes a time when rebellion is necessary.' Then again, Kanner was talking with McGoohan during filming, and asked, 'Pat? Isn't this a pacifist programme?' McGoohan replied, 'Fuck it. Do you want to keep coming back here month after month?'

CHRIS: One can look at this as neutralising the parts of your personality that are holding you back: doubt, laziness, apathy, lethargy etc, rather than mass murder.

Regardless of one's take on the violence, it's certainly terribly exciting. In an episode that deliberately eschews any vestiges of spy-show cliché, this late burst of energy is a brief reminder of the genre that *The Prisoner* notionally belongs to. Frantically cut together, we have gunfire, fighting, stampedes in the Village, a countdown and finally a rocket launch. Several helicopters take off (one of which, we reckon, has 'Arrival' director Don Chaffey[52] in the passenger seat) and for some inexplicable reason there are frogmen scooting away on mini-tractors. Finally the sky above the Village is filled with departing helicopters, and all of this set to a thrilling Ron Grainer score. For about 60 seconds, it all feels like a Gerry Anderson show.

CHRIS: The rocket launch at the end of the episode is footage of the de Havilland Propellers Blue Streak launch. Does this allude to self-destruction?

---

[52] At the *Prisoner at 50* celebrations in Elstree, editor John S. Smith said that there were absolutely *loads* of helicopter shots in the can, almost all shot during Chaffey's tenure as a director.

We can create weapons of such immense power, so why aren't we using the same technology for altruistic purposes? Why must it always be weaponry? Look at Jonas Salk. Came up with a cure for polio and just gave it away for the good of humanity. Why aren't there more Jonas Salks instead of people whose first thoughts are either to make tons of money from their discovery or turn it into a means of military gain?

It's unclear what the point of the rocket launch was or why the Villagers are all evacuating. One assumes that Number 6 is making good on his promise in 'The Chimes of Big Ben' to 'Escape, come back, and wipe this place off the face of the earth.' Yet there are no scenes of devastation as the missile hits the Green Dome, destroying the Village in an explosive inferno. Perhaps, with Lew Grade's chequebook under lock and key, there simply wasn't the money available for such an expensive sequence. Then again, as we will soon see, the Village as a metaphor for the prisons we construct inside our own minds *can't* be destroyed. Instead, we get a shot of Rover shrivelling away into nothing.

As Rover whittles away, we hear a burst of the Carmen Miranda song *I Yi Yi Yi Yi, (I Like You Very Much)*. It's something of a leftfield choice but Eric Mival said that McGoohan chose the song deliberately; Mival conceded that 'it worked brilliantly.'

CHRIS: It echoes the message of *All You Need is Love*. If you can love yourself you can be a stronger person and have a more focused life experience. That ditty, 'I like you very much,' is an acceptance of self-love. It's a moment of victory. The three (or four) parts of him have now come together as one to escape.

At precisely the same time that the rocket launches, a truck driven by the Butler, pulling the trailer from 'Once upon a Time', emerges from a tunnel and crashes through a gate. It has been made clear throughout the series that the Village's position on the map changes so often that it really could be anywhere. However, in this instance the tunnel leads directly onto the A20.

Six of One co-founder Dave Barrie told us that he'd been to the mouth of the tunnel in Mayfield, Sussex and had his photograph taken there. "Fall Out' is wonderful; a real statement,' he said. 'When I first saw it, I thought I'd never seen anything like it before. It's Patrick throwing down the gauntlet and saying, 'Are you still with me?' In my own *Prisoner* book, I score very conservatively with the maximum being five stars. 'Fall Out' gets six. I think it's magnificent.'

There's a wonderfully staged comic scene when a 1960s businessman from central casting, driving down the A20 in his Rolls Bentley, passes the trailer unaware that Number 6, Number 48 and Number 2 are inside enjoying an impromptu dance to *Dry Bones* behind the bars. There was a bit of cost-saving there as the Bentley apparently belonged to McGoohan.

The truck pulls over and they drop Number 48 off. There's a very subtle touch here: he crosses the road and thumbs a lift in one direction before changing his mind and hitch-hikes in the opposite direction. This ties in with the President's verdict that youth is uncoordinated with no sense of direction.

CHRIS: Young people live almost solely in the present. They don't think about next week or the years ahead. You can do that when you're completely invulnerable!

Ant Brierley, the co-ordinator of the Six of One conventions at Portmeirion, told us that Alexis Kanner was in the running to take over from Patrick McGoohan in a proposed follow-up to *The Prisoner*. 'The way Alexis explained it, it would be a Village outside the Village. It would follow Number 48 as he globe-trotted around the world, but at every turn he's being followed and is battling the Village. The opening scene was going to be set at the Rome Olympics, during the marathon. The runners would make their way past, then at the back you'd see Number 48 and the Butler running too, being chased by a hearse with the undertaker in it!'

We make it now to Westminster and the *actual* chimes of Big Ben. Number 2 bids his farewells and Number 6 walks off to speak to a policeman while the Butler looks on. It's an extraordinary, mind-boggling scene. Beautifully framed, with Muscat in the foreground with his back to us and McGoohan's twisted gyrations taking place in the distance. The relative positioning of the two men is arguably deliberate, in giving Muscat the same presence and size as McGoohan.

CHRIS: Just as McGoohan famously didn't give explanations, he is explaining the situation to the policeman in a frantic mime performance, talking through the narrative of the episode. The policeman looks on blankly.

CAI: If the Butler is 'the body,' then perhaps this is an out-of-body experience?

Number 6 and the Butler then scarper onto the Westminster bridge to catch a bus. Angelo Muscat looks like he's never run so fast in his life! Thenceforth, it's home sweet home. They arrive at 1 Buckingham Place. Number 6 hops into his Lotus 7 and drives off. The door opens in exactly the same mechanised, automatic way that they do in the Village, and the Butler enters the house.

CHRIS: It's what *everyone* picks up on: the door. A lot of people read that as, 'Oooh, the Village is one step ahead of him…' which is nonsense. It's a reminder that you take the Village with you everywhere you go.

You can never escape. You are never free. Freedom is a myth. But should we be free? If we were there'd be chaos. McGoohan himself said, 'Too much of that and society would be overrun by rampant extremists and there would be anarchy. The intention was simple. Be as free as possible within our situation, but the war is with Number One.'

CAI: I think Kenneth Griffith's description of McGoohan as a 'gentleman rebel' is spot on. He wants to be left alone and have society give him the courtesy to allow him to be who he wants to be. He's not for anarchy or destruction; you can count him out.

CHRIS: We've talked about Plato and Socrates, but we can bring people like Immanuel Kant here and talk about ethics. Utilitarian ethics, meta-ethics, virtue ethics, all these branches of normative ethics can be applied to *The Prisoner*, in that his morals throughout are always consistent. Once he picks up the machine guns, it becomes meta-ethics.

Perhaps making up for the fact that he hasn't had much in the way of credit, Angelo Muscat now gets two. One in the end titles and another as he disappears into the house at the end. Leo McKern and Alexis Kanner also get on-screen credits in the final moments of the show. McGoohan, though, is credited as 'Prisoner.' No definite article.

CAI: If you missed the symbolism of the door, here's another for good measure. He's driving around, free as a bird… Prisoner. He's *a* prisoner, not *The* Prisoner and it is inescapable.

CHRIS: It's also a nod to the celebrity aspect that we've alluded to. No matter where he went, what he was wearing or who he was with, people would see him as John Drake. Even off-camera, he's been treated like John Drake or Number 6 or Red from *Hell Drivers*. Who is the real Patrick McGoohan? Is he just a coat hanger?

As McKern returns to the Houses of Parliament, his Number 2 paraphernalia replaced by an umbrella, a trilby hat and a splendid three-piece suit, a clap of thunder rings out. It's the same thunderclap that begins *The Prisoner's* title sequence. Suddenly, we're back on the Elstree aerodrome watching a Lotus 7 approaching us at great speed before the iconic first shot of McGoohan at the wheel, so familiar from all those opening titles. It's the beginning again, back where we first started.

The End.

'You still want to know its message? It's this.
The most dangerous thing in the world is an attitude of mind.'
Patrick McGoohan

Scores

CAI: I actually ummed and ahhed about how to give this a unique score; it seemed inappropriately normal to simply give it a 6 out of 6. Dave Barrie gave it 6 out of 5, maybe he had the right idea. I even thought about giving it a 5 to reward it for being so special. Ultimately it can only be full marks. It's one of the most astonishing pieces of television art ever conceived and the fact that nothing like it will ever be made again only serves to emphasise its value. 6 out of 6.

CHRIS: Like any work of art, you can gain something new from this episode each time you watch it. This is an outstanding piece of television, ahead of its time and certainly too cerebral for television audiences in 1968. I didn't understand it in 1992 but I was essentially a child, with the advantage of 30 years of life experience I now appreciate it for what it is; a masterpiece. 6 out of 6.

Cai: 6 out of 6
Chris: 6 out of 6

Conclusion

There should be what one might call a *Wall-E* protocol. When any new invention is created and set before the world for its approval, we should always ask the question: will this hasten humankind's transformation into the bloated, sedentary, slug-like creatures in the classic 2008 Pixar animation, floating on hoverboards because generations of sloth have made walking both unnecessary and now impossible? If the answer is yes, then the new innovation in question should be destroyed at source.

We never question it though. Ever. We laugh at *Wall-E*'s pampered porcine humanoids and marvel at the satire, and then we install an Alexa in our living room so that we never have to deal with Sisyphean labours like light switches or volume controls ever again. We check in at automated hotels so that we don't 'have to' bother dealing with a concierge, and in the same way we use a self-service till that purports to make our shopping experience easier, when all that's happened is that an employer has cut down on staff). Using a steering-wheel is the next exhausting travail we'll soon be done with as driverless cars become ubiquitous.

Someone invents Facebook and we *have* to be on it. Then Twitter comes along and we *have* to be on that. By the time anyone even started to consider their lasting and game-changing effects on society politically and psychologically, these things have become an inescapable part of our lives and made us all the playthings of multi-billionaires.

It's this critical element of *The Prisoner* that has always resonated and it's something McGoohan, for all his love of obfuscating bluff and misdirection, was never ambiguous about. We're evolving too fast and we need to stop and take a moment to evaluate what we have and assess what our cart wheeling, Promethean technological development has done to us. Perhaps if we take stock, we might better channel our great skills for the betterment of everyone. How's that for deluded optimism?

It's important to try and hold onto optimism, mainly because cynicism is too easy a position to take. It's the sarcasm to optimism's genuine sense of humour, a cheap, unearned sophistication. But Christ, it's hard to be an optimist in the 21st century, especially if you're a confirmed Luddite who would have been quite happy for technology to have peaked in 1999 and then taken a long sabbatical (Cai wrote that bit).

Clearly, this position is classic middle-aged-man harrumphery and should be treated with suspicion by anyone under 30. However, concerns about technology's grip on us all and the kind of human beings we are becoming are not unreasonable. *The Prisoner* (in common with many such shows from the 1960s) saw it all coming years ago and has been shouting out a warning from the television schedules ever since.

We're all living in a post-internet world of numbers, passwords and algorithms, often self-curated digital avatar versions of ourselves that better live up to our idea of our best selves. Instead of seeking wisdom from those who don't agree with us, we're now encouraged to fight them into submission. YouTube clips of political disagreements are invariably described as one party 'destroying' the other, as though dynamite was involved.

On the horizon, Mark Zuckerberg is convinced that virtual, as opposed to actual reality, is the way forward and millions will agree with him. The AI innovations currently stampeding our way: novels, screenplays and examination essays all being written by computers, music being created by computers, lifelike human interaction being created by computers, all the things science fiction has been warning us about for decades will be old hat even by the time this book is published.

McGoohan wasn't alone in being fearful of all this stuff by any stretch, and it isn't just grumpy fortysomethings like us, still banging on about the superior sound quality of vinyl records, who are worried about it. Even the man who was known as 'The godfather of artificial intelligence,' Geoffrey Hinton quit his job at Google in 2023 citing his fears about where AI was taking us.

Matthew Syed penned a fine article this year about technology's ability to distract us with limitless nonsense while infantilising us at the same time. 'The great biologist EO Wilson wrote: "We are drowning in information, while starving for wisdom." Look around the world, the way we are surrounded by mind-bending technology while our creaking political and social institutions struggle to function coherently, and you'll see the profundity of this insight. With limited attention spans and endless distractions, we may be moving into a new phase of history envisioned by Aldous Huxley, when he wrote of societies "whose members spend a great part of their time, not on the spot, not here and now and in the calculable future, but somewhere else, in the irrelevant worlds of... mythology and metaphysical fantasy". The metaverse, anyone?'*

*The Sunday Times. February 12th 2023

The Prisoner was many things, and among them was a warning that this was the direction of travel unless we changed things. Then again, perhaps it's a bit much to have expected Western society to have heeded the warnings of a television show famous for its impenetrable enigmas. As Christian Durante said of *The Prisoner* 'The problem is that, like all truly great works of art, it has not really been understood, and has not changed anything...'

The fact that McGoohan didn't spare himself from his criticism is something that helped the medicine go down, at least for us. We're surely not alone in our distaste for ranting demagogues whose only answer to all the world's problems is that it's someone else's fault. Number 6 by contrast is a man of great complexity, often undone by his own failings. McGoohan's ultimate message in 'Fall Out', that we are our own jailers and the prison we create for ourselves in our minds is inescapable, is a world away from the blame and retribution peddled by inflexible ideologies.

However, I don't think that his conclusion is a cynical surrender. 'We're all bollocksed anyway so who cares?' On the contrary, I think it's an optimistic message. Once you realise and accept that the problem is probably you, you can empower yourself to do something about it or at least try. There is no hopelessness of defeat.

We've both found ourselves considering this on occasions where things have got on top of us and found ourselves drowning in despair. It might just equate to hearing Windsor Davies' voice in our heads shouting at us to pull ourselves up by our bootstraps, but it's *The Prisoner's* message of hope, that we *can* do something about it, that has frequently been the hand that reached down to pull us up out of the murk.

Ultimately, it's been a relief to discover that something we loved so much when we were 17 has not just survived in our affection over thirty years but has swelled in importance. If only we could say the same thing about *Manimal*, which Cai would have happily described in 1983 as the greatest TV show ever made now or at any time in the future (reader, it's terrible).

We think that *The Prisoner* is a masterwork. Unique within its lifetime, it only grows in stature as it becomes increasingly clear that nothing like it will ever be made again. It is also, as we can personally attest, limitlessly re-watchable. Enjoying its many pleasures once again, this time with each other as fine company, and getting to know it anew has been one of the most rewarding experiences of our lives. We can't wait to see what we'll discover about *The Prisoner* the next time we see it.

The Final Scores

Now, this isn't a competition… but since we *have* been keeping scores, here's how the episodes ranked, with 12 being the maximum.

1.	'Fall Out'	12
	'Free For All'	12
	'Once upon a Time'	12
4.	'The Chimes of Big Ben'	10.5
5.	'Arrival'	10
	'Checkmate'	10
	'Hammer into Anvil'	10
	'Many Happy Returns'	10
9.	'The Girl Who Was Death'	9.5
10.	'Dance of the Dead'	9
11.	'A. B. and C.'	8
	'Living in Harmony'	8
	'The Schizoid Man'	8
14.	'The General'	7
15.	'Do Not Forsake Me Oh My Darling'	6.2
16.	'It's Your Funeral'	6
17.	'A Change of Mind'	5

The Free For All Running Order

One of the most vexed questions that often comes up in *Prisoner* fan circles is, 'What is the best order to watch the series?' As we've discovered, all manner of different issues meant that it would have been impossible to broadcast the episodes in the order that they were shot. Andrew Pixley that the UK running order was decided upon 'To balance out accessible plots and Portmeirion-heavy episodes.' This led to some notable discrepancies, largely regarding how long Number 6 has been kept in the Village. 'I'm new here!' he bellows… in episode 8!

This has led many people to create what *they* think is the definitive running order. The US-based KTEH channel 54 re-jigged the schedule when they broadcast the series, as did the Sci-Fi Channel in the UK. In his book *I Am (Not) a Number*, Alex Cox reviewed the episodes in production order to help him unlock some of *The Prisoner's* secrets.

Frankly, apart from episodes 1, 16 and 17, the running order is largely irrelevant, just as Lew Grade would have wanted when he extended the series for syndication purposes. Also, after years of broadcasts / videos / DVDs / Blu-rays, all regimented in the official ITC broadcast order, it just feels… right. It's like accidentally listening to *Revolver* with the shuffle option on and hearing *Taxman* after *And Your Bird Can Sing*. It just feels somehow wrong.

Of course, that hasn't stopped us from having a go! These aren't our insistent, gate-keeperish demands for a new way to watch the series, we couldn't even agree on an order between the pair of us. These are merely our suggestions for an interesting *other* way to enjoy this extraordinary series. Why not try them on the *Prisoner* newbie in your life?

Cai's Running Order

The first thing to note is that I have separated my running order into two seasons. Maybe take a two-month break in between them? All the better to let the questions and mysteries percolate.

Series 1

'Arrival'

'Dance of the Dead'
Like many people, I think this one is tailor-made for a second episode. He's still very naïve about the ways of the Village, but by the end of it, he's in no doubt where he stands, or how hard he's going to have to work to escape.

'Free For All'

'The Schizoid Man'

'Checkmate'

'It's Your Funeral'

'A Change of Mind'

'The Girl Who Was Death'
I've pulled this one further in to rescue it from its undeserved reputation as silly filler.

'The Chimes of Big Ben'
Knowing that this is the final episode of the series, viewers might be half-expecting an escape bid, and the shock ending is a perfect way to blindside the audience and leave them wanting more.

Series 2

'Living in Harmony'
The absence of the title sequence is a deliciously playful way to disorientate viewers from the very start of the second series / season.

'The General'

'A. B. and C.'
Two fun episodes to let viewers bed in again, and now Colin Gordon's character arc makes more sense.

'Do Not Forsake Me Oh My Darling'

'Hammer into Anvil'
His success in this episode gives him a sense of confidence and false hope that he carries all the way through to the next episode... right up until the pilot pulls the ejector switch.

'Many Happy Returns'
He's so dejected at the end of this that the only way to go now is Degree Absolute. Putting this after 'Hammer' does mean that Patrick Cargill is clearly not playing his old Number 2 character here, which is a pity since I always enjoyed the inference that he was.

'Once upon a Time'

'I know your voice.'

'I've been here before.' Those lines are the reason I ended Season 1 with 'Chimes' and not 'Many Happy Returns', but the return of McKern after a gap makes more sense and is a huge treat for the audience.

'Fall Out'

Chris' Running Order

I have separated my running order into four phases, but all within one season.

Phase 1: New To The Village (December to January)
Learning the rules with the Village pushing back against him.

'Arrival'

'Dance of the Dead'

'Checkmate'

…because he's still figuring out the world. Who are the prisoners and who are the jailers?

'The Girl Who Was Death'

There's no malice here on the part of the Village, no escape attempt, just voyeurism. They're starting to work out that his compassion for people might be a weakness.

Phase 2: Messing With His Sanity (January to March)
He's still quite new, but they really turn up the heat on him now.

'Free For All'

'The Schizoid Man'

Set on February 10th, though after all those days of captivity, moustache-growing and rewiring, we don't really know when it's actually set.

'The General'

'The Chimes of Big Ben'

Later than originally scheduled because, strangely, he shows nostalgia for his own captivity. At this point, he doesn't know the location of the Village so it must be before 'Many Happy Returns'.

'Many Happy Returns'

It's March. Now he knows where the Village is.

Phase 3: The Village Starts To Get Desperate (March to August)

He's given up, after 'Chimes' and 'Returns'. He knows escape attempts are futile so how does he now win? This is where he turns the tables on the Village.

'A. B. and C.'
'A Change of Mind'
'Living In Harmony'

Phase 4: Number 6 Gets The Upper Hand (September to January)

The Village has eased up on their mind games, no longer even trying to find out why he resigned. These are altruistic episodes in which he uses his skills to benefit other people. It's been over a year now. The dinner party scenes at night in 'Forsake Me' are dark, suggesting it's autumn and the clocks have gone back.

'Hammer into Anvil'
'It's Your Funeral'
'Do Not Forsake Me Oh My Darling'
'Once upon a Time'
'Fall Out'

Further Reading

Books

The Prisoner: The official companion to the classic TV series by Robert Fairclough
Published by Carlton Books

If you don't have any *Prisoner* books, this is the first port of call. Fairclough is an illustrator too and the book looks suitably vibrant and beautiful. Packed with information, trivia and insight, it remains the most concise and entertaining book ever written about *The Prisoner*. The illustrated plan of the Village alone, locating all the subterranean offices and chambers, even the Embryo Room, is worth the purchase price. If you don't have it, you need it.

The Prisoner: An Illustrated History by Andrew Pixley
Published by Network

Originally this came with the 40th anniversary set and it's the technical bible for the show. Full of dates, information and trivia. It's not for the casual reader and is aimed more at the completist or those who enjoy detail. As far as historical accuracy is concerned, this is the argument-ender.

The Prisoner: A Televisionary Masterpiece by Alain Carrazé & Hélène Oswald
Published by Virgin

This was my Christmas present in 1992 when Channel 4 were showing *The Prisoner* again and my obsession first took hold. God only knows how many times I read it that year. For a while, this was pretty much the only major companion book out there. The bulk of it is made up of transcripts of the episodes, but there are excellent essays from Issac Asimov, Roger Langley and Jacques Sternberg among others, glorious photographs, and a fine section on the history of the production. There's also the rare bonus of an interview with McGoohan himself.

Inside The Prisoner by Ian Rakoff
Published by Batsford

South African-born Ian Rakoff had insider knowledge of *The Prisoner* from the very early days, initially assisting John S Smith with the editing. He was promoted to scriptwriter when McGoohan liked the look of his 'Western' script which, through a rather tortuous process, became 'Living in Harmony'. With a foreword by Nicolas Roeg, his memoirs take in not just *The Prisoner* but his time spent with Lindsay Anderson, for whom he worked on the 1968 classic *if...* Some great tales from the horse's mouth.

I Am (Not) a Number by Alex Cox
Published by Kamera Books

Acclaimed director, host of the indescribably influential *Moviedrome* seasons on BBC2 and, it turns out, a devoted *Prisoner* fan, Alex Cox's look at the series works as a fascinating episode guide full of the kind of informed observations that one would expect from him. Uniquely, he goes through the episodes in production, rather than broadcast order, to help decipher their many mysteries. His conclusion, regarding Number 6's pre-incarceration job, divided many *Prisoner* fans, which we're sure would have delighted Patrick McGoohan.

Not a Number: Patrick McGoohan - A Life by Rupert Booth
Published by Supernova Books

McGoohan made it clear in interviews that anyone waiting for an official autobiography was wasting their time. There would never be a *Village Life: My Story*. McGoohan fans keen to know more about their idol are perhaps best served by this biography, first published two years after McGoohan's passing. As well as being a writer, Rupert Booth is also an actor and cites McGoohan as an influence and a hero. In this snappily written and well researched book, he makes a convincing argument for McGoohan's exalted status, without sidestepping the low points and disappointments.

George Markstein and The Prisoner by Roger Goodman
Published by Pandqmedia

It might seem from our book that we are a bit 'Team McGoohan,' but there's no doubt that *The Prisoner* would not be the series it is without the help of George Markstein. This excellent book by *Prisoner* expert Roger Goodman (and other notable voices, including Dave Barrie and Rick Davy) gives Markstein some much-needed space to put his side of the story across, which he does with much good humour, revealing that in many areas, he and McGoohan were actually in complete agreement.

Websites

There are many websites dedicated to *The Prisoner* to say nothing of the countless number of fan sites and videos on YouTube and all have their merits, but the one site you *must* follow on all your social whatevers is **TheUnmutual.co.uk**. Devoted, informative, unmissable; the one site that has been instrumental in gathering our research.

Special Thanks

Thank you to all our Twitter and Facebook followers for your kind words and encouragement. Thanks especially to Dave Barrie, John Bleasdale, Ant Brierley, Alex Cox, Rick Davy, Mark Dawidziak, Andy English, Robert Fairclough, Christopher James, Ian Killick, Robin Llywelyn, Rodney Marshall, Jane Merrow, Gordon Milton, Alison Murray, Derren Nesbitt, Ian Rakoff, Glenys Siefers, Lucy Tomblin, Susan Uphill, Ren Zelen… and of course Patrick.

Especially special thanks to Alan Hayes for his magnificent work in putting this book together so beautifully and correckting all our typos (apart from that one).

ILLUSTRATIONS BY JEMIMA DUNCALF
www.jemimaduncalf.com

WHERE HAVE I BEEN ALL MY LIFE?

A MEMOIR BY ANNETTE ANDRÉ

"Annette Andre's memoir is a vibrant tapestry, woven of eloquent and engaging words that – in equal measure – inspire, intrigue and entice."

Karl Frunz, Glass in Hand Productions

For someone who has professed "terminal shyness," Annette André has written her memoir with arresting honesty and generosity. From a lonely childhood in Sydney, Australia, and overcoming a chronic illness to become a professional ballet dancer, *Where Have I Been All My Life?* reveals the truth behind her storybook romance with a famous bullfighter, how Benny Hill proposed marriage, and why a chance conversation with Prince Charles helped to change the course of her life.

Guest starring with Roger Moore in more episodes of *The Saint* than any other actress, Annette quickly became one of the most popular TV actors of Britain's "Golden Age," in such classic series as *The Avengers, The Prisoner, The Persuaders!* and her most memorable role of all, as Jeannie in *Randall and Hopkirk (Deceased)*. From her fly-on-the-wall view of Burton and Taylor's romance while filming *Cleopatra* to the perils of shooting *A Funny Thing Happened On the Way to the Forum*, and her appearances on the West End stage, Annette found writing the story of her life "excruciatingly hard work, but like a good orgasm, damn well worth the effort."

240mm x 160mm   Hardback, 272 pages, with 16 pages of colour and black and white photos

ISBN: 978-1-911537-10-6

Available from www.quoitmedia.co.uk

the prisoner
the essential guide

The Prisoner television series is regarded as one of the finest, yet most bizarre and controversial, programmes ever made. Starring Patrick McGoohan, Britain's highest paid television actor at the time, and filmed at the Italianate village of Portmeirion, it has achieved cult status and has entertained and beguiled viewers since it was screened in 1967/68.

Who was Patrick McGoohan?
Why Portmeirion?
How was The Prisoner made?
What car did Number Six drive?
Why the giant balloon?
And what was it all about?

All these questions, and more, are answered in *The Prisoner – The Essential Guide*, a handy guide to everything that made the series such a cult favourite which is still examined, discussed and loved half a century after it was made.

Also included is an easy reference guide to each episode, plus a wealth of behind the scenes photographs, many previously unpublished.

Written by renowned *The Prisoner* historian and researcher Rick Davy.

Paperback Book | 36 pages

ISBN: 978-1-911537-16-8

Available from www.quoitmedia.co.uk

'Be seeing you...'